스킬라와 카리브디스 그 너머

국가경영의 예술

글 모음집
김 진 우

추천사

1994년 가을 예일대학에서 저자(김진우 박사)를 처음 만났다. 처음 대면한 장소는 정확히 기억나지 않지만 분명히 도서관은 아니었다. 국민(초등)학교 시절 어린 나이에 미국 이민을 떠난 교포학생 신분이었지만, 한국말을 어찌나 잘 하던지 유학생인 줄 알았다. 저자는 역사학, 그것도 현대 서양사를 전공하는 박사 과정 대학원생이었고 영어 실력은 정말 탁월했다. 한국 유학생 중 여러 명이 그의 영어 실력에 신세를 진 것으로 기억한다. 김 박사는 술도 아주 잘 마시고, 테니스와 골프 등 스포츠도 아주 수준급인 친구였다. 같이 자주 어울렸지만 김진우 박사와는 근본적으로 친해지기 어려운 점이 있었다. 명석한 두뇌 소유자인데다 책도 많이 읽은 그 똑똑한 친구는 정치적으로 매우 보수적이었을 뿐만 아니라 열혈한 공화당 지지자였기 때문이다. 아이비리그 대학, 그것도 역사학 박사 과정 재학 중인 20대 보수주의자라니! 나 같은 얼치기 진보주의자에게는 지금도 그것은 상상이 잘 가질 않는다. 아무튼 그는 지적으로, 정치적으로 내가 지금까지 결코 본 적이 없는 참으로 독특한 사람이다. 그 당시 여럿이 어울려서 김진우 박사와 정치 관련하여 적잖이 많은 언쟁을 할 때마다, 그는 다음과 같이 자주 반문했다. "왜 다들 똑똑한 사람은 반드시 좌파일 것이라고 착각하는가?" 지금 돌이켜 보면 그 발언은 그의 단순한 냉소적 일성을 넘어서, 그의 강력한 정치적 신념에 대한 우회적인 표현이었다.

1996년경 나는 귀국하였고, 김진우 박사와 서로 연락한 적이 끊어지다시피 했었다. 나의 기억이 정확하진 않지만 2003년경 김진우 박사가 한국에 출장을 왔다. 이라크 전쟁 관련 이야기를 나누다 아주 크게 다투었다. 김진우 박사는 그 당시 나에게 "핵과 전쟁에 대해서 무엇을 안다고 그러는가? 정치학자도 아닌 언어학자인 노암 촘스키(Noam Chomsky) 책이나 몇 권 읽고서 미국 정치에 대해서 이야길 말라!"고 일갈했다. 지금 돌이켜 보니 김 박사는 그 당시에도 이미 핵 관련 업무에 깊이 관련하고 있었던 것 같다. 3년 전부터 한국에 다시 귀국한 그를 다시 만나게 되었고, 그 이후 그와 매우 긴밀하게 연락하는 사이를 유지하고 있다. 물론 지금도 나는 김진우 박사로부터 그가 2000년경부터 10년 동안 무엇을 하였는지 결코 제대로 말하는 것을 들어 본 적이 없다. 도대체 그에게는 무슨 비밀이 그리도 많은 것이지 나는 잘 모르겠다. 다만 신문 칼럼과 기고문, 논문 등을 통하여 그가 가슴 속에 품고 있는 비밀과 생각의 단편을 읽어 낼 뿐이다. 참고로 나는 이제껏 그저 평범한 회사원으로 지냈고, 정치 영역에 발을 들여 놓은 적도 없다. 다만 '신과 야수마저도 정치로부터 자유스러울 수 없다'는 격언을 신봉하여 정치 관련 비판적 관심을 가지고 살아갈 뿐이다.

    이번에 출판하는 그의 책 내용을 미리 읽어 볼 기회가 있어서 몇 마디 덧붙이고자 한다. 일단 그의 유려한 영어가 한국어로 명료하게 번역될 수 있을지 심히 우려한다. 그가 펼치고 있는 핵 관련 전문 용어와 국제정치사의 사건과 유명 인사들, 그리고 설명을 위한 문학적 비유 등이 한국어 번역을 통하여 과연 독자들에게 제대로 전달될 수 있을까 의문이다.

    김진우 박사가 이 책에서 주장하고자 하는 가장 핵심적인 사항은 다음과 같다. 즉, 그는 한국과 일본의 핵무장 문제를 중국과 북한에 대한 미국의 '확장억제력' 강화와 연결하여 풀어 가자는 논리 전개를 하고 있다. 그의 정치 성향과 핵 무장의 필요성 주장에 동의하지 않는다 하더라도 그리고 나와 같은 핵과 국제 정치 관련 문외한이 읽어 보더라도 그의 논리 전개는 너무 적절하고 확실히 탁월하다. 나는 그가 특히 글에서 결코 객관적인 사실과 개인적인 의견을 혼돈하는 법이 없음을 높이 평가한다. 김진우 박사와 같은 핵전략 전문 인재가 북핵 및 일체의 핵 문제 관련 공론장 밖 재야에 머물러 있는 현실이 너무 안타깝고 국가적인 손실이라는 생각마저 든다.

이 책의 출판으로 지금까지 전혀 주목 받지 못한 그의 주장이 정치 현장에서 관련 정책 담당자들과 전문가들을 통하여 재론되는 반전을 간절히 소망한다.

리어왕의 독백이 패러디로 떠오른다. "이 땅 대한민국에서 핵(핵무기)이 무엇인지 말할 수 있는 자는 누구인가?"

대한민국 핵무장은 과연 한반도 평화의 보증수표인가 아니면 망상인가? 이것에 대한 답을 진정으로 알고 싶은가? 비록 이 책은 한국어로 거칠게 번역되었지만, 그의 완벽한 영어 원문과 비교, 참고하면서 글 전체를 일단 찬찬히 읽어보자.

수림문화재단 사무국장
김정본

서문

　가톨릭(catholic)이라는 단어는 두 가지 의미를 지니고 있다. 천주교에서 Catholic은 'C'가 알파벳 대문자로 쓰인다. 알파벳 'c'를 소문자로 사용하는 catholic은 보편적이라는 것을 의미한다. 필자는 독실한 천주교(Catholic) 신자이며, 그 누구보다도 보편성(catholic)을 지향한다. 즉, 필자는 유년기부터 인간 관점과 사고의 '보편성'이라는 것을 배웠다. 물론 이는 그 무엇이든 상관없다는 것을 의미하지 않았다.

　라틴어로 '논 포수무스(Non possumus)'라는 말이 있다. 논 포수무스(Non possumus)의 진정한 의미는 '우리는 그렇게 할 수 없다'라는 의미를 가지고 있는 종교적인 문구로서, 아비티나에(Abitinae)의 순교 관련 이야기에서 유래하였다. 로마의 황제였던 디오 클레티아누스(Diocletian)가 기독교의 일요일 성찬례를 금지시키자, 아비티니에는 '우리는 주일 없이 살 수 없다(Sine dominico non possumus)'고 부르짖었다. 즉, '어떤 것들은 결코 받아들일 수가 없다'는 것이다. 필자는 누구보다도 보편성을 추구하지만, 과거의 이 라틴어 문장처럼 원칙 없이 시류에 편승하여 이루어진 그 어떤 지식 사회의 합의에도 단호히 반대한다. 필자는 본질 없는 겉치레에 불과하거나, 확인되지 않는 사항과 관련된 집단 합의에 대하여 일부분이라도 의견을 양보하거나 마지 못해 동조하는 일은 하지 않을 것이다.

　필자는 텍스트(text)없는 세상이나 삶을 상상할 수 없다. '텍스트(Text)'라는 단어는 '짜다(texere)'라는 라틴어에서 파생되었다. 우리가 천을 짜서 옷을 만드는 것처럼 단어를 짜고 꿰매어 말과 글을 만들기 때문이다. 헤라클레이토스는 "같은 강물에 발을 두 번 담글 수는 없다"라고 했다. 이는 인간의 '텍스트'와 일맥상통한 점이 있다. 이전에 읽었던 텍스트를 다시 읽을 때 인간은 새로운 시각으로 다른 차원에서 읽을 수 있다. 동일한 텍스트, 그리고 새로운 시각. 이것은 가장 처음으로 '텍스트'를 작성하는 '그 누군가'는 고된 창작의 고통을 겪게 된다는 것이다. 그리고 독자들이 다른 맥락으로 읽거나, 이들의 더 깊은 이해를 돕기 위하여 '그 누군가'는 적절한 단어들을 거듭하여 조합 나열하고 다듬는 지난한 과정을 거쳐야 한다.

필자는 과거 미국 정부에서 근무하는 동안 수많은 기밀 정보를 취급하고 비공개 프로젝트에 참여 했다. 필자의 수많은 단독 브리핑과 한 페이지 분량의 압축 보고서들은 상사들로부터 뛰어나다는 평가를 받았지만, 그 특성상 정부 기밀문서로 분류되어 아직까지 세상의 빛을 보지 못하고 있다. 이러한 사정으로 미국에서 활동한 40년간, 예일대 박사학위 취득을 위하여 작성한 이승만 전 대통령에 대한 논문을 제외하고, 필자의 제대로 된 저서나 학술 논문은 사실상 전무 하다시피 하다. 한국으로 귀국한 2016년 이후에도 필자 명의의 저서는 여전히 찾아볼 수 없었다. 하지만 클라라와 프란체스, 정본 형의 끈질긴 독촉과 격려로 필자는 마지못해 펜을 들기로 결심했다. 그 후 아프가니스탄 이슈부터 핵무기, 우크라이나 전쟁 등 많은 이슈와 관련하여 다양한 글을 썼다.

필자는 글을 쓸 때 세가지 사항을 유념하였다. 첫 번째는 정치지도자들이 직면했던 끊임없는 딜레마인 스킬라와 카리브디스 사이, 즉 '어떻게 하면 국제관계라는 위험한 바다의 거친 파도 속에서 국가라는 배를 안전하게 항해할 수 있을까?'라는 그 질문을 너머서 위대한 국가 지도자들은 그 이후에 펼쳐질 또 다른 바다를 안전하게 항해하기 위해 지속가능한 합의를 이끌어내야 한다고 생각한다. 따라서 지도자는 고통스럽더라도 지금 당장 해결해야 하는 일상적인 딜레마를 너머, 미래에 펼쳐진 세상을 제대로 만들어 놓아야 한다고 생각하며 글을 썼다.

두 번째는 진정성에 기반한 글쓰기 스타일과 관련이 있다. 필자는 직설적이고 솔직한 화법으로 정평이 나 있지만, 오히려 그 평판을 자랑스럽게 여기고 있다. 뿐만 아니라 '직설적'이라는 단어마저도 매우 친숙하게 느낀다. 물론 필자는 글을 아주 유려하게 쓸 수 있지만, 직접적인 접근을 더 선호한다. 그래서 필자는 1차 자료를 소중히 여기며, 직선적인 비판 방식을 취한다. 또한 필자는 아부하는 표현을 싫어할 뿐만 아니라 정치적 외풍에 휩쓸리는 것을 단호히 거부한다. 많은 사람들이 수 차례 당부하였음에도 불구하고, 필자는 최선이라고 생각하는 사고와 의견, 발언 등을 적당히 타협하거나 누그러뜨리는 일은 결코 하지 않았다.

마지막으로 필자가 유념한 것은 로마의 시인 유베날리스(Decimus Junius Juvenalis)의 "*Quis custodiet ipsos custodes?*"라는 문구이다. 이를 직역하면 "감시자들, 그 자신들은 누가 감시하는가?"라고 할 수 있다. 우리 시대의 감시자들은 오피니언 리더, 학자, 경찰, 검사, 관료 그리고 마지막으로 정치인이다. 그들은 일반 사람들의 삶과 인식에 많은 영향을 미친다. 그런데 누가 그들을 감시하는가? 누가 그들의 행동을 교정할 것인가? 누가 그들에게 잘못을 물을 것인가? 누가 그들에게 책임을 묻는가? 권력을 가지고 있는 감시자들의 행동을 통제하는 문제에 대해 플라톤(Plato)은 『국가(The Republic)』에서 논의하였고, 필자는 글을 통해 스스로 그 역할을 수행하리라 다짐했다.

필자가 글을 쓰기로 결심한 것은 진리 추구의 필수적인 요소라 할 수 있는 의견의 풍부한 다양성에 작은 기여라도 제공하고자 함이다. 존 스튜어트 밀(John Stuart Mill)은 『자유론(On Liberty)』을 통해 "(그러므로) 행정과 사법 체계의 압제로부터의 보호만으로는 충분하지 못하며, 지배적인 여론과 감정의 압제로부터도 보호하는 것이 필요하다"고 설득력 있게 주장했다. 정부의 검열은 위험하다. 하지만 어느 국가, 어느 사회적 맥락에서 잘못 이루어진 사회적

합의가 이보다 더 폭압적일 수 있다.

　필자의 정치적인 성향은 소수 중에서도 아주 소수에 속한다고 할 수 있다. 하지만 제대로 조직된 소수의 사람들은 귀족정치, 군주제, 신권정치, 과두정, 고대 민주주의와 공화정, 현대 자유 민주주의 체제에 이르기까지 조직화된 다수의 사람들에게 언제나 승리하였다. 그리고 진정한 리더십은 언제나 소수의 사람들로부터 나온다. 현대 외교의 거장인 헨리 키신저(Henry Kissinger)는 리더의 5가지 자질을 제시했다. 진정한 리더는 비정한 진실을 말할 수 있고, 비전을 제시할 수 있으며, 불의에 맞설 수 있는 용기를 가지며, 고독 속에서 홀로 시간을 보낼 수 있고, 논쟁이나 분열을 두려워하지 않아야 한다는 것이다. 나는 내 글들이 이러한 특징들을 보여주고 있음을 믿는다.

　필자는 모든 인간이 논리적인 사고 능력을 가지고 있다고 믿는다. 하지만 논리적인 사고보다 생각해야 할 도덕적 의무가 더 크다고 생각한다. 또한 필자는 보수주의를 믿는다. 즉, 인간의 합리성과 위대한 성취 결과를 보존하며, 그것을 훼손하려는 그 어떠한 시도 또한 강력히 저지하고자 한다. 필자는 펠라기우스(Pelagius)보다 아우구스티누스(Augustine)를 더 좋아하며, 윌슨(Woodrow Wilson)보다 메테르니히(Klemens von Metternich)를 더 선호하고, 레닌(Vladimir Lenin)보다 밀턴(John Milton) 쪽으로 더 기울어져 있음이 분명하다. 무엇보다 진리와 합리성 그리고 인류애를 믿는다. 비록 그 동안 기록된 역사가 그 믿음을 훼손한 것처럼 보일지라도 말이다. 아마도 그것은 믿음이 아니라 신념일 수 있다. 내가 기꺼이 기쁜 마음으로 붙들고 있는 신념!

　터키의 저항 시인으로 잘 알려진 나짐 히크메트(Nazim Hikmet)는 감옥에서 '진정한 여행'이란 제목의 시를 썼다.

가장 훌륭한 시는 아직 쓰여지지 않았다
가장 아름다운 노래는 아직 불려지지 않았다
최고의 날들은 아직 살지 않은 날들
가장 넓은 바다는 아직 항해되지 않았고
가장 먼 여행은 아직 끝나지 않았다
불멸의 춤은 아직 추어지지 않았으며
가장 빛나는 별은 아직 발견되지 않은 별
무엇을 해야 할지 더 이상 알 수 없을 때
그때 비로소 진정한 무엇인가를 할 수 있다
어느 길로 가야 할지 더 이상 알 수 없을 때
그때가 비로소 진정한 여행의 시작이다

진정으로. 나의 참된 여행은 이제 막 시작됐다.

---- 차례 ----

추천사 ·· 2

서문 ··· 5

억지가 실패하면 ·· 12

트럼프의 팬더 죽이기 ··· 15

레이건의 베를린, 트럼프의 판문점 ·· 18

사우디 공격: 정확성과 정교함에 주목해야 한다 ······························ 21

트럼프 탄핵의 진실게임: 답은 원출처에 있다 ································· 23

상상하기 싫은 것도 상상해야 한다: 억제가 실패한다면 ··············· 28

트럼프 2020 - Part 1. 2016년 대선으로부터 얻을 수 있는 교훈들 ········ 34

트럼프 2020 - Part 2. 2020 대선으로 가는 길 ································· 43

핵 억지력의 본질 ··· 50

2060 동아시아: 대한민국의 핵, 일본의 핵,
태평양동맹조약기구와 새로운 미국의 확장억제력 ························ 60

옹호와 진실 ·· 75

핵 억지력, 선택의 순간 ·· 78

독이 든 성배 ·· 80

모든 눈물은 똑같다 ·· 82

공허한 자들의 빈말 ·················· 84

바로 군인이다 ·················· 86

반격의 시작 ·················· 88

사이버 외교관을 찾습니다 ·················· 90

아프간 철군 사태를 통해 본 미국 리더십의 위기:
바이든 대통령의 직무유기 ·················· 92

스냅백은 없다 ·················· 98

악마는 디테일에 있다 ·················· 100

軍, 그들은 그들답게 ·················· 102

2048년, 발칙한 상상 ·················· 104

2048년, 끔찍한 악몽 ·················· 106

힘의 상관관계 ·················· 109

무기와 사내를 노래하다 ·················· 111

기획자의 변(辨) ·················· 120

참고문헌 ·················· 122

* 글은 날짜 순으로 되어 있습니다.

억지^{Deterrence}가 실패하면*

한반도에서 억지(deterrence)는 실패했다. 억지력은 북한이 핵무기를 획득하고 개발하는 것을 막지 못했다. 하루가 다르게 북한의 핵 능력은 강해지고 있다.

억지라는 단어는 라틴어 *de*(떨어져서)와 *terrere*(겁주다)에서 유래되었다. 억지력은 적이 상대방의 의지와 능력을 신뢰할 수 있다고 인식할 때 작동한다. 그 신뢰가 무너지면 억지는 실패하게 된다.

북한은 대한민국을 두려워하지 않는다. 북한의 의사결정자들의 마음 속에 그런 두려움을 다시 심어줄 때다.

빼앗는 힘, 획득하는 힘, 설득하는 힘은 현대인에게 매력적일 수 있다. 그러나 폭력을 가하는 원초적인 힘(능력)과 그것을 관철 시킬 수 있는 의지(신뢰성)는 여전히 국가권력의 본질로 남아 있다. 말(words)은 권력을 구현하거나 국익을 증진 할 때 그리고 막강한 권력이 부재한 공백기에 더 중요해진다. 그러나 말은 결코 행동과 폭력적 힘의 배치를 대체할 수 없다. 강력한 재래식 전력을 확대하고 전쟁을 준비하는 것은 대한민국의 생존을 위해 필수적이다.

북한은 핵 보유국이다. 하지만 한국은 핵 보유국이 아니다. 만약, 한국이 독자적 핵 능력을 추구할 준비가 되어 있지 않다면, 즉시 재래식 공격 능력의 대대적인 증강에 나서야 한다. 즉, 신속하고 방대한 군사력 증강을 말이다.

구체적으로 현무-3C 순항미사일{TERCOM(지형대조)과 DSMAC(영상대조) 능력을 갖춘 사거리 1,500km}의 조속한 대량 생산뿐만 아니라, 현재 한국이 보유하고 있는 15척의 디젤 잠수함에 추가적인 신형 핵잠수함 도입 역시 하루속히 이뤄져야 한다. 그러기 위해서 한국은 신형 핵 잠수함의 연료인 고농축 우라늄(HEU)의 제한된 생산을 위해 미국과 협상이 필요하다.

---

* 본고는 2016년 9월 1일에 작성한 미발표 글입니다.

몇 년 안에 북한은 훨씬 더 향상된 핵 능력을 갖게 될 것이다. 북핵을 미연에 방지함으로써 한국이 군사력 증강을 위해 벌 수 있는 약 20년의 시간이라는 기회의 창은 점점 줄어들고 있다. 바로 지금이 북한을 타격해야 할 때다. 지상 발사대가 없는 미사일은 무용지물이다. 북한의 이동식 발사대를 찾아 파괴하는 것이 어렵다고 우리가 이미 알고 있는 것에 대해 공격하는 것을 단념해서는 안 된다. 그 목표물은 바로 북한의 서해와 동해에 있는 두 개의 발사대와 SLBM을 탑재할 수 있는 2,000톤의 신포급 잠수함 한 척이다.

3개의 목표물에 각각 2발의 미사일을 계산하면 이 목표물을 파괴하기 위해서는 순항 미사일 6발만 사용하면 된다. 북한의 발사 능력을 선제적으로 제거한 후, 한국은 반드시 전쟁 준비를 해야 한다. 북한의 보복을 예상하고 광범위한 방공망 제압(Suppression of Enemy Air Defenses, SEAD) 작전수행을 준비하여 한국 전투기가 전방에 배치된 북한 포병부대에 압도적이고 결정적인 융단폭격을 수행하게 해야 한다. 그 후, 한국은 신속하고 은밀하면서도 파괴적인 공격으로 북한의 주요 지휘 · 통제 목표물에 대한 보다 광범위한 작전을 준비해야 한다. 믿을 수 없을 정도로 유능한 한국의 특수부대는 북한 참수작전 성공에 핵심적인 역할을 할 것이다.

이러한 북한에 대한 선제공격의 여파로 한국에 퍼붓는 국제적인 비난은 국익이라는 명분으로 짊어져야 한다. 이라크의 오시라크(Osirak) 원자로와 알 키바르(Al Kibar) 핵시설에 대한 공습은 이스라엘과 국제사회의 실존적 위협을 제거했고, 이들에게 핵 위협을 억제할 수 있도록 귀중한 시간을 벌었다. 북한이 이미 핵무기를 보유하고 있는 상황에서 영변 핵시설에 대한 폭격은 폭격의 여파로 잠재적인 방사능인 낙진(radioactive fallout)으로 인해 오히려 역효과를 낼 것이다. 하지만 미사일만으로 3개의 목표물을 폭격하는 것은 북한의 즉각적인 핵 위협을 무력화하고 좌절시킬 수 있는 시간을 한국에게 준다. 선제적인 공격을 통해 주어진 시간은 한국이 독자적 핵 능력을 추구하기 위한 복잡한 결정을 숙고하면서 동시에 공격적인 군사력을 강화할 수 있게 할 것이다.

한국의 국가 안보는 동맹국에만 의지할 수 없고, 적에게 볼모로 잡혀서도 안된다. 고고도미사일방어체계(Terminal High Altitude Area Defense,

THAAD) 배치는 환영한다. 하지만 한국은 새로운 방패와 함께 더 날카롭고 강력한 검이 필요하다. 강력하고 진전된 재래식 전력 증강과 즉각적이고 실체적이며 가시적인 위협인 북한의 3개 목표물에 대한 선제타격은 핵무장한 북한에 대한 대한민국의 국익에 부합한다. 이를 통해 억지 방정식의 균형을 회복하게 한다. 로마 장군 베게티우스(Publius Flavius Vegetius Renatus)가 말한 "평화를 원한다면, 전쟁에 대비해라"처럼 제대로 된 국가는 국가의 생존을 보장하고 국익을 증진시키기 위해 전쟁을 준비해야 한다.

트럼프의 팬더 죽이기*

　미・중 무역전쟁에서 중국은 패배할 것으로 보인다. 트럼프(Donald Trump)는 이를 알고 있고 중국도 이미 알고 있을 것이다.
　두 사람이 사막에서 표류하고 있다고 가정해보자. 물 한 통을 가지고 있는 사람이 쌀 한 되를 가지고 있는 사람보다 사막에서 더 오래 버틸 수 있다. 현재 물 한 통을 가지고 있는 쪽은 경제적으로 훨씬 자립도가 높은 미국이다. 중국은 쌀 한 되만 믿고 미국에 맞서고 있을 뿐, 싸움의 주도권은 미국이 가지고 있다.
　미국의 전체 경제규모는 중국보다 여전히 크며 수출품목 뿐만 아니라 금융・경제 주체 역시 훨씬 다양하다. 이에 반해 중국은 독자적인 기술이 부족하고 아직 공산품 및 식품 모두 자급자족을 할 수 있는 능력을 갖추지 못하고 있다.
　중국 지린대학교의 리샤오(李曉) 교수는 2018년 6월 2일 졸업식 축사에서 중국 전체 무역에서 대미 무역이 차지하는 비율이 매우 높고, 핵심기술과 농산물에 대한 중국의 대미 의존도가 특히 높음을 언급하며 중국 경제의 자립성 부족을 지적한 바 있다.[1]
　만약 중국이 위안화의 가치를 떨어뜨린다면, 결국 자국이 보유한 달러 가치에 큰 타격을 입힐 것이고, 글로벌 공급망에서 중요한 위치를 차지하는 중국 공장들이 문을 닫으면 더 많은 실업이 발생해 노동 불안을 초래할 것이다. 뿐만 아니라 애플, 보잉, GM과 같은 미국의 글로벌 기업들은 중국 내 경제활동이 여의치 않게 된다면, 언제든지 다른 나라로 이전할 수 있다.
　2019년 5월 5일, 트럼프가 트위터로 포문을 연 관세 전쟁에서 중국은 미국에 대한 보복 관세 조치로 응수했다.[2] 이에 트럼프는 5월 15일, "미국 국가 안보에 용납할 수 없는 위협에 대응 한다"는 명분 하에, 미국 기업의 해외 통신장비

---

* 본고는 2019년 6월 4일에 작성한 미발표 글입니다.

사용을 금지한다는 내용의 행정 명령을 내렸다.[3] 이는 물론 화웨이를 겨냥한 것이다. 공화당의 마르코 루비오(Marco Antonio Rubio)와 민주당의 마크 워너(Mark R.Warner) 상원의원 모두 화웨이의 통신장비기술 뿐 아니라, 에너지 장비 사용도 금지해야 한다는 서한을 미 국토부와 에너지부에 보낼 만큼 이 사안에 대해 초당적 지지를 얻고 있다.[4]

화웨이와 무역 관세를 통한 압박 이전에 이미 트럼프는 대중 무역 불균형을 해소하고 중국과의 패권 다툼에서 이기기 위한 정교한 움직임을 보여왔다. 북미자유무역협정(NAFTA)을 수정한 새로운 미국·멕시코·캐나다협정(USMCA)의 핵심은 제32조 10항 비시장경제 국가 조항이다. 이 조항은 협정 당사국이 만약 비시장경제 국가와 FTA를 체결하는 경우, 다른 당사국들이 협정을 종료할 수 있다는 내용을 담고 있다. 이는 캐나다와 멕시코가 중국과 FTA를 체결하는 것을 방지함으로써 중국의 북미 경제권 진출을 저지하는데 그 목적이 있다.

USMCA 협정이 타결된 후, 트럼프는 브릭스(BRICs: 브라질·러시아·인도·중국·남아프리카공화국 등 신흥경제 5국) 국가들 중 브라질과 인도를 먼저 정조준했다. 문제가 되어 왔던 고관세와 불공정무역을 양자협상으로 해결할 것이라는 압박을 지속하며, 중국이 포함된 BRICs의 힘을 약화시키려는 의도였다. USMCA 협정을 새로 체결하고 BRICs를 흔들며 트럼프는 중국의 경제성장에 제동을 걸고 있는 것이다.[5]

2025년까지 첨단 산업을 집중 육성하여 제조 초강대국으로 성장하겠다는 '중국 제조 2025(Made in China 2025 Strategy)' 계획에 트럼프는 "그런 일은 절대로 일어나지 않을 것"이라며 공언했다.[6] 이를 허언(虛言)으로 받아들여서는 안된다. 많은 사람들은 여전히 트럼프를 과소평가하고 있다. 이는 매우 심각한 실수다. 시진핑 주석 역시 트럼프를 과소평가하는 우를 범하고 있다. 그러한 어리석음으로 인해 시진핑(Xi Jinping)과 중국은 무거운 대가를 치르게 될 것이다.

가열되고 있는 미·중 무역전쟁이 북핵문제에는 어떤 변수로 작용할까? 무역전쟁이 심화될수록 중국이 훨씬 더 교묘하게 뒤에서 북한을 조정하리라는 것을 트럼프는 알고 있다. 하지만 중국의 경제 위기가 심해질 수록 중국은 트럼프와 더 나은 거래를 위한 조치를 취할 수 밖에 없다. 트럼프는 중국이 경제 생존을 원한다면 북한에게 핵포기를 종용하라고 요구할 것이다. 트럼프에게 중국과의 무역전쟁은 북핵문제 해결을 포함해서, '미국을 위대하게' 만들 수 있는 만병통치약인 것이다.

레이건의 베를린, 트럼프의 판문점*

1987년 6월 12일, 미국의 로널드 레이건(Ronald Reagan) 대통령은 베를린의 브란덴부르크 문 앞에서 역사에 길이 남을 연설을 하였다. 레이건은 당시 소련 공산당 서기장 미하일 고르바초프(Mikhail Gorbachev)에게 "이 장벽을 무너뜨리시오!(Mr. Gorbachev, tear down this wall.)"라고 말한 구절은 지금도 회자될 만큼 유명하다.[7] 트럼프가 2019년 6월 말에 방한하여 남북 분단과 전쟁의 고통을 상징하는 판문점에 방문할 것으로 예상하는 이 시점에 트럼프가 레이건만큼이나 설득력 있고, 감동적이고, 중요한 연설을 하지 않을지 기대해 본다.

판문점은 아시아의 베를린 장벽으로 냉전의 마지막 상징이자 유일한 잔재이다. 판문점은 한반도의 물리적, 정신적 분열을 상징한다. 분단은 시간으로 치유할 수 없는 영원한 상처다. 한국인들에게 판문점은 쉽게 지울 수 없는 국가적 기억으로 비핵화 여부와 관계없이 이 분열은 언젠가 반드시 끝나야 한다.

레이건의 베를린 연설 중에서 "이 장벽을 무너뜨리시오!"라는 문장만큼 유명하지는 않지만, 그만큼 눈 여겨 볼 한 대목이 있다. 그 단락에서 몇 개의 단어만 대체한다면 이 연설은 당장 트럼프가 판문점에서 해도 될 만큼 한반도의 현재 상황과 맞아 떨어진다.

"내 뒤로는 이 도시의 자유로운 부분을 둘러싼 장벽이 서 있으며, 이는 유럽대륙 전체를 둘로 나누는 거대한 장벽의 일부입니다. 이 장벽은 발트해에서 시작하여 남쪽으로 내려와 가시 철조망, 콘크리트, 순찰견, 초소 등으로 독일을 가로지르고 있습니다. 남쪽으로 더 내려가면 눈에 보이는 장벽은 없을 것이지만, 무장 초병과 검문소가 남

---

* 본고는 2019년 6월 26일 세르모국제연구소에 게재된 글 입니다.

아 있습니다. 이는 여행할 권리를 제한하는 존재이자, 보통 사람들에게 전체주의 국가의 뜻을 강요하는 수단이 되고 있습니다. 그러나, 이 장벽이 가장 두드러지는 곳은 바로 여기 베를린이며, 여기서는 뉴스 사진과 TV 화면이 이 야만적인 대륙 분단의 모습을 전 세계인의 뇌리에 각인 시켰습니다. 브란덴부르크 문 앞에 서면 누구나 동포들로부터 떨어진 독일인이 됩니다. 모두가 상처를 돌아 보아야 하는 베를린 시민이 됩니다."

– 레이건의 베를린 연설 중 일부분

이 단락에서 대한민국 상황에 맞게 단어 몇 개를 한번 바꾸어 보겠다.

"내 뒤로는 이 자연의 자유로운 부분을 둘러싼 '철조망'이 서 있으며, 이는 '한반도 전체'를 둘로 나누는 거대한 '분단선'의 일부입니다. 이 '분단선'은 '서해'에서 시작하여 '동쪽'으로 가로질러와 가시 철조망, 군인, 순찰견, 초소 등으로 '한반도'를 가로지르고 있습니다. '동쪽'으로 내려갈수록 무장 초병과 검문소가 남아 있습니다. 이는 '통행할' 권리를 제한하는 존재이자, 보통 사람들에게 전체주의 국가의 뜻을 강요하는 수단이 되고 있습니다. 그러나, 이 '분단선'이 가장 두드러지는 곳은 바로 여기 '판문점'이며, 여기서는 사진과 TV화면이 이 야만적인 '한반도 분단'의 모습을 전 세계인의 뇌리에 각인 시켰습니다. '판문점' 앞에 서면 누구나 동포들로부터 떨어진 '한국인'이 됩니다. 모두가 상처를 돌아 보아야 하는 '대한민국의 시민'이 됩니다."

몇 개의 단어만 바꿨을 뿐인데, 30여년 전 베를린 브란덴부르크 문 앞과 지금 판문점 앞의 상황은 소름 끼칠 만큼 서로 잘 맞아 떨어진다. 그래서 한걸음 더 나아가 트럼프가 만약 이런 연설을 한다면, 그 이후의 상황은 어떻게 될지 그려본다.

당시 레이건의 연설은 지나치게 자극적이고 도전적인 것으로 여겨졌지만 그의 연설은 이후 새로운 물꼬를 터, 거스를 수 없는 거대한 흐름을 만들었다. 2년 후인 1989년 11월, 동독이 마침내 장벽을 개방하여 사람들은 자유롭게 서독과 왕래할 수 있게 되었고, 그로부터 다시 2년 후인 1991년 12월 26일, 소련은 붕괴되어 기나긴 냉전이 종식되었다.

어쩌면 레이건의 연설처럼 트럼프의 판문점 연설이 신호탄이 되어 대한민국에 평화와 화합의 기류가 흐르게 될 지도 모른다. 남과 북이 자유롭게 왕래하고, 마침내 민족의 분단과 대립에 종지부를 찍을 수 있을 지도 모른다.

물론 트럼프가 나의 상상에 찬물을 끼얹 듯, 헬리콥터를 타고 판문점까지 와 잠시 사진만 찍고 다시 돌아가 버릴 수도 있다. 하지만 판문점과 베를린 장벽이 같은 운명의 길을 가는 것을 싱싱해 보는 것은 돈이 드는 것도 아닌데, 한 번 해보는 것이 뭐 어떤가? 2019년 6월의 트럼프가 못한다 하더라도 미래의 그 누군가는 할 수 있을 것이고, 해야만 한다. 지금이 아니라도 언젠가는 반드시 이 분열의 아픔을 끝내야 한다고 믿는 것은 필자만의 지나치게 순진한 생각일까?

사우디 공격:
정확성과 정교함에 주목해야 한다*

2019년 9월 14일, 사우디아라비아 압카이크에 있는 국영 석유회사 아람코의 정유시설의 50%가 사우디의 방공망을 조롱하듯한 대담하고도 전문적인 공격으로 파괴되었다.

이번 공격은 모하메드 빈 살만(Mohammed bin Salman) 왕세자와 사우디 국방 관계자들에게 큰 충격을 안겨 주었다. 사우디 정부가 어떻게 맞대응해 나아갈지 아직 아무도 모르지만 그들이 독자적으로 행동할 가능성은 매우 낮다.

우리는 누가 이러한 공격을 자행하였는지 아직 확실히 알지 못한다. 하지만 결정적인 자료와 시각적인 증거들을 통해 배후에는 이란이 있음을 충분히 의심할 수 있다. 물론 오바마(Barack Obama) 전 행정부의 벤 로즈(Ben Rhodes)는 이번 공격이 예멘 후티 반군의 소행이라고 하며 이란과 선을 긋는 모습을 보이고 있지만 후티 반군이 이란 정부의 지원을 받고 있는 것은 잘 알려진 사실이다.

현재까지 나온 이야기들은 중동의 정치 역학을 중심으로 한 분석이 대부분으로, 그 분석들은 여전히 추측이나 추정에 불과하다. 오히려 주목해야 할 부분은 이번 공격의 성격이다.

우리가 현재 알고 있는 것은 이번 공격에 드론과 크루즈미사일이 동원되었다 것이다. 최소 17개 지점을 타겟으로 하였는데 특히 공격의 정확도와 정밀도를 눈여겨 보아야 한다. 2019년 9월 15일, 미국 정부와 디지털글로브가 제공한 사진을 보면 요구충격점(DMPI)이 믿을 수 없을 만큼 매우 정교하고 정확히 그 지점만 조준하였음을 확인할 수 있다.[8]

---

* 본고는 2019년 9월 23일 세르모국제연구소에 게재된 글 입니다.

예멘 반군이 과연 이러한 공격을 계획하고 실행할 만한 기술과 장비를 가지고 있는지 의심되는 부분도 바로 이 지점이다. 국가의 지원을 받고 있는 단체들만이 이처럼 정교한 공격을 설계하고 실행에 옮길 수 있다. 국가만이 이런 공격에 필요한 실시간 정보, 정밀 GPS 및 군사적 작전을 지휘하고 통제할 수 있는 C2(Command and Control) 능력을 가지고 있기 때문이다.

현재 사우디와 미국은 드론과 크루즈미사일 파편을 수거하여 정확한 공격 발사 지점을 분석하고 있다. 필자가 예멘 후티 반군의 소행이라는 주장에 동의하지 않는 또 다른 이유는 만약 미사일이 예멘에서 발사뇌었다면, 그 사성거리가 아람코의 정유 시설까지 절대 미치지 못하기 때문이다.

사우디 정부가 군사적 보복 대응을 고려하고 있을지 모르나, 미국의 암묵적인 승인 없이는 불가능할 것으로 보인다. 트럼프가 선뜻 이란을 공격하지 않는 이유는 지난 부시(George W. Bush) 대통령 때 이라크가 대량살상무기(WMD)를 가지고 있다는 잘못된 분석을 바탕으로 이라크 공격을 감행했던 전철을 밟지 않으려는 것으로 풀이된다.

사우디나 미국이 어떤 반응을 보이던지 결국에는 정치적인 결정이 될 것이다. 하지만 이번 사우디 공격에 대한 기술적인 평가는 그 어떠한 국내 혹은 국제정치에도 좌우되지 않는 중요한 팩트임에 틀림없다.

트럼프 탄핵의 진실게임:
답은 원출처^{primary source}에 있다*

'가짜 뉴스(fake news)'라는 용어는 그 자체로 이미 모순적이다. '가짜인 진실(뉴스)'은 존재하지 않는다. 가짜이거나 아니면 진실이거나 둘 중 하나다. 뉴스도 마찬가지다. 뉴스이거나 아니면 뉴스가 아니거나 둘 중 하나이다. 가짜와 뉴스라는 두 가지 단어를 마치 요즘 유행하는 것처럼 그저 대칭적으로 배열한다고 해서 그 용어가 합법적인 의미를 가지는 것은 아니다.

트럼프 대통령의 탄핵 조사를 둘러싸고 민주당과 공화당은 첨예하게 대립하고 있다. 여기에 언론까지 가세하며 미국은 지금 요란한 야단법석을 치루고 있다. 하지만 이러한 소동은 오히려 '가짜 뉴스'가 불러오는 파장을 되돌아 볼 수 있는 기회가 될 수도 있다.

최근 CNN 여론조사에 따르면, 트럼프 탄핵에 대한 찬성 여론이 더 우세한 것으로 나타나고 있다. 하지만 이 여론조사의 표본 집단을 살펴보면, 민주당원의 비율이 더 높은 것을 알 수 있다.[9] 마치 2016년 대선 여론조사와 데자뷰처럼 일치한다. 한국 언론들은 이러한 미국 언론들이 이야기하는 것들을 앵무새처럼 그대로 반복하고 있다. 문제는 미국 언론들이 현재 미국의 심장부에서 진짜 무슨 일이 일어나고 있는지 잘 모르고 있다는 것이다. 상황을 제대로 보지 못하는 미국 언론 매체들의 말을 그대로 받아 적기 때문에 한국 역시 지금 미국의 상황을 제대로 보지 못하는 악순환이 계속되는 것이다.

하지만 미국의 중심지에서 트럼프 재선 캠프는 3분기에만 무려 1억 2천 5백만 달러(한화 약 1,500억 원)를 후원금으로 모금하며 이전의 모금 기록들을 모

---

* 본고는 2019년 10월 7일, 세르모국제연구소에 게재된 글 입니다.

두 깨뜨렸다.[10]

도대체 왜 낸시 펠로시(Nancy Pelosi) 하원의장과 민주당은 서둘러 트럼프의 탄핵을 추진했을까? 빠르게 탄핵을 추진한 펠로시 의장은 탄핵 절차 승인을 위한 공식적인 하원 의원 투표조차 하지 않았다. 이러한 행위는 매우 정치적이고 당파적이다. 하원 의원의 투표 없이는 탄핵 조사를 위해 트럼프 대통령을 소환할 수도 없다.

펠로시와 민주당 그리고 미국 언론들이 근거로 삼았던 2차 자료들은 말 그대로 2차직인, 즉 부수적인 사료들일 뿐이다. 문제의 핵심을 제대로 보고 정확히 판단하기 위해서는 정보의 1차 출처(primary source)를 확인해 보아야 한다. 그렇다면 1차 출처들을 무엇일까? 바로 ① 2019년 7월 25일 트럼프 대통령과 우크라이나 젤렌스키(Volodymyr Zelensky) 대통령 간의 통화 녹취록,[11] ② 2019년 8월 12일 내부 고발자의 고발장,[12] ③ 2018년 바이든(Joe Biden) 전 미 부통령의 인터뷰 영상자료,[13] ④ 2019년 9월 4일 전 우크라이나 검찰총장 빅토르 쇼킨(Victor Shokin)의 진술서이다.[14]

먼저 트럼프와 젤렌스키 간의 통화 녹취록을 보면, 트럼프 대통령이 요구한 부탁이란 뮬러 수사가 어떻게 시작되었는지, 구체적으로 러시아가 민주당 전당대회를 해킹했을 때 사용했던 것으로 알려져 있는 크라우드스트라이크 서버에 대한 진상 규명에 대한 평이한 부탁이다. 민주당이 주장한 대가성 보상도 없었다. 우크라이나에 대한 군사적 지원을 유보한다는 위협도 없었다. 비밀스러운 거래도 없었다.[15]

내부고발자의 고발장에도 이상한 점은 한 두가지가 아니다. 첫째, 내부고발자는 자신이 대통령의 위법 행위에 대한 직접적인 목격자가 아님을 인정하고 있다. 문서 전반에 걸쳐 그/그녀는 언론 기사와 같은 대중에게 공개된 자료를 통하여 대통령의 위법행위를 알거나 듣게 되었다고 이야기하고 있다. 즉, 기밀문서나 자료를 직접 보고 알게 된 것이 아니라는 것이다. 둘째, 내부고발자는 '나는 모릅니다'라는 말을 6번이나 하고 있다. 셋째, 고발자는 트럼프 대통령이 트럼프-젤렌스키의 대화 녹취록을 별도의 잠금 장치에 넣었다고 주장하고 있다. 하지만 이는 2017년 백악관이 트럼프 대통령과 멕시코, 호주 대통령의 대화가 누출되었던 사건을 계기로 시행했던 관행이지 이번을 위해 갑자기, 특별히 만들어진 장치가 아니다. 마지막으로 고발장의 내용에도 잘못된 팩트가 상당수 포함되어 있는 것을 보아 '내부 고발자는 대통령의 통화를 직접 듣거나 혹은 그 녹취록을 직접 보지 못했다'는 사실을 확인할 수 있다. 한 가지 예로 고발장에는 "트럼프 대통령은 우크라이나 검찰총장 '유리 루센코(Yuriy Lutsenko)'를 칭찬하였다"고 나와있지만, 녹취록과 비교해보면 트럼프는 루센코가 아닌 쇼킨에 대해 이야기했음을 알 수 있다.[16]

조 바이든 전 부통령은 2018년 미국 외교위원회(CFR) 행사에서 청중들에게 2016년에 있었던 이야기를 다음과 같이 공개하였다. 발언 내용은 영상 자료를 통해서도 확인할 수 있다.

> "우크라이나에 가서 우리 팀을 설득한 기억이 난다 … (중략) 미국은 우크라이나에게 대출 보증을 해야 한다 … (중략) 10억 달러의 대출 보증을 하기로 되어 있지만 나는 당시 우크라이나 대통령이었던 페트로 포로센코와 당시 총리였던 야체뉴크에게 검찰총장인 쇼킨을 해임하지 않으면 대출 보증을 받을 수 없을 것이라고 했다. … (중략) 이 말을 듣고 그들은 기자회견장을 박차고 나가려고 했다. 하지만 나는 '10억 달러를 주지 않을 것이다'라고 이야기 했고 그들은 나에게 '대통령도 아닌데, 너에게는 권한이 없다' 라고 대꾸했다. 그래서 내가 다시 이야기 했다. '대통령한테 그럼 전화해봐라. 내가 말했듯이 너희는 10억 달러를 받을 수 없다. 나는 6시간 후에 우크라이나를 떠난다. 그 사이에 쇼킨이 해고되지 않으면 돈을 받을 수 없을 것이다'라고 말했다. 자, 그리고 그 망할 쇼킨이 결국 해고 되었다. 쇼킨의 자리에는 확실한 우리 편을 앉혔다."[17]

조 바이든이 발표한 발언에서는 그 어떠한 모호함이 없을 뿐만 아니라 해석이 어려운 애매모호한 단어들도 없다.

마지막으로 빅토르 쇼킨 전 우크라이나 검찰총장의 진술서를 한번 살펴보자.

"여러 차례에 걸쳐 포로센코(Petro Poroshenko) 대통령이 부리스마에 대한 형사 사건을 살펴보고 이 회사를 건들이지 말고 수사를 종결시킬 수 있는 방법을 고려해 달라고 요청하였습니다. 하지만 나는 이를 거부하였습니다. 이를 거부했기 때문에 나는 조 바이든 부통령과 미국 행정부의 직접적이고 강한 압력을 받으며 검찰총장의 자리에서 물러날 수 밖에 없었습니다. 당시 포로센코 대통령은 나에게 부리스마에 대한 조사를 중단해야 한다고 강조하였습니다. 그리고 내가 이를 거부하자, 포로센코는 미국이 바이든을 통해 약속한 10억 달러의 대출 보증을 중단하겠다며 압박하고 있나고 이야기 하였습니다. 그래서 나는 사퇴할 수 밖에 없었습니다."[18]

쇼킨은 계속해서 다음과 같이 이야기하였다.

"조 바이든은 내가 해임된 후 공개적으로 성명을 내면서까지 나를 해고했다고 자랑했습니다. 이를 통해 내가 해고된 진짜 이유가 부리스마와 부리스마의 사외이사였던 아들 헌터에 대한 바이든의 개인적인 이유 때문이라는 점이 분명해졌습니다. 이는 아래에서 좀 더 명확히 드러납니다.
a) 나 쇼킨이 그 자리에서 해고된 것은 포로센코의 결정이 아니라 바이든의 지시였고 소망이었습니다.
b) 그 이유는 정확히 미국 오바마 대통령의 행정부의 관리들 – 특히 조 바이든 – 은 우크라이나 사법부 윗선에게 조사 방법과 조사 대상을 직접 지시하고 간섭하고자 했으므로 나는 그 자리에서 없어져야만 했습니다.
c) 본 사안은 포로센코 대통령이 애국자임을 보여주는 것이 아닙니다. 바이든 부통령의 개인적 이익과 오바마 행정부의 정치, 경제적인 요구에 포로센코가 복종한 것입니다."[19]

쇼킨, 바이든, 트럼프, 내부 고발자 중 누군가는 거짓말을 하고 있다. 그리고 누가 거짓말을 하고 있는지는 우리가 스스로 판단해야 한다.

트럼프 탄핵론이 급물살을 타면서 오히려 국민과 언론들은 오바마 행정부와 우크라이나 정부 사이의 거래에 대해 더 깊이 들여다보게 되었다. 인터넷에서 확산되는 '가짜 뉴스'나 '음모'에 대한 호기심과 동조는 정보의 가장 기본 출처가 되는 1차 출처를 살펴보면 충분히 사라질 수 있다. 더 많은 정보가 반드시 더 나은 정보를 보장하지는 않는다. T.S. 엘리엇(T.S. Eliot)은 "정보 안에서 길을 잃는다면 지식은 어디에서 찾을 수 있는가?"라고 했다.

탄핵은 중대한 사안이다. 이것은 본질적으로 국민들이 직접 참여한 선거의 결과를 뒤집는 것이므로 매우 심각한 일이다. 2016년 트럼프를 당선시킨 국민의 뜻을 뒤집기 위해서는 법적, 정치적 기준을 모두 충족해야 한다.

탄핵은 신중하고 투명해야 하며 탄탄한 증거를 바탕으로 해야 한다. 참된 민주주의는 중우정치(mob rule)에 의해 지배되거나 유지될 수 없다. 많은 사람들이 원한다고 그것이 다 옳은 일은 아니다. 이성을 잃은 대중들의 외침과 요구는 민주주의라는 제도 안에서 냉정하고 철저한 심의를 통해 걸러져야 한다.

트럼프가 탄핵 된다면 앤드류 존슨(Andrew Johnson)과 빌 클린턴(Bill Clinton)처럼 역사 속에서 그의 명성에 오점을 남길 것이다. 만약 트럼프가 하원에서 탄핵 소추가 될지언정, 최종적으로 탄핵되지 않는다면 이 싸움에서 가장 큰 패배자는 민주당 뿐만 아니라 미 의회가 될 것이다.

상상하기 싫은 것도 상상해야 한다: 억제가 실패한다면*

"평화를 원한다면, 전쟁에 대비해라"
— 베게티우스(Vegetius) —

현재 북한에 대한 논쟁은 비핵화를 중심으로 진행된다. 대화를 하고 있는 상황은 칭찬할 만 하지만 비핵화의 내용과 맥락이 불안한 가정에 의존하고 있는 것이 문제다. 대부분의 사람들은 북한이 핵무기를 보유하는 목적이 체제 유지를 위해서라고 주장한다. 하지만 자기 자신과 자신의 체제를 보장하는 수단을 누가 과연 쉽게 포기하겠는가? 이러한 가정 하에서 비핵화는 사실상 불가능하다. 하지만 북핵의 목적이 북한의 국력을 키우는 것이라고 한다면 완전한 비핵화, 혹은 부분적 비핵화의 가능성은 작게나마 존재한다.

그러나 지금 진행되고 있는 비핵화에 대한 집착에서 벗어나, 한국을 둘러싼 안보의 기본을 전체적으로 한번 살펴보자. 전체적인 시각에서 조망해본다면 우리는 전쟁도 안보의 기본 안에 존재하고 있다는 것을 알게 된다. 우리는 지금 평화의 분위기에 도취되고 있지만 전쟁의 위험은 보이지 않게 언제나 우리 주변에 도사리고 있다. '북한과의 전쟁 가능성'이라는 상상하기 싫은 상황도 우리는 생각해야 한다. 물론 이런 생각이 어떤 사람들에게는 끔찍할 수도 있다. 많은 사람들이 전쟁을 생각하는 것 자체를 싫어한다. 그러나 한국의 국가안보정책에 대해 진지하게 고민해보고자 한다면 이러한 상상이 반드시 필요하다.

2017년 11월 29일, 북한이 발사한 대륙간탄도미사일(ICBM)이 고도 4,475km, 사거리 950km를 53분동안 비행한지 어느덧 2년이 다되어 간다. 표

---

* 본고는 2019년 11월 15일, Exclusive by 중앙일보 8호에 게재된 글 입니다.

준 궤도에 안착한 이 미사일은 추정 사거리는 8,100마일을 상회하는데 이는 뉴욕과 워싱턴 DC가 모두 북한의 탄도미사일 사정권 안에 들어갔음을 의미한다. 물론 대기권 재진입(re-entry) 기술에 대한 의구심은 여전히 존재하지만, 미국과 한국의 군사전문가들도 북한의 ICBM 프로그램이 완성 단계에 있음을 심각하게 받아들이고 있다. 이러면서 강경 매파들이 지금까지 주장하던 군사적 옵션이 훨씬 더 설득력을 얻게 되었다. 니키 헤일리(Nikki Haley) 당시 UN주재 미국대사는 "만약 전쟁이 일어난다면, 미국은 확실히 북한 체제를 철저하게 파괴할 것이다"라고 경고하였다.[20]

북한 문제에 대해서는 여러 가지 의견이 분분하지만, 한반도의 전쟁이 어떻게 시작될지에 대해서는 대체로 한 목소리를 낸다. 제1차 세계대전처럼 작은 사건이 빌미가 되어 한반도 전쟁으로 확대될 수 있기 때문에 북한을 자극하고 긴장감을 고조시켜 통제할 수 없는 상황이 오는 것을 막아야 한다는 것이다. 하지만 만약 군사적 옵션을 고려하고 있는 중이라면, 적대적 행위가 발발한 이후 전쟁을 어떻게 종결할 것인지 엄정하게 고려하는 것 역시 정책가와 분석가 모두에게 똑같이 필요하다. 핵무기가 존재하고 있는 현재의 상황에서 전쟁을 어떻게 종식시켜야 할지, 바로 지금 – 핵 억제력이 실패로 돌아가기 전에 – 우리는 심각하게 고민해야 한다. 모두가 전쟁의 시작에 대해 이야기하고 있지만, 정작 모든 정책이 실패로 돌아가 전쟁이 발발했을 때 그 이후에 어떻게 해야 할지에 대한 논의는 전무하다.

북한 문제를 바라보는 시각은 김정은에 대한 모순된 분석에 크게 좌우된다. 냉철한 살인자부터 정신 나간 젊은 날라리까지 김정은은 서로 상반된 평가를 받고 있다. 하지만 1948년 10월, CIA는 또 다른 한국인인 이승만 대통령에 대해서도 이렇게 부정확하고 모순적인 평가를 내렸다. CIA는 이승만 대통령을 "약하고, 비이성적이고, 유치하지만, 놀랄 만큼 빈틈이 없다"라고 평가하였다.[21] 어쩌면 지금 세계도 북한의 젊은 지도자를 이처럼 잘못된 바라보고 있는 것은 아닐까?

이렇게 모순된 평가는 북한에 대한 분석을 어렵게 하지만 다행인 것은 이것이 핵 억제력의 계산과 논리와는 상관이 없다는 것이다. 북한에 대한 정책은 다를 수 있지만, 핵 억제력의 논리는 정책과 별개다.
 비둘기파와 매파 모두 같은 가정에서 출발하고 있다. 그것은 '김정은이 예측불가능하고 비이성적이며 서울, 도쿄, 뉴욕을 상대로 핵무기를 사용할 만큼 미쳤기 때문에 그를 막을 수 없다'는 것이다.

분류	기본 전제	정책 논리	한계
비둘기파	김정은은 예측불가능해서 억제할 수 없다.	북한을 핵보유국으로 인정하고, 외교국가로 인정한다면, 김정은과 그 체제를 유화시킬 수 있으니 그 이후에 억제할 수 있을 것이다.	하지만 협상 이후, 다시 김정은이 예측 불가능하게 나온다면 그 때는 어떻게, 무엇을 가지고 억제할 수 있는 것인가?
매파	김정은은 비이성적이기 때문에 억제할 수 없다.	이성적인 판단을 하지 못하는 김정은을 제거해야만 전쟁을 억제할 수 있다.	김정은을 제거한 이후, 발발한 전쟁을 종식시킬 수 있는 권한자가 없으면 어떻게 할 것인가?

 김정은과 협상을 계속 하자고 주장하는 비둘기파들은 김정은의 예측불허성을 강조한다. 미국이 군사적 옵션을 고려하기에는 그 예상되는 피해가 너무나 끔찍하기 때문에 북한을 핵보유국으로 인정함으로써 군사적 적대행위를 피하고 지속적으로 협상을 해야 한다는 논리이다. '선 협상, 후 억제' 라는 기본 전제 아래, 미국과 국제사회가 북한의 핵무기와 핵 비축량을 인정한 후에만 북핵을 억제할 수 있다는 것이다.
 하지만 비둘기파의 이 주장은 2015년 오바마가 했던 이란과의 핵 협상에서 드러난 약점을 그대로 보여준다. '일시 중지'나 '축소'를 요구하는 모든 핵 협상 자체가 체제를 유화시키는 것을 전제로 하고 있다. 평화협정과 북한을 공식 외교국가로 인정해주는 것 만으로 김정은의 예측불허성이 과연 갑자기 사라질 수 있는 것일까? 북한이 핵무기를 보유했다는 자체로도 김정은을 억제하지 못하고 있는데, 협상 이후 김정은이 핵무기로 세계를 위협한다면 그 때는 어떻게 그를 억제할 수 있는 것인가?
 반대로 군사적 옵션을 주장하는 매파는 김정은의 '비이성적 측면'을 강조한다. 그들은 김정은의 광기를 저지할 수 없다고 본다. 매파들은 전쟁이 일어난 후 북한이 직접적인 피해를 본다면 김정은이 사태의 심각성을 깨닫고 이성을 되찾을 것이라 가정하지만 과연 그럴 수 있을까? 북한 내 정권교체를 희망하는 사람들은 이 시나리오에 편승한다. 이들은 김정은만 제거 된다면 북한은 합리적이고 이성적으로 변할 것이라고 믿는다. 하지만 여전히 딜레마는 있다. 만약 김정은이 제거된다 할지라도 북한 핵이 여전히 남아있는 상황에서 과연 매파가 기대하는 만큼 북한을 억제할 수 있을까?

김정은 그 자체를 억제할 수 있는가에 대한 의문은 지금 당장 해결할 수 없는 것이므로, 타협이 안 보이는 그 이슈에서 벗어나 우리는 억제력이 실패하여 만약 전쟁이 일어났을 경우를 가정하고 궁극적인 전략목표를 구상해야 한다. 만약 북한과 전쟁을 할 경우, 콜린 파월(Colin Powell)이 1차 걸프전에서 선언했던 것처럼 미국과 한·미·일 동맹국은 '뱀의 머리만' 제거하면 되는 것인가? 김정은 만 제거한다고 모든 것이 해결이 되는 것일까? 이미 언론에서도 보도된 바 있는 미국의 작전계획 5015(US Operations Plan 5015 - OPLAN 5015)와 한국의 킬체인 그리고 대량응징보복(KMPR) 구상은 북한의 지도층에 대한 참수공격(decapitation strikes), 즉 김정은을 제거하는 것을 제1차 목표로 하고 있다.

그러나 핵무기를 사용할 수도 있는 전쟁에서 전쟁을 시작할 수 있는 능력보다는 전쟁을 끝낼 수 있는 능력이 더 중요하다. 2017년 9월, 북한의 마지막 핵실험 위력은 140~250kt으로 추정한다.[22] 추정치는 다양하지만 북한이 적어도 증폭 설계장치 혹은 최소한 열핵 장치를 보유하고 있다는 것은 의심의 여지가 없다.

북한이 핵실험을 통해 폭발 능력을 과시하고 최근 ICBM 시험 발사를 성공한 이 시점에서 미국과 동맹국들이 김정은 혹은 북한 군대와 '가볼 때까지 끝까지 가보겠다'라고 위험을 감수하기는 이제 어려울 것이다. 끝까지 가보겠다는 것은 전쟁에 대한 공포를 거부하는 것이다. 하지만 이 공포는 전쟁을 종식시키는데 가장 중요한 요소로 특히 핵무기가 수반된 전쟁에서는 반드시 필요하다. 바로 이 공포가 바로 전쟁을 끝낼 수 있는 가장 큰 원동력이기 때문이다.

김정은을 제거하고자 하는 욕망은 정치적으로, 전략적으로 혹은 도덕적으로 매우 강할 것이다. 하지만 전쟁을 종식시키기 위해서는 그 전쟁을 끝낼 수 있는 힘과 권한을 가진 누군가와 반드시 협상해야만 한다. 만약 김정은이 제거된다면, 일어난 전쟁을 끝내기 위해서 우리는 누구와 협상을 해야 할까? 북한 인민들은 전쟁을 끝낼 수 없다. 김정은은 전쟁을 일으킬 위험요소인 동시에 전쟁을 끝낼 수 있는 권한자이기도 하다는 사실을 기억해야 한다.

이성적인 판단이 불가능한 전쟁의 소용돌이에서 명확함과 냉철함은 더 중요하다. 필자의 의견이 물론 비난을 받을 수는 있지만, 북한군이 완전히 제압된 상황에서 오히려 김정은의 생존을 보장하고 김정은 자신에게 전쟁을 종식할 수 있는 선택의 기회를 주는 것이 더 나을 수 있다. 필자는 김정은이 이런 패배를 감당할 능력이 있다고 본다. 하지만 만약 그가 전쟁을 종식시키지 않거나 그럴 의지가 보이지 않는다면, 북한 군부의 누군가가 김정은을 제거하고 그의 권한을 이어 받아 전쟁을 끝내는 수순으로 갈 수도 있다. 어떤 경우가 됐던 권한을 가진 사람만이 전쟁을 끝낼 수 있다. 핵무기가 사용될 수 있는 전쟁에서 대량 살상 이후 적대적 행위를 어떻게 종식시켜야 하는 지에 대한 논의는 현 시점의 한·미·일 안보전략계획에서 중요하게 다루어져야만 한다. 다시 한번 강조하건대 전쟁은 대부분 감정에 의해 시작되지만 언제나 이성에 의해서 종식된다.

너무나 끔찍해 상상하기 조차 싫은 것을 상상해야 하는 상황이 매우 불편할 수 있다. 하지만 필자는 반드시 필요하다고 본다. 비핵화는 칭찬할 만한 목표지만 정책이 될 수는 없다. 로마 장군의 말처럼 우리가 진정한 평화를 원한다면 전쟁을 대비해야 한다.

전쟁을 계획한다고 당장 국가가 전쟁을 일으키는 것이 아니다. 전쟁을 계획한다고 평화가 가져오는 행복을 무너뜨리는 것이 아니다. 오히려 전쟁을 계획하는 것은 평화에 대한 기대를 높이는 것이다. 왜냐하면 계획을 수립한다는 자체가 전쟁을 억제할 수 있기 때문이다. 그리고 한국의 정책가들이 만약 억제가 실패로 돌아가 전쟁이 발생할 경우에 전쟁을 종결시킬 수 있는 방안에 대해 미리 생각해 볼 수 있기 때문이다. 언젠가 전쟁이 발생했을 때 끔찍한 대량 살상과 손 쓸 수 없는 혼란을 겪는 것 보다는 지금 상상하기 싫은 것을 상상하는 것이 더 낫다. 이것이 현재를 살고 있는 우리가 미래를 위해 가져야 할 도덕적인 의무이다.

트럼프 2020:
Part 1. 2016년 대선으로부터 얻을 수 있는 교훈들*

> *"아, 이런 또야"*
> – 요기 베라(Yogi Berra) –[23]

2020년 11월 3일 미국 대선을 1년여 앞 둔 지금(2019년 11월 27일 기준), 민주당과 언론, 선거전문가들은 2015년과 2016년 그들이 했던 실수를 되풀이하며 여전히 도널드 트럼프 대통령을 과소평가하고 있다.

여론 조사, 각종 보도, 여러 진술이 계속되면서 정보와 사실, 데이터가 눈덩이처럼 불어나고 있지만 결국 그 모든 것들은 트럼프 대통령이 재선에 실패하리라는 것을 가리키고 있다. 트럼프를 반대하거나 과소평가하는 사람들은 이를 그대로 믿고 싶을 것이다. 하지만 적어도 선거 전문가들과 오피니언 리더라는 사람들은 현실을 제대로 보기 위해서 일하는 사람들이다. 최소한 그들은 지금 현 상황을 보고 싶은 대로가 아니라 있는 그대로 봐야 하는 의무가 있다.

트럼프에 대한 무조건적인 증오와 경멸은 이성적인 판단을 어렵게 한다. 2016년 대선 당시 사람들이 저질렀던 실수는 요기 베라가 "아, 이런 또야"라고 외칠 만큼 2020년 대선에도 그대로 반복되고 있다.

민주당과 공화당의 기성 정치인들이 보여주었던 구태의연한 태도에 대한 미국민의 분노와 원망이 트럼프를 대통령으로 당선시켰다. 정치 비평가들은 트럼프가 국민의 분노를 자극하고 미국을 분열시켜 포퓰리즘을 일으킨 원인이라고 비판한다. 하지만 이미 국민들의 분노는 트럼프 등장 이전부터 자리하고 있었다. 트럼프와 트럼피즘은 포퓰리즘의 원인이 아니라, 포퓰리즘의 한 증상

---

* 본고는 2019년 11월 27일, Exclusive by 중앙일보 9호에 게재된 글 입니다.

인 것이다.

　미국민의 분노와 원망은 2008년 9월 15일 리먼 브라더스의 파산이 불러온 경제 위기에서 시작된, 10년 이상 축적된 뿌리 깊은 것이다. 미국발 글로벌 경제위기가 가속되면서 헨리 폴슨(Henry Paulson) 당시 재무부 장관은 7,000억 달러 규모의 부실자산구제프로그램(TARP)을 내놓았다. 국민의 세금으로 이루어진 공적 자금으로 대형 은행을 구제하는 것이 프로그램의 주요 골자였는데, 2011년 제임스 펠커슨(James Felkerson)은 실제 투입된 구제금융 자금이 약 29조 달러에 달한다고 추산하였다.[24]

　동네의 작은 꽃집도 언제나 파산의 위기를 안고 있다. 하지만 과연 그들이 이런 구제프로그램의 혜택을 받을 수 있었을까? 미국 경제의 국유화라고 불러도 될만한 부실자산구제프로그램의 혜택은 오직 대형은행에게만 돌아갔다. 정부는 대형은행들이 파산하도록 그냥 두기에는 그 규모가 너무 크다고 주장했다. 매년 그 은행들이 정치권에 후원하는 후원금도 무시하지 못할 정도로 너무 거대했다. 무엇보다 관련 전문가들은 월 스트리트가 미국 국가 경쟁력의 핵심 원동력이므로 그대로 둘 수 없다면서 대형은행을 구제해야 한다고 앞장섰다.

　하지만 당시 정부와 전문가들은 모두 틀렸다. 월 스트리트가 정부로부터 구제를 받고 있는 동안, 거리에 방치되어 있는 수많은 일반 시민들이 머리를 긁적이며 "그럼 우리들은?"이라고 의문을 제기했다. 하지만 아무도 그들의 구슬픈 외침에는 대답하지 않았다. 대통령도, 의회도, 언론도, 지식인도 그들의 질문에는 답하지 않았다. 언론은 부실자산구제프로그램을 마련한 폴슨 장관의 선견지명에는 찬사를 보냈지만, 길가에서 생계를 위해 애쓰고 있는 일반 국민들의 목소리에 귀기울이지는 않았다. 그들을 대변해 줄 사람은 아무도 없었다. 아무도.

　이런 상황은 7년이 지난 2015년, 뉴욕의 부동산 업계에서 성공가도를 달린 퀸즈 출신의 억만장자 도널드 트럼프가 대통령 후보로 출사표를 던질 때까지 계속 되었다.

　트럼프는 과잉(excess)의 전형이다. 그는 상류층인 척 하거나 억지로 예의 바른 척 하지 않는다. 그는 닳고 닳은 정치가가 아니다. 그는 다듬어 지지 않았고 거칠다. 그는 아주 쉬운 언어를 사용하여 반복해서 이야기하고 과장해서 말한다.

이것이 바로 미국 국민들, 즉 스스로 잊혀진 사람들이라고 생각하던 사람들이 기다리고 있었던 바로 '그 것'이다. 2016년 트럼프와 유권자들 사이의 이러한 유대감은 여전히 강하게 남아있는데, 트럼프를 반대하는 많은 사람들은 2016년 대선의 교훈을 벌써 잊은 것 같다.

2016년 거의 모든 사람이 왜 대선 결과를 잘못 예측했는지 그 정황과 역학관세, 내용을 다시 한번 우리는 살펴보아야 한다. 그래야만 똑같은 우를 범하지 않고 지금 현 실상을 제대로 보며 2020년 대선 결과를 올바로 관측할 수 있기 때문이다.

1. 첫번째 교훈: 계층적 갈등과 잊혀진 사람들

2016년 선거는 미국 포퓰리즘 계층이 승리한 첫 번째 선거였다. 보다 정확하게 말하자면, 포퓰리즘이 자신이 속한 계층에 대해 우월감을 가지는 속물주의를 이긴 선거였다. 생색내는 것을 좋아하는 오만한 계층과 평범하고 잊혀진 사람들과의 대결에서 포퓰리즘이 계층적 우월주의를 이긴 것이다.

트럼프는 2016년 7월 공화당 대선 후보 지명 연설에서 노동 계층을 거론하며 "미국에서 잊혀진 사람들 - 열심히 일하지만, 더 이상 목소리를 낼 수 없는 사람들 - 내가 바로 여러분의 목소리이다"[25]라면서 그들을 대변하겠다고 선언하였다. 잊혀진 사람들이란 퇴역한 군인, 경찰, 군인, 소방관, 구급대원, 정비원, 농부, 트럭운전사, 공장노동자, 청소부, 가정부, 석탄 광부 등 미국의 근대화와 산업화를 위해 헌신했지만 제대로 인정받지 못한 사람들을 의미한다.

2016년 트럼프의 승리는 동·서부 해안가에 살면서 자신들만의 세계를 구축하던 해안 엘리트들의 자만과 그러한 자만이 불러온 정책의 실패 그리고 엘리트들에게 분노한 수 백만 노동자 계층의 집결이 만들어 낸 결과였다.

2. 두번째 교훈: 트럼피즘(Trumpism)

트럼프주의는 反엘리트, 反체제 운동이며, 거대한 세계화에 반대하는 운동이다. 글로벌 자본주의는 막대한 이익을 가져다 준다. 하지만 모든 사람이 동일한 혜택을 받을 수 없다는 데 그 허점이 있다. 글로벌 자본주의는 마치 소금과도 같다. 소금은 어떤가? 모든 음식에 반드시 필요하고 소금 없이는 맛을 낼 수 없지만 너무 많이 먹으면 건강을 해친다.

글로벌 자본주의가 극단으로 치우칠수록 타인에 대한 공감과 배려, 공공선(善)에 대한 추구는 무시된다. 그리고 이러한 현상을 인해 사람들이 겪는 아픔과 분노를 건드려 영리하게 이용하는 정치인이 선거에서 승리한다.

트럼프는 전 미 하원의장이었던 팁 오닐(Tip O'Neill)이 말했던 "모든 정치는 지역적이다"라는 말을 직감적으로 이해했던 것 같다.[26] 트럼프와 그의 선거운동본부는 특정 카운티를 목표로 삼았다. 잊혀진 사람들의 상처 입은 자존심은 정부가 나눠주는 유인물 몇 개가 아니라 좋은 일자리를 통해서 가장 잘 치유될 수 있다고 생각했다. 트럼프가 교황 레오 13세(Pope Leo XIII)의 『레룸 노바룸(Rerum Novarum)』을 직접 읽어본 적은 없겠지만, 이미 1891년 노동 보호를 위해 자본주의가 가져야 할 의무에 대해 이야기했던 레오 13세의 견해를 누구보다 잘 이해하고 있었다. 그는 글로벌 자본주의라는 거대한 그림자 뒤에 가려진 사람들의 고통에 관심을 갖고 보살펴주는 것, 이 것이 대선 승리를 위한 중요한 열쇠가 될 것이라 판단하였다.

J.D. 밴스(J.D. Vance)는 그의 책인 『힐빌리의 노래(Hillbilly Elegy)』에서 트럼피즘의 등장을 예견하였다. 트럼프가 호소하는 잊혀진 사람들의 슬픔과 고통은 누구에게나 깊은 울림을 줄 수 밖에 없을 것이다. 밴스는 그의 책에서 미 동부와 서부의 최고 엘리트들이 보여주는 미국 중산층에 대한 무시와 차별을 신랄하게 묘사하였다. 힐빌리는 미국의 남동부 산악 지대에 살던 '촌뜨기'를 뜻하는 말로 밴스 자신이 바로 이런 촌뜨기 출신이었다. 책에서 밴스는 예일대 로스쿨 재학 시절, 다른 학생들이 자신의 보잘 것 없는 배경을 무시하면서 자신을 마치 2등 시민처럼 느끼게 했던 일을 씁쓸하게 떠올렸다.[27]

아버지에게 버림받고 약물중독인 어머니의 보살핌도 받지 못했던 밴스는 좋은 직업이나 사회적인 지위를 가질 수 있는 기회가 거의 없는 오하이오 주의 한 시골 마을에서 할머니 손에 자랐다. 그는 백인이고, 중-하류층이었으며, 인종 차별을 하거나 이민자들과 함께 일했던 경험도 없었다.

미국 중서부 공업지대에 주로 거주하던 노동자들은 미 산업 발전에 지대한 역할을 했음에도 불구하고 그 동안 공정한 대우를 받지 못하고 있었다. 소위 '해안가 엘리트'라고 불리던 백인 엘리트계층이 백인 노동자 계층을 무시해오면서, 백인이 같은 백인을 무시하는 모순적인 상황이 지난 수십 년간 계속 되었다. 하지만 백인 엘리트와 백인 노동자 간의 문화적 경제적 분열은 대부분 무시되었다. 밴스가 『힐빌리의 노래』라는 책으로 소외되었던 그들의 목소리를 처음 대변하기 시작하였고 이제 트럼프가 그들을 직극직으로 끌어 안게 된 것이다.

거의 대부분의 언론과 전문가들이 이 현상을 제대로 보려 하지 않았지만 예외도 있었다. 뉴욕 포스트의 프리랜서 기자인 살레나 지토(Salena Zito)와 같은 사람이다. 그녀는 많은 미국인들이 방치되고 잊혀진 느낌을 받고 있으며 오히려 트럼프처럼 이해관계로부터 아웃사이더 억만장자가 그들의 이익을 대변해 줄 것이라 여기고 있는 사실을 서술하며, 주요 언론들이 거의 다루지 않은 트럼프의 장외집회 규모와 열기에 대해 보도하였다.[28]

한발 더 나아가 2016년 대선 당시 트럼프가 불러온 현상을 좀 더 자세히 들여다 보았다. SNS를 통해 본 트럼프의 장외집회 현장에서 트럼프가 하는 말들은 곧 밴스의 고통과 같았다. 그리고 그 집회에 참석한 사람들의 구성을 살펴보았다. 백인들, 흑인들, 히스패닉들, 아시아인들… 보고도 믿을 수가 없었다. 그곳에는 오바마가 폄하했던 총에 목숨 거는 백인 인종주의자들만 있는 것이 아니었다. 그곳에는 힐러리가 무시했던 한심하고 무식한 백인 노동자들만 있는 것이 아니었다. 그리고 무엇보다 필자는 집회 참석자들의 놀라운 열정을 보았다. 트럼프의 연설을 보기 위해 어떤 사람은 300마일을 운전해서 오고 비가 오는 밖에서 8시간이나 기다렸다고 한다. 만약 그들이 트럼프를 뽑을 생각이 없었다면 이렇게 하지도 않았을 것이다.

필자는 이들 사이에서 확산되는 트럼프의 메시지를 좀 더 깊이 살펴보았다. 대부분의 미국인들은 건강보험을 원하고 있고 더 많은 보험 보장을 받기 위해서라면 기꺼이 더 높은 비용을 지불할 것이라 생각했다. 하지만 오바마케어의 가장 치명적인 단점은 바로 그 시행 절차였다.

물론 그 누구도 오바마케어의 비싼 보험료를 좋아하지 않았지만, 미국인들이 정말 싫어하고 두려워하는 대상은 보험료를 징수하고 집행을 담당하는 국세청(IRS)이었다. 알려진 바와 같이 미국 대법원은 오바마케어의 건강보험이 '세금'이라는 판결을 내렸다.

세금은 비자발적으로 납부하는 것이다. 세금을 제 때 내지 못하면 국세청으로부터 조사를 받게 된다. 국세청은 미국인들이 가장 증오하는 정부기관으로, 세금으로 구분된 건강 보험은 이제 제 때 납부하지 못하면 처벌을 받게 되는 요소가 된 것이다.

여기서 잠깐 트럼프에 향한 지지를 설명하기 위해서 실력(성공)에 대한 미국인들의 믿음을 먼저 언급하고자 한다. 미국인들은 실력을 찬양하고 성공한 사람들은 winner(승자)라고 기꺼이 부른다. 특히 자수성가한 사람들에 대해서 미국인들은 성공한 사람의 실력과 결과에 도덕적 잣대를 들이대며 공격할 거리를 찾으려 하지 않는다.

예를 하나 들자면 뉴욕 맨하탄에는 많은 노숙자들이 있고 그들 중 일부는 5번가와 57번가 사이의 트럼프 타워 앞에서 노숙을 한다. 그들에게 누군가 "당신은 트럼프를 증오하나요?"라고 질문 한다면, 그들은 이렇게 대답할 것이다. "아니요. 저는 트럼프처럼 부자가 되고 싶습니다. 분명 트럼프는 지금의 억만장자가 되기 위해 정말 열심히 일했을 겁니다" 자신들은 가질 수 없는 부와 명예를 가지고 있다고 트럼프를 미워하고 질투하기 보다, 노숙자들은 트럼프처럼 되길 원하고 있고, 언젠가 그들도 트럼프처럼 성공하기를 바라고 있는 것이다.

요즘 대부분의 미국인들에게 있어 아메리칸 드림이란 노력과 실력에 의한 성공을 원하는 미국인들을 위한 것이 아니라, 정식 이민 시스템에서 벗어나 불법으로 미국에 정착한 사람들을 위한 구호일 뿐이라는 인식이 팽배하다. 미국인들은 새치기 하는 사람들을 굉장히 싫어한다. 미국인들에게 아메리칸 드림을 외치는 불법 이민자들은 새치기를 하는 사람과 다를 바 없고, 결국 이는 미국인들 사고에 깊숙이 뿌리 박힌 'fair play(정정당당한 승부)' 인식에 반하는 것이다.

특히나 미국의 노동 계층들은 이러한 불공정한 규정들에 대해 매우 분노하고 있었다. 사실, 흑인들은 불법 이민자들의 값싼 임금으로 인해 미국 내 일자리를 점점 잃어가며 누구보다 가장 큰 피해를 보고 있었다. 민주당은 이런 흑인들의 투표권이 자신들에게 올 것이라고 계산했지만 이는 대단히 오만하고 게으른 생각이었다. 민주당은 완전히 틀렸다.

당시 언론은 트럼프의 강경한 反이민정책으로 히스패닉계 지지층이 대거 이탈했다고 연일 보도했다. 하지만 사실 트럼프가 주장한 것은 反불법이민정책이었다. 합법적으로 미국에 이민 온 히스패닉계 미국인들은 민주당이 아닌 드림프를 지지하였고 오직 최근 미국에 들어온 불법 이민자들이 트럼프를 반대했다. 하지만 이들 중 상당수는 투표 등록을 하지 않았거나 정식 미국인이 아니므로 투표권 자체가 없기 때문에 정작 그들의 영향력은 미비할 수 밖에 없었다.

3. 세번째 교훈: 문화적 분열

트럼피즘을 이해하는 데 걸림돌로 남아 있는 요인 중 하나가 아이러니하게도 트럼프의 높은 인기를 설명해 줄 가장 큰 요인이 된다. 바로 트럼프 지지자들과 반대자들 사이의 사회 · 문화적 격차이다.

대부분의 학자들과 언론인들은 대체로 진보와 민주당에 편향되어 있다. 비록 원래 시골 출신이라고 할지라도 유수의 대학과 대학원을 졸업하고 대도시나 좋은 직장에 취업하여 점점 성공의 사다리를 오르게 되면서 어느새 정체성의 정치와 사회적 평등을 믿는 진보주의자로 변모하게 된다.

이들은 자신들의 국제적이고 세련된 세계관을 반대하는 사람들을 촌스럽고 인종차별주의적이라고 힐난한다. 이들에게 트럼프에 대해 질문을 한다면 대부분은 "정상적인 사람이라면 어떻게 트럼프를 좋아할 수 있나요?"라고 대답한다. 이러한 엘리트들은 미국 서부와 동부의 해안도시에 주로 거주하며 그들끼리 만의 견고한 네트워크를 구축한다. 그들에게 미국 중부 지역은 미국이 아니다. 그들이 살고 있는 동부와 서부 대도시 이외의 지역은 '갈 일도 없고, 갈 필요도 없는 곳'으로 생각하기 때문이다.

4. 네번째 교훈: 트럼프라는 개인의 매력

확실하게, 아마도, 어쩌면 트럼프의 당선에 가장 결정적인 요인은 트럼프 그 자신일 것이다.

트럼프는 뉴욕 출신의 억만장자다. 그는 맨해튼에 아파트를 가지고 있지만 뉴욕 시 외곽 자치구인 퀸즈에서 자랐다. 브롱크스, 브룩클린, 스테이튼 아일랜드, 퀸즈는 뉴욕의 대표적인 외곽지역으로 기본적으로 사람들이 거칠고 공격적인 성향을 가지고 있다. 트럼프는 수많은 글로벌 비즈니스의 경험에도 불구하고 여전히 퀸즈에서 자란 소년처럼 보인다.

뉴욕 외곽지역 사람들은 말을 할 때 자신들의 발언을 강조하기 위해 과장하는 경향이 있다. 예를 들어, 만약 기다리고 있는 버스가 조금 늦게 도착했다면 뉴욕 외곽지역 사람들은 "왜 여기 오는데 400년이나 걸린거야?"라며 운전기사를 놀린다. 무엇을 칭찬할 때도 마찬가지다. "이것은 그냥 맛있는 햄버거가 아니라, 세계 어느 곳에도 없는 최고의 햄버거야!"라고 과장한다.

트럼프가 말하고 표현하는 방식은 뉴욕 출신이라면 단번에 알아 볼 수 있는 뉴욕의 변두리, 퀸즈 특유의 성향을 보여주고 있다. 말하는 형식을 통해 자기를 어떻게 홍보하는지를 알 수 있다. 트럼프는 본인의 주장을 과장하거나 과시한다. 그의 이야기는 허풍과 자칫 모욕을 줄 수 있는 내용으로 가득 차 있다.

트럼프는 닮고 닮은 정치인들처럼 애매모호하고 조심스럽고 계산된 어투로 말하고 대화하지 않는다. 아마도 그는 그렇게 얘기할 수 없을 것이다. 그는 다채로운 언어를 사용하고 중요한 점을 강조하기 위해 반복적으로 말하며 종종 이전의 단어와 문단을 바꾸어 더 강조해서 말하기도 한다. 트럼프는 다른 정치인들처럼 매끄럽게 다듬어진 사람이 아니다. 이러한 자질 때문에 오히려 그의 지지자들은 트럼프가 신선하고 정겹다고 생각하고 특히 언론이 그를 비난하는 것에 대해 혐오감을 느낀다.

살레나 지토는 "언론은 트럼프의 말을 말 그대로 받아들이고 진지하게 받아들이지 않았다. 하지만 그의 지지자는 말 그대로 받아들이지 않고 오히려 훨씬 더 진지하게 받아들였다"라고 중요한 지적을 하였다.[29]

오늘날까지 많은 사람들은 "나는 정말 트럼프를 이해할 수 없다"라고 말한다. 하지만 진정으로 트럼프를 이해하기 위해서는 그의 말투, 억양, 퀸즈라는 뉴욕 변두리에서 자란 그의 배경과 그를 지지하고 있는 잊혀진 사람들의 사회, 경제, 문화적 상황을 총체적으로 이해해야 한다.

물론 이러한 관찰이 그저 재미있는 이야깃거리에 불과하다고 일축하는 사람도 있을 것이다. 대부분의 사람들이 그렇다. 하지만 미국정치학자인 레이몬드 울핑거(Raymond Wolfinger)는 데이터, 통계, 수치에만 의존하는 분석을 냉소적으로 비판하며 다수의 사람들이 많이 주고 받는 이야깃거리라면 충분히 데이터가 될 수 있다고 말했다. 2016년 대선 당시 수치만 이야기하는 사람들은 틀렸지만 사람들의 이야기를 통해 얻은 데이터와 분석은 정확히 들어 맞았다. 여러 가지 이야기들이 숫자로 확인이 되면 우리는 그것을 fact(사실)라고 부른다.

추측과 뻔한 이야기, 피상적인 관찰은 이제 덮자. 진지하게 정치를 분석하고자 한다면 사실과 증거가 반드시 필요하다. 작가 크리스토퍼 히친스(Christopher Hitchens)가 했던 "증거 없이 증명할 수 있다면, 증거 없이도 부정할 수 있다"라는 말처럼 사실과 증거는 중요하다.[30]

트럼프의 낙선을 예측했던 언론과 전문가들은 여론조사 같은 수치 게임에만 집중한 채, 진짜 사실이자 증거인 사람들과 그 사람들이 하는 이야기들을 무시했다. 그들은 글로벌 자본주의와 주류 사회를 이끄는 엘리트주의 뒤에서 잊혀진 채 신음하던 미국인들의 목소리를 듣지 못하였다. 트럼프를 지지하는 사람들과 반대하는 사람들 사이의 문화적·경제적 분열을 보지 못하였다. 그리고 잊혀진 미국인들을 사로잡을 수 밖에 없었던 트럼프 개인의 특징들을 파악하지 못하였다.

앞으로의 대선을 예측하기 위해서는 2016년 대부분의 사람들이 무엇을 놓쳤는지 다시금 살펴보아야 한다. 그것은 교훈이 되어 지금까지도 여전히 유효하며, 우리에게 많은 것을 시사하고 있기 때문이다.

트럼프 2020:
Part 2. 2020 대선으로 가는 길*

Part 1에서 살펴 본 것처럼 2016년 대선에서 얻은 교훈은 2020년 대선에서도 유효하다. 거기에 대통령으로서 트럼프가 여러 방면에서 이루어 낸 성과들이 덧붙여진다. 만약 대통령 선거에서 경제 분야가 제일 중요한 부분이라면 우리는 다음의 자료를 잘 살펴 보아야 한다.

경제적 성과

부시 대통령의 평균 중위소득은 8년 간 400달러 증가에 그쳤고, 오바마가 집권한 8년 동안에는 약 975달러가 올랐다. 트럼프가 대통령으로 취임한 이후, 불과 2년 반 남짓한 기간 동안 무려 5,000달러가 증가했다.[31] 물론 트럼프를 싫어할 수는 있다. 하지만 그렇다고 해서 이런 경제적 수치들을 무시해서는 안 된다.

2019년 1월 집계된 가용 일자리 수는 760만개로, 이는 실업자수보다 약 100만개 더 많은 수치이다.[32] 미국 역사 상 실업자 수보다 가용 일자리수가 더 많았던 적은 유례를 찾기가 힘들다. 2018년 미국에서는 약 1억 5천 5백만 명의 사람들이 직업을 가지고 있었고, 2019년에는 그보다 약 2만명 더 늘어날 예정이다.[33] 또한 2018년 9월, 미국 실업급여 신청건수는 약 203,000건으로, 1969년 12월 6일 이래 최저치를 기록하였다.[34] 동 월 실업률은 49년 만에 최저치인 3.6%를 기록했는데, 이는 2년 전 오바마 정부에서 자랑하던 4.9%보다도 훨씬 더 낮은 수치이다.[35] 흑인, 히스패닉계, 아시아인들 모두 역대 최저 실업률을 기록했다.

---

* 본고는 2019년 12월 6일, Exclusive by 중앙일보 10호에 게재된 글 입니다.

뿐만 아니라 소득지표를 살펴보면 2017년 미국의 가계중위소득은 61,372달러로 역대 최고치를 경신하였다. 2018년 9월, 시간당 임금은 27.24달러를 기록해 2016년 10월 시간당 임금인 25.88달러보다 5% 상승하였다. 2019년 6월, 미국의 평균 가구의 순자산은 97,300달러로, 전체 미국인의 순자산은 사상 최대인 100조 달러를 기록했다. 기업 법인세는 35%에서 21%로 인하되었고, 스탠더드앤드푸어스(S&P) 500지수는 트럼프가 취임한 이후 600여일 동안 약 32% 상승했다.[36] 경제상황의 뚜렷한 회복세와 더불어 미국은 75년 만에 처음으로 석유 순수출국이 되어 현재 세계 최대의 원유 생산국이 되었다.[37]

이는 어떠한 정치인들도 인정할 수 밖에 없는 놀라운 경제적 성과들이다.

대선의 향방을 가늠할 주요 카운티와 州의 동향

위스콘신, 아이오와, 오하이오, 펜실베니아, 미시건, 인디애나 주는 2020년 미 대선에서 주요 격전지가 될 것이고, 이 주들 가운데 일부 카운티들이 특히 대선의 향방을 좌우할 주요 지역이 될 것이다.

1) 위스콘신:

2019년 11월 20일, 위스콘신 마르케트 법학대학원 여론조사는 위스콘신의 유권자들을 대상으로 트럼프 대통령과 민주당 내 주요 대선주자들과의 가상 대결을 진행하였다.[38]

트럼프: 47% vs 바이든: 44%
트럼프: 48% vs 샌더스: 45%
트럼프: 48% vs 워렌: 43%
트럼프: 47% vs 부티지지: 39%

4명의 민주당 후보들과의 대결에서 트럼프가 모두 3~8% 차이로 앞서는 것을 확인할 수 있다.

2) 아이오와: 2012년 미 대선에서 버락 오바마는 아이오와 주의 리(Lee) 카운티에서 공화당의 미트 롬니 후보를 상대로 2배가 넘는 압도적인 표를 얻어,

대통령 당선 가능성을 한층 높였다. 2016년 대선에서 이곳은 트럼프의 우세를 보여주었고, 2020년에도 여전히 리 카운티는 트럼프의 우세를 보여줄 것으로 예상한다.

3) 오하이오: 오하이오 주는 대선의 향방을 가늠할 수 있는 가장 중요한 풍향계이다. 특히 클락(Clark) 카운티가 매우 중요하다. 1860년 링컨 대통령(Abraham Lincoln) 당선부터 지금까지 그로버 클리브랜드(Grover Cleveland)와 존 F 케네디(John F. Kennedy) 단 2명을 빼고는, 오하이오주에서 승리한 후보들은 모두 대통령에 당선되었다.

4) 펜실베니아: 루체른(Luzerne) 카운티와 체스터(Chester) 카운티가 핵심이다.

5) 미시간: 매콤(Macomb) 카운티를 주목해야 한다.

6) 인디애나: 비고(Vigo) 카운티가 중요하다.

필자는 트럼프가 앞서 살펴본 이 카운티들에서 승리할 것이라 예상하고 있다.

탄핵

혹자는 트럼프가 탄핵 때문에 2020년 대선에서 낙선할 것이라고 주장한다. 물론 탄핵이 민주당의 주장대로 진행될 수도 있겠지만 탄핵 때문에 트럼프가 재선에 실패하지는 않을 것이다.

2019년 7월 25일	트럼프와 볼로디미르 젤렌스키 대통령 통화
2019년 7월 26일	커트 볼커와 빌 테일러, 젤렌스키 대통령 회동
2019년 8월 27일	존 볼튼과 젤렌스키 대통령 회동
2019년 9월 1일	펜스 부통령과 젤렌스키 대통령 회동
2019년 9월 5일	상원의원 론 존스(공화당)과 크리스 머피(민주당), 젤렌스키 대통령 회동

보시다시피 2주 동안 5번의 회의가 있었다.[39] 그리고 그 회의 내내 군사 원조와 정치적인 수사를 연결시키는 직접적 언급은 단 한번도 없었다. 모든 언론에서 일제히 떠들고 있는 *quid pro quo*는 원래 '대가성'을 뜻하는 라틴어이다. 하지만 2019년 11월 14일, 바딤 프리스타이코(Vadym Prystaiko) 우크라이나 외무장관은 "나는 바이든 전 부통령의 수사와 군사원조에 대한 직접적인 연관을 보지 못했다"고 증언했다.[40] 현지시간으로 12월 2일, 젤렌스키 대통령 역시 타임지와의 인터뷰에서 "트럼프 대통령과 대가를 주고 받는 입장에서 말한 적이 없다 … (중략) 나는 우리가 구걸하는 것처럼 보이는 것을 원하지 않는다 … (중략) 이것은 정당성에 대한 것이지 대가성에 대한 것이 아니다" 라고 명확히 밝혔다.[41]

*Quid pro quo*를 가장 잘 설명할 수 있는 실제 예를 보고 싶은가? 2012년 3월 핵안보정상회의에서 오바바는 러시아 메드베데프(Dmitry Medvedev) 대통령에게 폴란드에 배치하려 했던 미국의 미사일방어체제(MD)를 검토 할테니, 재선에 성공할 수 있도록 자신에 대한 비난을 중단해 달라고 부탁하였다.

> 오바마: "이번이 나의 마지막 선거이다. … 당선된 이후에 좀 더 유연성을 가질 수 있을 것이다."
> 메드베데프: "이야기를 블라디미르 푸틴(Vladimir Putin)에게 전달하겠다."[42]

오바마가 개인의 이익과 정치적 승리를 위해 다른 외국 정부에게 부탁한 것을 두고 그를 탄핵해야 한다고 주장한 사람은 그 어디에도 없다.

마찬가지로 대통령 특사였던 루돌프 줄리아니(Rudolf Giuliani)가 문제라는 주장하는 쪽도 있다. 이러한 주장을 하는 사람들은 역사책을 먼저 읽어보길 바란다. 특사는 미국의 초기 대통령 시절부터 있었다. 초대 대통령인 조지 워싱턴(George Washington)은 영국과 프랑스 양국 간 전쟁 해결을 위해 존 제이(John Jay)를 본인을 대신하는 특사자격으로 파견하여 양국 관계 개선을 도모하였다. 이는 당시 국무부 장관이었던 토마스 제퍼슨(Thomas Jefferson)의 질투를 불러 일으켰다. 프랭클린 루즈벨트(Franklin Roosevelt)는 해리 홉킨스

(Harry Hopkins)를 백악관에 머물게 하며, 특사자격으로 윈스턴 처칠(Winston Churchill)과 함께 무기대여법과 조셉 스탈린의 전후 처리를 협의토록 하였다. 당시 코델 헐(Cordell Hull) 국무장관과는 상의하지도 않았다. 루돌프 줄리아니를 문제 삼는 사람들의 논리라면 조지 워싱턴과 루즈벨트도 탄핵되었어야 한다.

마지막으로 대통령은 언제 어떤 이유로든 대사를 해고할 수 있다. 2008년 12월 3일, 새로 당선된 오바마는 부시 대통령 시절의 모든 대사를 해임했다.[43] 이를 이유로 그 누구도 오바마를 탄핵하려 하지 않았다.

2주간의 청문회 기간 동안 12명의 증인이 출석했지만, 스모킹 건이라 부를 만한 어떠한 구체적 실체도 나오지 않았다. 청문회 직후 실시된 에머슨 여론조사를 보면, 무당층 안에서 트럼프 탄핵에 반대하는 쪽이 무려 49% 달하는 것으로 탄핵을 찬성하는 쪽보다 15%p 높게 조사되었다.[44]

탄핵 절차

탄핵 소추안이 하원을 통과하더라도 공화당이 과반을 차지한 상원에서 거부될 가능성이 크다. 낸시 펠로시 하원의장과 민주당이 생각하는 최악의 시나리오는 대선이 치러지는 2020년에 상원에서 트럼프가 무죄 판결을 받는 것이다. 만약 탄핵 소추안이 하원을 통과하여 상원으로 가게 된다면 그 곳에는 다른 문제가 있기 때문이다.

상원은 헌법에 따라 탄핵 심판을 열 것이다. 공화당 상원 원내대표인 미치 맥코넬(Mitch McConnell)은 뛰어난 전략가다. 만약 하원이 2020년 1월이나 2월에 탄핵 소추안을 통과시킨다면, 맥코넬은 민주당 의원들이 가장 불리한 시기로 상원 심판 일정을 잡을 것이다. 상원에서 이루어지는 탄핵 심판은 통상 6~8주가 걸리는데, 이 심판에는 사실상 모든 상원의원이 배심원으로 반드시 출석하도록 되어 있다. 즉, 민주당 대선후보이자 동시에 상원의원인 버니 샌더스, 엘리자베스 워런, 코리 부커, 카말라 해리스, 에이미 클로부차 의원은 재판이 진행되는 그 기간 동안 선거운동을 할 수 없게 된다. 이 과정에서 유일하게 혜택을 받는 사람은 끊임없는 말 실수와 감동 없는 토론회로 지지율이 휘청거리고 있는 조 바이든 전 부통령뿐일 것이다.

한층 더 공고해진 트럼프 지지층

입장을 바꾸어 '내가 만약 트럼프 지지자라면'이라고 생각하면 모든 이해가 더 쉬워진다. 트럼프를 지지하는 사람들 두고 오바마는 미저리처럼 집착증에 시달리는 사람들이라고 했고, 클린턴은 개탄스러운 사람들이라고 불렀다. 바이든은 사회의 찌꺼기라고 폄하했으며 민주당은 인종주의자들이라고 비난하고 있다. 하지만 트럼프는 이들을 '미국인들'이라고 부른다.

2017년 2월 보수정치행동회의(CPAC)에서도 트럼프는 공화당이 '잊혀진 사람들'을 대변하겠다고 힘주어 이야기했다. 트럼프는 그들에게 갈채를 보내며, "글로벌 국가, 세계 통화, 세계 국기 같은 건 존재하지 않습니다. 나는 세계를 대표하지 않습니다. 나는 바로 여러분의 조국, 미국을 대표하고 있습니다"라고 발언을 이어갔다.[45]

트럼프는 손꼽히는 억만장자이지만 그를 대통령으로 만든 사람들은 소외받았던 중·하류층 유권자라는 사실을 기억해야 한다. 일례로, 2019년 1분기 트럼프 캠프는 3,000만 달러의 선거 자금을 모았는데 이는 정치후원금으로 역대 최고 금액이다. 하지만 이 중 99%가 200달러 이하인 소액 기부금들로 이루어져있고, 1인당 평균 기부금은 34달러에 불과했다. 트럼프의 취임 후 지금까지 100만 명 이상의 온라인 기부자가 새로 가입하여 트럼프를 응원하고 있고, 2019년 한 해 동안의 신규 가입자만 약 10만 명으로 추산된다.[46] '샤이 트럼프'라고 불리는 그의 지지자들은 감소하기는커녕 점점 증가하는 추세고, NBC 뉴스는 트럼프 지지자들의 충성도가 근대사에서 최고 수준이라고 이야기할 정도다.

우리가 살고 있는 지금, 사회지도층과 엘리트, 각 분야의 전문가들은 그들이 봉사로 섬겨야 하는 국민들로부터 더욱 멀어졌다. 그들은 국가는 항상 국민의 일꾼이 되어야 하고, 결코 국가 자체가 주인이 되어서는 안 된다는 결정적인 교훈을 완전히 잊어버린 듯 하다. 엘리트들의 가장 큰 문제는 민주주의의 주권자인 '국민'들을 위하지 않고, 오히려 그 반대편에 있다는 점이다. 이것이 바로 그들의 아킬레스 건이다. 여전히 엘리트들은 트럼프를 비웃고 그를 보며 한심한 듯 혀를 차고 있다. 하지만 많은 '미국인'들은 지금도, 오히려 예전보다 훨씬 더 단단하게 트럼프를 지지하고 있다.

2019년 11월, 살레나 지토는 그녀의 책 『위대한 반란(The Great Revolt)』을 집필하기 위해 2016년 대선을 앞두고 인터뷰했던 사람들을 다시 찾아갔다. 그 사람들은 놀랍게도 트럼프의 트윗이나 시끄러운 탄핵 이슈에 절대 흔들리지 않는 모습을 보여주었다. 오히려 그들은 3년 전보다 지금 트럼프를 훨씬 더 강하게 지지하고 있다고 밝혔다. 러스트 벨트 출신의 한 유권자는 지토와의 인터뷰에서 이렇게 답했다.

"두 번 생각해 볼 것도 없이 난 트럼프를 다시 뽑을 겁니다."[47]

대선을 1년 여 앞둔 지금, 우리는 이 말을 결코 가볍게 들어서는 안될 것이다.

핵 억지력의 본질*

제 1부
이론적 기초

데이비드 포스터 월러스(David Foster Wallace)는 우리에게 다음과 같은 이야기를 남겼다. 새끼 물고기 두 마리가 함께 헤엄치고 있는데 우연히 그들을 향해 헤엄치는 나이 많은 물고기를 만났다. 나이든 물고기는 고개를 끄덕이며 "안녕, 애들아. 물은 어때?"라고 물었다. 어린 두 물고기는 잠깐 동안 말없이 헤엄쳐 가다가 결국 그들 중 한 마리가 다른 한 마리를 쳐다보며 물었다. "그런데 도대체 물이 뭐야?" [48]

그들에게 물은 우리가 숨쉬는 공기와 같이 알아채지 못할 정도로 익숙한 것 아닐까? 우리는 공기가 언제나 존재하고 생존에 필수적이라는 것을 알고 있지만, 우리는 그것에 대해 생각조차 하지 않고 살아가고 있다.

'핵 억지력'도 비슷한 맥락으로 이해될 수 있다. 이 개념은 대부분 일반 사람들의 일상적 관심에서 아주 벗어나 있다. 다시 말해, 대다수 사람들은 '핵 억지력'이 무엇인지 전혀 생각하지 않고 살아가고 있다. 그러나 '핵 억지력'의 영향력은 실로 엄청나다. 심지어 '핵 억지력'이란 단어에 대한 정의가 너무 많아 오히려 낯설게 느껴지기도 한다. 그 개념 자체 또한 정확하지 않다. 그러기에 이 단어에는 과도한 공포가 수반되어 있다.

확장핵억제(extended nuclear deterrence)는 '적용된 억지(applied deterrence)'라는 의미이며 이것을 자세히 설명하는 데에는 상당한 어려움이 뒤따른다. 기본적인 '억지' 자체만으로도 이미 너무 어렵지만, '적용된 억지'는 인간 합리성에

---

* 본고는 2020년 1월 3일에 작성된 미발표 글입니다.

대한 한 없는 신뢰와 인간 비합리성에 대한 깊은 두려움 양쪽 모두를 요구하는 개념이다. 우선 쉽게 설명하자면 '확장핵억제'는 한미상호방위조약의 핵심 사항이다. 한마디로 북한이 한국을 공격하면 파괴적인 핵 반격으로 응징하겠다는 미국의 약속이라고 할 수 있다. 이는 얼마 전까지는 믿을 수 있는 약속이었을지도 모른다. 하지만 북한이 실질적인 핵을 보유하고 ICBM 프로그램 기술을 터득함에 따라 이제는 확장억제의 유효성에 심각한 의문이 제기되고 있다. 즉, 과연 미국은 서울을 위해 샌프란시스코를 희생할 수 있을까?

이 질문에 정확한 답을 하려면 핵 억지력과 관련한 철학적, 역사적, 심리적인 근원을 전반적으로 재검토해 보아야 한다. 그리고 한국의 안보전문가들은 핵 억지력에 대한 미국의 이해와 관점을 완벽하게 파악하고, 철저하게 익숙해져야 한다. 오직 이것만이 대한민국으로 하여금 국가안보를 관리할 수 있는 정신적, 물리적 준비태세를 갖추게 할 것이다.

핵 억지력에 대한 전제적인 개요 밑바탕에는 미국식 색채와 구조가 넓게 깔려 있다. 미국은 과거 소련뿐만 아니라 다른 국가들과 관련한 핵 억지력에 대해 가장 많이 생각하고 고민할 수 밖에 없었다. 냉전 시대에 만들어진 미국의 핵 억지 논리는 냉전이 종식된 후에도 그 위상과 중요성을 유지하고 있다.

국제법과 국제사회의 윤리는 여전히 전통적인 전쟁 개념과 결부되어 있다. 전쟁에 있어서도 개전 정당성(*jus ad bellum*)과 아울러 전시 행위의 정당성(*jus in bello*) 제한이라는 문제가 항상 뒤따른다. 무력충돌법(Law of Armed Conflict, LOAC)의 주된 4가지 기본원칙인 '구별의 원칙, 비례성의 원칙, 군사적 필요성, 불필요한 고통'은 여전히 유지되고 있다. 이러한 지침들과 개념들은 핵전쟁에서도 의미가 있는 것인가? 우리는 핵전쟁을 단지 더 파괴적인 재래식 전쟁이라고 생각하면 되는 것인가? 아니면 핵 억지력에 대한 새로운 정의, 기준, 이해가 필요한 것인가?

핵 억지란 무엇인가?

핵 억지는 핵 활용 자체가 사실상 전멸하는 힘인 동시에 핵으로 인한 전멸을 막을 힘, 모두를 가지고 있다고 가정한다. 이 가정은 앞뒤기 전혀 맞지 않고 매우 비논리적이다. 필자가 핵에 대한 연구를 할 때마다 이 문제들은 매일 나의 뇌리를 떠나지 않았다. 물론 지금 이 순간까지도 말이다. 하지만 대부분의 사람들과는 다른 방식으로 필자를 괴롭힌다. 필자는 핵무기가 두렵지 않다. 생각할 수 없는 것을 생각한다는 것도 두렵지 않다. 핵무기 사용을 고려하는 정책을 수립하는 것 역시 두렵지 않다. 하지만 필자는 인간이 두렵다. 즉, 가장 본질적인 두려움을 압축해서 말하자면 억지력은 오로지 인간의 이성을 믿고 베팅한 거대한 도박이라는 것이다.

미국 케네디 행정부에서 국방장관을 지냈던 로버트 맥나마라(Robert McNamara)는 "핵무기는 그 어떤 군사적 목적도 없으며, 단지 상대방이 그것을 사용하지 못하도록 막는 것 외에는 전혀 쓸모가 없다"고 했다.[49]

'전쟁은 단지 정치의 또 다른 연장'이라는 클라우제비츠(Carl von Clausewitz)의 말은 핵전쟁에 적용될 수 없다는 주장도 있다. 즉, 이성이 마비되거나, 대량살상에 대해 희열을 느끼거나, 이론을 너무 맹종하여 현실 감각을 완전히 상실하지 않는 한 말이다. 하지만 이들의 비판은 과연 타당한가?

물론 핵전쟁은 확실하게 다르다는 것이다. 핵전쟁에서 군사적인 수단은 항상 정치적 목적을 초월할 것이다. 전략이란 정치적 목적을 위해 군사적 수단을 의도적으로 사용하는 것을 의미한다. 그렇다면 상호확증파괴(MAD)는 전략의 부정(否定)이라고 할 수 있다. 하지만 이는 한가지 의문을 갖게 한다. 그렇다면 핵 억지전략이란 무엇인가?

상호확증파괴(MAD)에 대한 잘못된 생각

어떤 사람들은 핵무기는 안정을 위한 힘이라고 주장한다. 이에 더 나아가 케네스 왈츠(Kenneth Waltz)는 실제로 핵 확산을 주장한다.

> "세계는 1945년 이래 지금까지 오랜 세월 동안 평화를 누려 왔다. … (중략) … 역사가 보여주듯이 핵무기는 핵전쟁을 현실 가능한 전망으로 만들지 않았다. … (중략) … 핵무기의 확산에 관한 많은 글들은 다음과 같은 독특한 특징이 있다. 그것은 과거에 일어나지 않았던 일이 미래에 일어날 가능성이 높다고 말한다. … (중략) … 행복했던 핵의

과거는 많은 사람들로 하여금 불행한 핵의 미래를 기대하게 한다. … (중략) … 핵 보유국들이 많아질수록 세계는 더 나은 미래를 갖게 될 것이다. 핵무기는 억지력의 그 이상을 가능하게 만든다."[50]

억지력을 비판하는 자들은 '단지 핵무기 사용에 대해 생각 하는 것만으로도 핵무기 사용 가능성이 훨씬 높아진다'고 주장하다. 즉, 억지가 실패할 가능성을 고려하는 것 자체가 그것의 실패 가능성을 높인다는 것이다.

억지력을 옹호하는 자들은 '묵시적인 절멸 위협이 상호확증파괴(MAD) 논리의 필수적인 부분'이라며 반박한다. 하지만 이 적나라한 취약성과 참담한 공포 없이 억지력은 신뢰할 수 없다.

인류의 존재론적 절멸 공포는 그 어떠한 수단으로써의 핵 사용에 대한 궁극적인 억지력이 되기때문에 보존되어야 한다는 논리가 가능하다면, 어느 쪽도 전쟁을 일으킬 합리적인 이유가 없을 것이다.

하지만. 그러나. 그럼에도 불구하고. 핵 억지전략은 실패할 수 있다. "핵전쟁은 절대 일어나서는 안 된다"는 미국 레이건 대통령의 말에 대다수 사람들은 동의할 것 이다. 그러나 이 논쟁 자체가 핵 억지력의 취약성을 드러내고 있다. 그 누구도 억지력이 실패하여 전쟁이 발생한다면 어떻게 해야 하는지는 알려주지 않는다.

전쟁의 종결

억지가 실패하여 우리가 핵전쟁의 한가운데에 있다면, 가장 우선순위의 계산과 목표는 그 전쟁을 종식시키는 것이다. 버나드 브로디(Bernard Brodie)는 세상을 떠나기 전 다음과 같이 말했다.

"전략적 핵공격(strategic nuclear exchange)이 시작되면, 전쟁의 주요 목표는 가능한 한 빨리 확실하게 그리고 양측 피해의 최소화로 끝내야 한다는 것이다."[51]

클라우제비츠의 주장을 재조명해 볼 필요가 있다. 전쟁 종식은 편익과 손실의 계산 결과이기 때문이다.

핵전쟁 시 최대한 빠른 종식만이 모두에게 절대적인 이익이다. 핵전쟁의 확대 및 지속으로부터 이익을 얻을 수 있는 사람은 아무도 없다.

이것이 바로 합리적 관점이다.
이것이 바로 논리적 선택이다.
이것이 바로 도덕적 명령이다.

그러나 전쟁 종식 결정 관련한 가장 본질적인 문제는 사실 매우 철학적이라고 할 수 있다. 모든 것은 인간의 이성에 달려있다. 어떤 면에서 핵 억지력에 관한 필자의 기본 이론 지침서는 개개인의 자제력에 대한 논의로 끝을 맺는다. 그것이 옳고 적절하다. 억지에 대한 논의뿐만 아니라 그 어떤 실재 인간의 노력은 개인에서 시작하고 개인에서 끝나기 때문이다.

마치 물처럼 말이다.
결국, 그것이 바로 물이다.

제 2부
핵 억지의 실행

제1부에서는 핵 억지력의 이론적 토대를 다루었다. 이제부터 그 이론을 구체적으로 전개할 것이다. 북대서양조약기구(NATO)의 핵억지정책은 MC-48 (NORTH ATLANTIC MILITARY COMMITTEE DECISION-48, 1954. 11. 22) 에 수록되어 있다. 이 정책은 나토 헌장 제 5조의 기초를 이루고 있다.[52] 미국의 핵억지정책은 NSC-162에 명문화 되어 있으며 핵전쟁 발발 시 소련에 대해 즉각적인 대량보복을 담고 있다.

그러나 대량보복정책은 그 자체로써 신뢰성이 부족했다. 핵무기 사용이 모든 핵무기사용을 의미하는 것이 아니기 때문이다. 이에 '제한적인 핵전쟁 (limited nuclear war)'이라는 개념이 등장했다.

미국 로렌스 리버모어 국립 연구소(Lawrence Livermore National Laboratory)의 수소 폭탄 디자인은 복잡하고, 정교하며, 이해하는 것은 거의 불가능에 가까웠다.

1952년, 미국은 태평양 중서부의 섬나라 마셜의 비키니 환초에서 수소 폭탄 한 개를 실험하였다. 이 한번의 실험으로 그 섬을 문자 그대로 '지도상에서 지워' 버렸다. 이 무기는 그 누구도 실제 사용을 상상할 수 없을 정도로 가공할 파괴력을 가졌다.

1957년, 독일 악센트가 짙은 젊은 하버드대 정치학 교수는 제한적인 핵전쟁에서의 핵무기 사용을 주장하며 이름을 알렸다. 그는 케네디 행정부에서 일자리를 얻기 위해 고군분투하고 있었다. 그의 이름이 궁금한가? 그는 바로 그 유명한 헨리 키신저(Henry Kissinger)이다.

비록 그가 케네디 행정부에서 일자리를 얻지는 못했지만, 그의 사고는 쿠바 미사일 위기에 급속하게 휘말려 들어간 젊고 검증되지 않은 지도자 존 케네디의 생각에 지대한 영향을 미쳤다. 1962년 10월, 13일 동안 세계는 핵전쟁의 기로에 놓여있었다. 이 공멸의 위기를 겪은 뒤, 케네디는 '모든' 핵 지휘권을 미국의 통제 아래로 집중시켰다.

케네디는 전임 대통령인 아이젠하워(Dwight Eisenhower)가 당시 유럽동맹군의 최고사령관(SACEUR)에게 부여한 핵공격 권한위임을 철회하였고 핵탄두 통제권을 가진 동맹국들이 미국의 공식적인 허가 없이 핵탄두를 사용하거나 발사하는 권한을 부여하지 않는 권한입력코드제도(Permissive Action Link, PAL)를 도입하였다. 그 동맹국들로 하여금 핵전쟁 개시 여부를 통제하도록 허용하는 것이 이제 금지된 것이다. 그것은 쿠바 미사일 위기의 중요한 교훈에 근거하였다. 만약 핵전쟁이 일어난다면, 그것은 미국의 결정이고 미국 만의 결정일 것이다. 미국의 동맹국가라는 자체는 중요하다. 그러나 미국이 이렇게 모든 것을 통제 한다면 동맹국간의 신뢰, 헌신, 의존성, 든든함, 독립성은 다 어디로 사라진 것인가? 동맹국들의 국가 주권 역시 어디에 있는가?

사실, 이것은 미국이 미국 이외 그 누구의 핵무기 관련 지휘와 통제도 신뢰하지 않는다는 것을 의미했다. 그리고 미국과 소련의 양측 동맹국들, 위성 국가들, 피후견 국가들(client states)은 다음과 같은 냉혹한 교훈을 얻었다. 즉, 미국과 소련은 핵전쟁 발발 시 각자 동맹국들을 방어하겠다는 약속을 반드시 지키지는 않을 것임을 말이다.

소련이 핵 안정이라는 명목으로 쿠바를 사실상 포기한 것을 북한이 지켜보았고 이를 통하여 북한이 독자적인 핵 능력을 추진하도록 영감을 받았다라는 합리적인 주장을 누군가 할 수 있다. 1985년 미국의 인공위성에 포착된 북한 영변 원자로 기반 시설은 실제로 쿠바 미사일 위기 3년 뒤인 1965년에 만들어졌다.

1960년대 후반, 소련은 미국과 핵 균형(nuclear parity)을 달성하기 위해 노력했으며 본격적인 핵 경쟁에 돌입했다. 소련은 또한 모스크바 주변에 제한된 대탄도 요격 미사일(Anti-Ballistic Missile, ABM) 방어 시스템을 구축하려고 했다. 이러한 시도는 잠재적으로 상대방에 대한 선제 공격 가능성을 높일 수 밖에 없다. 한 쪽이 먼저 공격을 하면서 동시에 상대국에서 날아오는 미사일을 격추하여 상대방으로부터의 보복 공격을 방어할 수 있게 하기 때문이다. 미사일 방어체계(MD) 개념은 MAD의 상호 취약성에 처음으로 도전장을 던진 것이다. MD는 억제력에 신뢰성을 부여한 근본적인 두려움을 약화시키는 것을 넘어 아예 없애버리고자 했다.

미국은 1972년 당시 소련이 더 많은 수의 탄두를 보유할 수 있도록 하는 전략무기제한협상(SALT)을 수용하였다. 왜냐하면 당시 미국이 다탄두각개유도 기술에서 우위를 점하고 있었기 때문이다. 즉, 소련은 양을 선택한 반면에 미국은 질을 선택했다. 방어선을 구축하는 것보다 공격력을 높이는 것이 비용이 적게 들었다. 거기에 더하여, 방어 시스템 구축의 가속화는 오히려 핵 공포를 약화시킬 수 있었던 까닭에 얼마 동안은 미사일 방어체계의 본격적인 개발 움직임은 없었다.

세계가 핵의 벼랑 끝에 서 있다는 것을 미·소 양 국가 모두 인식하고 있었음에도 불구하고, 한동안 상호 취약성(안정성)에 대한 두려움이 방어의 편안함(불안정성)보다 우세했다. 안정성의 한 형태로서의 방어(예; 미사일 방어)는 아직 상상하지 못하였다.

1차 전략무기제한 협정(SALT)에서 남겨진 쟁점들은 2차 협정에서 다뤄졌다. 특히, 미국의 전진배치무기와 소련의 중거리탄도미사일(IRBM)을 전체 탄두 수에 포함시킬지 여부가 핵심 쟁점이었다. SALT-I 이후, 두 국가는 서로 다른 핵 전략을 추구했다. 미국은 더 정확한 미사일을 만드는 것에 소련은 더 큰 탄두를 만드는 것에 총력을 기울였다.

SALT-II 협상은 투사중량(throw weight)과 미사일 수를 세는 방법에 대한 견해 차이로 결렬되었다. 투사중량은 미사일에 장착할 수 있는 총 폭탄 무게로서 탄두의 중량, 미사일의 모든 장치 그리고 탄두들이 탑재되어 있는 소위 '버스'라고 불리는 중량 전부를 포함한다. 미국은 소련이 보유한 대형 지상 미사일의 높은 투척 중량에 대해 우려했는데, 이는 소련이 미사일에 추가 탄두를 장착하여 전체 무기 재고를 확장시킬 수 있었기 때문이다. 물론 미국은 원한다면 투척 중량이 큰 대형 미사일을 만들 수 있었다. 그러나 작지만 강력한 핵탄두를 제조할 수 있는 기술적 우위를 가진 미국은 소련의 SS-18과 같은 대형 미사일을 만들 필요가 없었다.

일부 전문가들은 소련이 탄두를 1개씩 탑재한 SS-25 미사일을 약간의 투척 중량의 확장만으로도 3개의 탄두를 탑재할 수 있는 새로운 형태의 미사일로 개발할 수 있다고 주장했다. 이러한 가능성에 대비해서 미국 협상가들은 소련이 개발한 새로운 종류의 미사일은 기존의 미사일과 다른 투척중량을 가진 것으로 평가되어야 한다고 주장했다. 그들은 새로운 유형의 미사일들이 SS-25보다 훨씬 더 큰 투척중량을 보유해야 한다고 주장했다.

놀랄 것도 없이 소련은 이 제안을 거절했다. 이 제안은 소련이 이전 시스템을 수정하는 대신 새로운 미사일을 처음부터 만들어야 하는 값비싼 과정을 거쳐야 하기 때문이었다. 그러나 그것이 바로 폴 니체(Paul Nitze)가 원하는 것이었다. 즉, 소련이 국방비를 과도하게 지출하다가 파산하도록 하는 것 말이다.

그렇다. NSC-68의 저자 폴 니체는 소련을 억지할 수 있는 유일한 방법은 미국이 재래식 무기와 아울러 핵무기의 대대적 확충 작업에 참여하는 것이라고 주장했다.

상호확증파괴(MAD)를 약화시키는 미사일 방어체계(MD)

냉전 시대의 가장 위대한 전사 로널드 레이건은 '핵무기는 부도덕하다'고 했다. 그는 또한 전멸의 두려움을 가지고 끊임없는 불안 속에서 사는 것은 미친

짓이라고 말했다. 상호확증파괴(MAD) 전략 자체가 '상호확증파괴적'인 미친 짓(mad)인 것이었다. 그는 그런 세상에서 살고 싶지 않았다. 그는 미국을 공격용 미사일로부터 보호할 수 있기를 원했다. 이에 전략방위구상(SDI)이란 아이디어가 탄생했다. 이것이 바로 미사일 방어체계(MD) 시스템의 원조였다.

그러나 MD는 MAD의 본질을 약화시켰다. MD의 비판자들은 만약 한 측이 적보다 덜 취약하다면, 적에게 치명적일 수 있는 선제 공격을 감행하려는 유혹이 더 매력적일 것이라고 주장했다. MD는 취약성(vulnerability) 축소를 통하여 핵전쟁으로 인한 죽음의 공포를 감소시킨 측면이 있었다. MD 비판자들은 이로 인해 전쟁의 가능성이 증가하는 더 위험한 세계로 나아갈 것이라 주장하며 레이건이 오히려 전쟁을 조장한다고 비난했다.

반면 지지자들은 MAD는 MD 개발에도 불구하고 핵탄두의 엄청난 위력 때문에 거의 손상되지 않았다고 주장했다. 그들은 MD가 사실상 국가 안보와 안정성을 높이고 전쟁 가능성을 낮춘다고 주장했다. 미사일 방어망을 갖춘 국가들은 날아오는 공격용 미사일을 격추할 수 있어 선제공격에 유리하지 않다는 점을 알고 있기 때문이다. 이들은 MD가 실제로 생존 확률을 높였으며 따라서 1차 공격을 저지할 수 있는 2차 타격 능력을 증강시켜, 사실상 1차 타격을 하고자 하는 인센티브를 억지할 수 있다고 주장했다. 그러므로 이들은 MD는 오히려 선제공격의 매력을 훼손함으로써 억지력을 강화한다고 주장했다.

미국 핵 독트린

미국의 핵 정책에 대해 깊은 오해와 달리, 미국은 '선제 사용'이라는 정책을 가지고 있지 않다. 더 정확하게 표현하자면 '선제 사용 금지'를 명시하고 있지 않다. 미국은 적(또는 동맹국)이 전쟁을 시작하고자 하는 욕망을 단념시키기 위해 분쟁에서 먼저 핵무기를 사용하겠다고 약속하지 않는다.

그러므로 핵심 이슈는 미국이 동맹국들에 대한 약속을 강화하고 핵무기를 결코 사용하는 일이 없도록 핵 문턱을 높이는 데 필요한 모든 재래식 수단의 개발 여부가 아니다. 당연히 미국은 재래식 무기 개발 능력을 강화하여야 한다.

가장 핵심적인 이슈는 미국이 가장 극단적인 상황에서도 절대 먼저 핵 문턱을 넘지 않겠다고 약속할 경우, 동맹국을 위해 핵 보복공격이 약화될 것인지 이다. 이런 상황이 실제로 발생할 확률은 매우 낮다. 그러나 동맹국들은 전쟁에서 미국이 그들을 위한 핵 보복의 보장이 필요하다. 그래서 핵 억지력은 기존의 재래식 전쟁에 대한 억지력을 약화시키기보다 오히려 강화시킨다.

핵 억지력의 이론과 실행은 너무도 본질적이고 실존적인 문제다. 그러므로 심사숙고와 비판적 사고를 바탕으로 한 정밀한 분석을 실행 가능한 정책으로 담아내는 것이야 말로 핵 억지력을 연구하는 전문가들에게 남아있는 진정한 임무이다.

평화는 희망이지만 전쟁은 현실이다. 핵 억지력 자체는 국제정치를 필요로 하지 않는다. 그러나 핵 억지력이 없는 국제정치는 공허하고 무의미하다. 결국 국제관계에 있어서 가장 핵심적인 문제는 핵무기이다.

2060 동아시아: 대한민국의 핵, 일본의 핵, 태평양동맹조약기구와 새로운 미국의 확장억제력*

미국중심 세계질서의 종식

심상치 않은 시기에는 비범한 발상이 필요하다. 지금이야말로 향후 40년간의 동아시아 현실을 예측하기 위한 국제질서를 재편하고 재형성 할 때이다. 새로운 태평양동맹조약기구의 일원이자, 새로운 미국의 확장억제력으로 뒷받침되는 한국과 일본의 핵무장은 북한의 핵을 억지하고 부상하는 중국을 견제할 수 있는데 최상의 방안이다.

역사는 우리가 가진 유일한 실제 '빅'데이터라고 할 수 있다. 심지어 그 데이터가 때때로 '난장판'에 가까운 데이터 일 수도 있다. 국제 관계를 연구하는 사람들의 임무는 현재와 미래를 위한 교훈 발굴을 위하여 그 너절한 데이터를 면밀히 살펴 보는 것이다.

'자유주의 국제질서'의 붕괴를 비통해 하는 전문가와 평론가들이 적지 않다. 그러나 신성로마제국이 '신성'하지 않았던 것과 마찬가지로 자유주의적 국제질서는 '자유주의적'이지도, '국제적'이지도, '질서정연'하지도 않았다. 그것의 붕괴 역시 아니다. 대략 100년의 사이클로 움직이는 많은 역사적 현상들과 마찬가지로 윌슨주의 국제질서의 쇠퇴 역시 한 동안 지속적으로 진행되어 왔다. 우리는 이제 국제 질서를 이루었던 벽돌 하나하나의 해체 효과가 우리 시대에 어떤 결과를 가져 오는지 목도하고 있다.

약 100년 전인 1914년 6월 28일, 오스트리아-헝가리 제국의 합스부르크 왕위

---

* 본고는 2020년 3월 7일에 작성한 미발표 글입니다.

계승자인 페르디난트 대공(Franz Ferdinand)이 사라예보에서 세르비아계 민족주의자에 의해 암살당했다. 이 사건은 고대 제국을 무너뜨리고 세계 지도를 다시 그리려는 윌슨(Woodrow Wilson)의 14개 조항(Fouteen Points)에 명문화된 민족 자결 원칙에 영향 받은 반제국주의 세력을 촉발하였다. 결국 이 사건은 제1·2차 세계대전, 드레스덴과 도쿄에 대한 무자비한 폭격에서 절정에 달했다. 일본에 투하된 '리틀 보이'와 '팻 맨'은 핵 시대를 열었고 전쟁의 법적 한계를 확장하였다.

약 100년 후인 2014년 3월 19일, 러시아는 크림반도의 얄타를 합병하면서 전후(戰後) 세계질서의 상징을 없애버렸다. 그로부터 2년 후, 도널드 트럼프가 미국대통령으로 당선되면서 '보통사람'의 물결이 국제질서의 제방을 완전히 무너뜨렸다.

제2차 세계대전의 종식은 미국중심 세계 질서의 서막을 열었다. 얄타 회담(Yalta Conference, 1945년 2월)이 국제 협력의 기준으로, 브레튼우즈 체제(Bretton Woods System)가 세계경제의 협정으로 공표되었고, 파리조약(1947년 2월)은 1951년 4월 18일 유럽석탄철강공동체(ECSC)를 탄생시켰다. 세계전쟁으로 확대된 유럽 지역 분쟁 발발에 가장 책임이 있는 프랑스와 독일이 이번에는 유럽 연합(EU) 창설의 주축이 되었고 유엔(UN), 국제 통화 기금(IMF), 세계 은행(World Bank) 등 거의 모든 '국제 기구'는 사실상 미국의 의지로 만들어졌다.

미국이 만든 이러한 세계질서는 한국 전쟁, 즉 북한 개성의 언덕과 한국 인천의 파도 위에서 만들어졌다. 검증되지 않은 시골 출신 지도자 해리 트루먼(Harry Truman)은 베를린 위기와 한국 전쟁 중에 단호한 행동을 통해 자신의 패기를 보여주었고 자신을 비방하는 사람들이 틀렸음을 증명했다. 딘 애치슨(Dean Acheson)의 멋진 우아함과 조지 마셜(George C. Marshall)의 냉철한 진실성에 힘입어 트루먼은 한반도 평화를 지켜냈다. 독일의 베를린 장벽이 냉전의 상징이었다면, 한반도의 38선과 비무장지대(DMZ)는 냉정한 현실이었다. 한국전쟁은 북대서양조약기구(NATO)의 '기구(Organization)'화에 결정적 역할을 하며 유럽의 결속력을 공고하게 만들었다.

두 명의 변호사, 두 명의 은행가 그리고 두 명의 외교관. 이 여섯 명의 주창자들이 마샬 플랜(Marshall Plan, 1947)으로 기획된 제2차 세계대전 전후 미국 중심 세계 질서의 청사진을 그렸다. 그들은 바로 딘 애치슨, 찰스 볼렌(Charles E. Bohlen), 에버렐 해리먼(W. Averwell Harriman), 조지 케넌(George F. Kennan), 로버트 로벳(Robert A. Lovett), 존 맥클로이(John McCloy)였다. 자부심과 재능을 겸비한 이 두뇌집단에 맥조지 번디(McGeorge Bundy), 유진 로스토(Eugene Rostow), 월트 로스토(Walt Rostow), 엘런 덜레스(Allen Dulles), 존 포스터 덜레스(John Foster Dulles)가 가세했다. 이 앵글로색슨 백인 남성들이 미국 중심 세계 질서를 창조한 것이다.

냉전은 억지력을 통해 전쟁과 같이 '뜨거운' 상태가 되는 것을 방지했다. 핵 아마겟돈의 위험마저 아랑곳 하지 않는 정신 나간 사람으로 선전된 '미친 사람'의 모습을 통해서 말이다. 이러한 계산된 비합리성의 신봉자인 커티스 르메이(Curtis LeMay) 장군은 소련이 궁지에 몰리도록 미 전략항공사령부(Strategic Air Command)에 압도적인 치사성을 명령했다. 그 두려움은 긴장을 고조시켰지만 이로 인해 평화를 유지했다. NSC-68의 해석, 게임이론의 발전, 허먼 칸(Herman Kahn), 버나드 브로디(Bernard Brodie), 토마스 쉘딩(Thomas Schelling) 그리고 프레드 이클레(Fred Ikle)의 선구적인 작업은 핵 억지력에 관한 수사학, 논리 및 논증을 발전시켰다. 새로운 세계질서는 베트남 전쟁의 라드랑(la Drang) 전투와 닥토(Dak To) 전투에서 그리고 인도네시아 반둥회의(1955년 4월 18~24일)에서 시험대에 올랐다. 곧 이어, 다탄두 각개목표설정 재돌입 비행체(MIRV), 투척무게 그리고 SLBM은 핵 전쟁의 알고리즘을 명료한 공포와 상호 취약성으로 바꾸어 놓았고 이로 인하여 지정학적 안정성이 지탱될 수 있었다.

이 안정은 베를린 장벽이 무너지고 소련이 붕괴될 때까지 약 50년 동안 유지되었다. 냉전 종식 후 핵무기에 대한 환원주의적 공포는 지속되었으나 과시적인 물질만능주의가 세계를 지배했다. 여러 국가들과 세대들은 유례없는 물질적 부를 축적하며 빈곤에서 벗어나며, 생활 및 보건 수준의 향상, 평균수명 연장 등 가시적 성과를 거두었다. 말라리아는 과학 교과서에서 사라졌다.

그러나 인간의 자만심이 글로벌리즘의 물질적 진보를 동반했다. 개인용 컴퓨터, 휴대전화, 금융 파생상품 등은 과잉 소비를 부추겼다. 2008년 금융 위기는 엘리트와 일반대중 사이의 갭(fault line, 단층선)을 심화시켰다. 1991년과 2008년 사이, 메인스트리트(Main Street)와 중산층은 글로벌리즘의 전리품을 거의 모두 빼앗겼다. 그리고 기득권층은 문화적·사회적 우월한 지위를 이용하며 대중의 지위가 상승하고 향상 되는 것을 막음으로써 대중들로 하여금 제자리를 고수하도록 만들었다.

제한적이고 억제된 정부는 이제 구시대적이라며 조롱 당했다. 그러나 『마그나 카르타(Magna Carta, 대헌장)』와 『연방주의자 논집(Federalist Papers)』을 뒷받침하는 원칙은 여전히 세계의 개개인들에게 경종을 울리고 있다. 다름 아닌 국가는 항상 일반 대중의 주인이 아닌 종이 되어야 한다는 사실이다. 이것은 스파르타쿠스(Spartacus)가 '이제 그만(no more)'이라는 단순한 말로 노예 해방 투쟁을 하던 그 시대 이래로 자유를 열망하는 사람들에게 정부와 종교의 수립에 앞선 간명하고 기본적인 원칙이었다. 하지만 이제 이 원칙은 글로벌 엘리트의 비대해진 국가 권력으로 인하여 철저하게 훼손되었다.

변화는 갑작스럽게 닥쳤다. 자유주의 엘리트들은 보고 싶은 것만 보았고 포퓰리즘 폭풍의 전조를 전혀 감지하지 못했다. 그들은 2014 러시아의 크림 반도 합병이 현재의 국제 질서를 위협하는 첫 포문을 열었음을 인식하지 못하였다. 2016년 11월 트럼프의 대통령 당선과 12월 시리아 알레포에 대한 폭격은 그러한 위협을 확정 짓는 최후의 일격이 되었다.

트럼프는 무시당한 대중의 고통과 상처 입은 자존심을 파고들었다. 에릭 호퍼(Eric Hoffer)는 『맹신자들(The True Believer)』에서 대중운동의 호소력이 시사하는 바에 대해 서술했다.[53] 내용 면에서 이 저서와 아주 대조를 이루는 호세 오르테가 이 가세트(Jose Ortega y Gasset)가 쓴 『대중의 봉기(Revolt of the Masses)』에서는 대중은 호소력이 없음을 가정하며 대중에 대해 비판적이었다.[54] 역설적이게도 가세트의 그 비판이 오히려 역설적으로 대중이 얼마나 중요한지를 의도치 않게 보여주었다. 미국은 패권국가로서 막강한 힘을 보유하고 있지만 더 이상 세계 질서 유지를 위한 서비스를 제공하려는 욕망은 없는 것처럼 보인다. 반면에 러시아와 중국은 군사적 현대화를 추구하며 1920년대 해군 군비 경쟁 시대를 상기시키고 있다. 지금 이 시대의 주요한 특징은 정보의 확산으로 촉발된 사회, 문화적 변혁에 군사력이 순응하고 있다는 점이다. 각국의 국가 지도자들에게 민족주의와 영토분쟁 문제는 여전히 골치 아픈 문제로 남아있다. 정보의 즉각적인 속성은 이러한 어려움을 더욱 악화시키고 있다. 윌슨의 14개 항목에 명시된 민족자결의 원칙은 전 세계적으로 민주주의와 국가 정체성의 확산을 촉발했다. 1945년 이전 독일만의 '특별한' 정치 체제를 의미했던 손디비그(Sonderweg)는 더 이상 독일에만 국한되지 않는다. 이제 모든 국가는 자신만의 '특별한 방법'을 주장한다.

전쟁에 대한 악몽으로 인하여 추동 되었던 유럽인이라는 공동 정체성의 형성도 약화되고 있다. 이탈리아 북부동맹(Lega Nord)의 부상, 프랑스판 나치즘인 '블랑주의(Boulangisme)'의 회귀, 그리고 '독일 대안당(Alternative for Germany)'의 출현 등은 전 세계를 두 번이나 전쟁의 소용돌이로 몰아넣었던 토착 민족주의의 악취를 내뿜고 있다. 1, 2차 세계대전 당시에도 이에 대한 준비가 되어 있지 않았고, 오늘날에도 여전히 준비되어 있지 않다.

우리는 유례없는 불확실성의 영역에 서 있다. 1683년 9월 12일, 비엔나 전투에서 얀 3세 소비에스키(John III Sobieski)가 이슬람 오스만제국이 비엔나 점령을 포기하게 만들었을 때와 유사한 전환점에 처해 있는 것이다. 그로부터 318년 뒤인 2001년 9월 11일, 19명의 이슬람 테러리스트들은 미국 항공기 두 대를 납치해 그때의 상실에 대해 앙갚음하고 역사의 흐름을 바꿔 버렸다

'역사의 종말'이라는 말 자체에 대한 신빙성은 확실히 떨어지고 있다. 오히려 역사는 경제와 문화를 뛰어 넘는다. 그리고 역사는, 지금 여기에 있다.

한반도만큼 '역사가 지금 여기에' 있는 곳은 없다. 국제관계 이론, 추론, 예측 관련한 격언들이 모두 이곳에서 만난다. 권력 정치와 국제 문제가 충돌하고, 융합하고, 궁극적으로 공존하는 곳이다. 여기에는 '둘 중 하나/또는(either/or)'이 없다. 오직 '둘 다/그리고(both/and)' 만 존재한다. 역사가 만들어져야 하는 곳 - 그것도 매우 긴급하게 만들어져야 - 바로 여기 한반도다.

제2차 세계대전 이후 지속되었던 미국 중심의 세계 질서가 쇠퇴하고 있다.

이제 동아시아에서는 비록 불편하고 어색할지라도 민족주의, 경제 포퓰리즘, 협동주의, 전체주의 그리고 자유선거, 개인의 자유, 자본주의, 민주주의가 공존하는 새로운 질서를 만들어야 한다. 북한의 비핵화 '또는' 한국의 핵무기 필요성을 부정하며 미국 핵우산 보호의 지속이라는, 즉 현재의 '둘 중 하나 모델'은 더 이상 유지 될 수 없다. 이러한 이분법은 환상일 뿐이다. 진정으로 안정적인 국제질서를 원한다면, 그 틀(framework)은 반드시 '모두/그리고'여야 한다. 북한의 핵과 한국의 핵, 이 '둘 다'를 인정하고, 동시에 미국의 확장억제를 강화하는 것. 이것이 바로 진정한 핵우산이고, 확장억제력이다. 그리고 이에 대한 새로운 셈법이 필요하다.

새로운 확장억제력

현대 국제 관계에서 MAD(상호확증파괴) 또는 MD(미사일 방어) 관련논쟁에서 뜨거운 열기는 그다지 느껴지지 않는다. 하지만 전면적인 핵전쟁에 대한 두려움이 줄어들었음에도 불구하고 억제력, 즉 핵억지력은 동맹이라는 단합의 상징이자 전략과 방위 계획을 위한 작전개념으로서 그 위상을 확고히 유지하고 있다. 핵억지력의 장점은 그 어느 때보다 현재와 같은 상황에 꼭 들어맞는다.

핵 전략가인 키스 페인(Keith Payne)은 다음과 같이 적절하게 언급했다.

> "냉전 종식 이후 20년이 넘는 기간 동안 미국의 핵 정책은 핵억지력과 핵무기의 가치가 급격히 하락하고 있다는 일반적인 믿음에 기반을 두고 있었다. 왜냐하면 국제 관계가 훨씬 더 온화해졌고, 역사는 지속되고 있기 때문이다. 미국 안보에 있어서 핵무기의 역할은 이제 거의 전혀 남아있지 않은 것으로 추측된다. 그저 남아있던 유일한 질문은 '어떻게 그리고 얼마나 빨리 미국이 세계를 비핵화로 이끌 수 있는가?'하는 것이었다. 그리고 냉전 종식은 미국을 유일한 초강대국으로 남게 하였고 역사, 핵 억제력, 핵무기 관련 미국의 시각에 많은 영향을 끼쳤다. 하지만 러시아의 핵 부활, 중국의 부상, 북한과 이란의 핵 위협으로 인하여 미국이 더 이상 핵무기에 대해 관심이 없어도 된다는 인식은 명백한 허구가 되었다. 이제 미국의 핵 정책은 매

우 다른 현실 직면하였고 그에 맞게 조정되어야 한다."[55]

아주 색다른 현실이 한반도에서는 매우 현실적으로 펼쳐지고 있다. 실제로 한미동맹의 결속력은 미국의 확장억제에 대한 신뢰성과 연결되어 있다. 2018년 ≪핵 태세 검토 보고서(Nuclear Posture Review, NPR)≫는 고위력, 저정밀 탄두를 사용할 필요가 없는 분쟁에서 저위력, 고정밀 핵탄두와 고정밀 순항미사일의 사용 채택을 고려한다.[56]

NPR 지지자들은 고위력 무기는 억지력(기본 및 확장)의 신뢰성을 떨어뜨리는 반면, 비록 저위력이지만 훨씬 정확한 무기가 확장억제의 신뢰성을 오히려 향상시킨다고 주장한다.[57]

드골(Charles De Gaulle)이 먼저 제기했고, 또 다른 맥락에서 트럼프 대통령에 의해 맥락하게 묘사된 동맹 신뢰성에 대한 정치적 의문은 여전히 부인하기 어려운 문제로 남아 있다. 즉, 과연 미국은 파리를 위해 뉴욕을 희생할 것인가? 한국 입장을 대입하여 보면 과연 미국은 서울을 위해 샌프란시스코를 희생할 것인가?

새로운 NPR의 논리에 따라 미국의 더 세분화되고 치명적인 대처 방안이 더 신뢰할 수 있는 선택지를 제공 할 수 있다는 신호를 적군과 아군에게 모두 보냈다. 이를 통하여 미국은 동맹의 신뢰성에 대한 딜레마를 피하려고 한다. 이러한 기조는 한국으로 하여금 과격한 접근 방식(maximalist approach)의 필요성을 느끼지 못하게 하고, 대신에 확장억제의 보장을 뒷받침한다.

비판가들은 NPR이 각국 지도자들로 하여금 전쟁에서 핵무기 사용 관련 방심을 부추길 것이라고 주장한다. 그들은 저위력 무기의 사용이 핵 사용의 문턱을 낮추는 것과 같다고 지적하면서, '핵전쟁은 너무 끔찍하고 상상할 수 조차도 없는 것으로 남아 있어야 하고, 결국 의사 결정권자의 마음에서 핵 사용 가능성 자체를 지워 버려야 한다'고 주장한다.

많은 발전과 변화에도 불구하고, MAD는 핵억지력을 연구하는 대다수의 사람들의 사고를 여전히 지배하고 있다. 이러한 현실에서 핵무기 사용이 훨씬 더 가능성 높은 고려 대상이 된다면, 한국과 일본 같은 동맹국들은 더욱 소외되고 긴장할 수 밖에 없다. 결국 미국과 북한 사이의 그 어떤 방식의 핵 교환이라도 동맹국 영토 내에서 발생할 확률이 높기 때문이다. 이것은 전쟁 공포에 대한 동맹국들의 우려를 악화시켜 확장억제를 강화시키기보다는 오히려 저하시킬 것이다.

어떤 측면에서 보면 지지자와 비판가 모두 잘못된 가정을 하고 있다. 저위력, 고정밀 무기를 지지하는 사람들은 적(敵)들이 저위력 또는 고위력 무기를 식별하여 구분할 수 있고 처음부터 분쟁 전반에 걸쳐 갈등의 확대를 통제할 수 있음을 가정한다. 반면에 이러한 저위력 무기에 대한 비판가들은 MAD보다 아주 조금, 아주 작은 것 조차도 전쟁을 불러일으킬 뿐만 아니라 선제 공격은 전면적인 핵전쟁으로 이어진다고 가정한다. 두 가정 모두 논리가 빈약하며, 추가적인 검토가 필요하다.

MAD의 취약성으로 다시 돌아가지 않으면서도 MD의 선제공격과 핵 생존 가능성에 대한 공격적 충동을 유발하지 않고 핵 무기로 위협하는 자들을 막을 방법이 있을까?

아마도, 답은 있다.

1995년, STRATCOM은 ≪냉전 이후 억지력의 본질≫이란 건조한 제목의 보고서를 발표했다.[58] 이것은 크게 주목 받지는 못했지만, 분석적이면서도 통찰력이 있으며 역사적 세부사항과 심리적인 판단까지 모두 녹여 쓴 것이었다.

이 보고서는 합리성에 대한 MAD의 핵심 가정을 뒤집었다. 미국은 잠재적 적대행위자의 눈을 통한 합리성을 이해함으로써 그들의 미국에 대한 행동(action)을 효과적으로 억제할 수 있다고 주장한다. 또한 적들의 감정과 가치를 공략하고 합리적이면서도 감성적이라고 여겨지는 리더의 의사결정 과정에 초점을 맞추고 있다.[59] 요컨대 적의 가치를 식별하고 표적화하여 위협할 때 억지력이 가장 잘 발휘 될 수 있다고 주장한다. 공격성을 억제하는 것은 특정 문화적 '가치'에 대한 이러한 이해와 위협이다.

이 주장에서 제시된 사례의 내용은 끔찍하다. 1980년대 레바논은 무법천지였고 여러 혁명단체가 이 혼돈 속에서 번성했다. 한 단체가 세 명의 소련 국민을 납치 살해하였다. 이틀 후, 소련은 아무 말을 하지 않고 해당 혁명 그룹의 지도자에게 그의 장남의 고환이 담긴 꾸러미를 보냈다. 그 어떤 말도 남기지 않았지만, 소련은 "다시는 우리 국민을 괴롭히지 말라"는 암묵적인 메시지를 전달한 것이다. 그 이후 레바논에 소련군이 주둔하는 기간 동안 소련 국민 그 누구에게도 손을 대지 않았다.[60] 그것이 바로 억지력이다. 소련이 보낸 메시지의 의미를 적(敵)은 분명하고도 명확히 이해하였고 이들은 마침내 억지된 것이다. 이 예시에서 보여준 것처럼 억지력은 핵무기 유무와는 상관이 없다. 가장 가치 있는 것에 취해진 위협과 행동이 핵심이었고 이는 그 이후의 공격이나 보복 행위를 저지(억제)하는데 중요한 역할을 했다.

이 새로운 억지력 개념을 북한에 적용한다면 적절한 질문은 무엇일까? 그것은 '김정은이 무엇을 가장 중요하게 생각 하는가? 그리고 그의 중요한 가치를 어떻게 위협할 수 있을까?'이다. 우리는 김정은의 핵무기를 평가하고 연구하며 주요 인사교체 동향을 면밀히 분석하기도 한다. 또한 우리는 북한 당국의 동기와 의도를 김정은과 그의 측근에게 대입하여 연구한다. 그러나 김정은이 정말로 가장 소중하게 여기는 것이 무엇인지에 대한 연구가 있는가? 김정은이 가치 있다고 여기는 것과 억지력의 함축성에 관련한 학술적 연구나 언론 보도 조차 찾아 보기 힘들다.

이 참신한 개념은 동맹국에도 적용될 수 있다. 이에 대하여 명시적으로 언급하지 않았지만, STRATCOM 문서는 이 중요한 사실을 강조한다. 확장억제력은 조약을 맺는 것 그 이상이다. 확장억제력이 제대로 작동하려면 동맹국 지도자들 사이에서 정서적·문화적 유대감이 있어야 한다. 하지만 이것은 앵글로색슨이나 서양이 아닌 동맹국들과 미국의 관계에는 그리 썩 좋은 징조가 아니다. 왜냐하면 양국의 가치관이 다르기 때문이다.

그렇다면 한국의 지도자들은 어떻게 하면 미국인들과 정서적으로나 문화적으로 더 강한 유대감을 가질 수 있을까? 반대로 미국 지도자들은 어떻게 하면 한국 사람들과 그럴 수 있을까? 한국과 미국 관계자들은 '공유 가치'에 대해 경쾌하게 이야기하며 한국어로 '같이 갑시다'를 힘차게 외친다. 물론 그것은 PR이나 외교적 수사로는 바람직하다. 그러나 이것만으로 한미 양국간 유의미한 신뢰관계를 구축하거나, 한국의 전략적 사고를 진전시킬 수는 없다.

진정한 신뢰를 구축한다는 것은 표면적인 환담만 주고받는 일련의 회의나 공적인 식사 그 이상을 의미한다. 핵무기와 관련된 갈등 해결에 있어서 신뢰는 가장 필수적인 요소다. 또한 이 신뢰 형성을 위해서는 진지한 상호 협의가 전제되어야 한다. 대부분의 미국 관료들은 한국 문화 관련 관용구에 대한 제대로 된 이해는 고사하고 한국어를 유창하게 구사하지도 못한다. 반면에 많은 한국 관료들은 유창하게 영어를 구사하지만, 미국의 문화적 레퍼런스(특히 어떤 상황을 스포츠에 비유하는 것)와 관련된 견고한 구사력을 찾아 보기 힘들며 미국의 핵억지 정책과 핵 전략에 대한 기본적인 이해조차 매우 부족한 실정이다. '식사를 함께 하는 것(breaking bread)'은 진부한 표현일 수 있지만 매우 중요한 일이다. 진정으로 식사를 같이 한다는 것은 음식과 술뿐만 아니라 가족, 전쟁과 같은 직장생활 같은 사적인 세부사항마저도 공유한다는 의미다. 언어적·문화적 차이에도 불구하고 서로 같은 언어를 유창하게 구사하거나 상대방의 '알겠다(gets it)'는 암묵적인 이해는 확장억제에 필요한 진정한 신뢰 구축에 중요한 역할을 할 것이다. 한·미 확장억제전략협의체(EDSCG)는 양측이 각자의 감성, 우선순위 및 불안감에 익숙할 수 있도록 훨씬 더 자주 그리고 더 장(長)시간 동안 만나야 한다.

북한의 핵무기라는 현실과 동아시아의 평화로운 미래라는 이상은 당분간 공존 가능하겠지만, 앞으로 지속하기 어려운 비정상적 조합이다.

지금은 동아시아와 세계의 안보를 강화하기 위해 미국의 확장억제 관련 진화된 사고(思考)가 필요한 시점이다. 뿐만 아니라 이제 한국의 독자적인 핵무기 개발 프로그램 추진을 심각하게 고려해야 할 시점이다. 미국의 동아시아의 정책 맥락에 한국과 일본의 핵 능력이 미국과의 더욱 긴밀한 관계를 통해 억지력을 강화 할 수 있다는 내용이 포함될 수 있다. 또한 이제 미국은 이 두 주요 비NATO 동맹국(한국과 일본)과의 동맹을 다른 차원으로 강화해야 할 시점이다.

'미국의 확장억제는 향후 40년 동안 신뢰할 수 있고 또 신뢰할 수 있는 상태로 유지 될 것인가?'라는 아주 근본적인 질문에 답을 하여야만 한다. 만약, 그 답이 부정적이라면 한국은 이제 해야 할 일들이 많아진다. 독자적인 핵 능력을 개발하고 유지하는 데 필요한 군사적 요구 사항과 재정안정성을 넘어, 한국은 전략, 억지, 핵 정책, 핵 사용 및 교전 규칙에 대한 깊은 사고(思考)에 있어서 큰 도약을 이루어 내야 한다. 이러한 문제들에 대하여 한국은 핵무기 관련 미국 워싱턴 당국의 비교 불가한 경험으로부터 많은 것을 배울 수 있을 것이다.

만약 한국이 실제로 핵무기를 개발·획득하는 것으로 결정한다면, 무엇보다 사전 준비가 매우 중요하다. 즉, 그러한 결정을 하기 전에, 우리는 먼저 기존한 미국의 확장억제 개념이 한국과 일본의 국익에 부합하는 정책인지 아니면 새로운 개념의 확장억제를 모색해야 할 것인지부터 고민해야 한다. 지금까지 우리는 북한체제의 붕괴를 통한 정권 교체라는 환상에 떠밀려 비확산과 비핵화라는 이름 하에 그 논쟁을 피해왔다. 지금 이 문제에 대하여 전반적이고도 직접 직으로 재고하여야 할 필요가 있다.

여기에 한가지 새로운 접근방식이 있다.

잭 니클라우스(Jack Nicklaus), 타이거 우즈(Tiger Woods) 등 최고의 골퍼들은 기존의 포워드(forward, 앞으로) 방식이 아닌 백워드(backwards, 거꾸로) 방식으로 각 홀을 플레이했다. 즉, 아마추어 골프 애호가들과 달리 골프의 최고의 전략가들은 그린까지 접근 비거리가 얼마나 될지 계산한 다음, 티에서 그 접근 목표 지점까지의 비거리를 역으로 계산한다. 이 접근 방식을 북한 핵문제에도 적용할 수 있다. 즉, 북한을 그린으로 상정하고 거꾸로 플레이 해보자.

김정은은 1984년 1월 8일에 태어났다. 36세인 그는 술과 담배를 좋아하는 것으로 알려져 있다. 그의 비만 체구는 왕성한 식습관을 표현하고 있다. 김정은이 언제 건강 문제에 직면할지 모르지만, 그가 76세까지 앞으로 40년 동안 북한을 통치할 것이라고 가정해보자. 트럼프, 아베, 문재인, 시진핑, 푸틴은 그때쯤이면 이 세상에 없을 것이다. 그 사이 이들 국가의 다른 지도자들이 북한의 핵무기에 맞서 싸워야할 것이다.

2060년에 예상되는 현실을 되짚어 보면, 우리는 지금 행동해서 다른 미래를 창조할 수 있을 것이다. 지금 세대의 한국인들은 미국 확장억제의 새로운 개념과 아울러 새로운 핵억지전략의 일환으로 북한의 핵무장에 대처하는 방법에 대한 전략을 모색하여야 한다.

향후 40년 동안 펼쳐질 미국과 중국의 경쟁은 동아시아의 지정학적 지형 윤곽을 형성하는 결정적 요인이 될 것이다. 중거리 핵전력 조약(INF)은 종료되었다. 미·러 신전략무기감축조약(뉴스타트, New START)은 2026년까지 5년 연장되겠지만 그 이후의 전망은 그렇게 밝지 않다. 1970년대부터 존재하였던 공식적인 군비통제조약들의 폐기에 대한 중국의 인식 향방이 미국, 러시아, 중국의 핵 정책 수립에 중요한 역할을 할 것이다. 북한의 핵 개발은 향후 수십 년 동안 미·중 관계 및 핵확산 금지 플랫폼의 지표라 할 수 있다.

다른 미래를 상상하고 실현하기 위한 노력이 없다면, 몇 가지 가정들은 40년 안에 결승점에 다다를 것이다. 비핵화 노력은 실패할 것이고, 북한은 현재의 핵 보유량을 증가시켜 핵 중견국으로 부상할 것이다. 미국과 러시아는 2026년 만료된 뉴스타트(New START) 외에 다른 협정을 찾아 나설 것이다. 중국은 핵과 미사일 능력의 지속적인 증대를 추구할 것이다. 물론 이 문제는 오직 중국의 경제 활력이 여하히 유지될 것인가에 달려 있다. 하지만 중국은 경제적으로나 군사적으로 미국을 추월하지는 않을 것이다. 미국은 여전히 세계에서 가장 강력한 국가로 남을 것이다. 그런 세계에서 한국은 전략과 정책을 조정하고 교정할 필요가 있다. 그리고 계획 역시 필요하다.

한국은 밝은 미래를 만들 수 있다. 2019년 US News & World Report에 따르면 한국은 세계에서 10번째로 강력한 파워를 지닌 국가로 명목 GDP 12위, 1인당 GDP 약 32,000달러 그리고 세계 7위의 강력한 군사력을 가진 나라가 되었다.[61]

그러나 이 통계 자료는 상당한 오해의 소지를 내포하고 있다. 더군다나 한국과 미국을 비교하는 데 있어서 한 가지 통계는 충격을 준다. 2017년 대한민국 정부 세입은 약 3,510억 달러였다.[62] 이는 미국 월마트의 2018년 매출액(약 5,000억 달러)에 한참이나 못 미치는 액수다.[63] 물론 한국은 세계 강대국의 사다리를 오르기 위해 엄청난 노력을 할 것이다. 그럼에도 불구하고 2060년경 미국과 한국 사이의 격차는 여전히 커다란 간격을 유지하고 있을 것이다.

그러나 이러한 이유들은 적극적인 국가 안보 의제 추진에 있어서 한국인들의 의욕을 꺾기보다는 오히려 강력한 동기로 작용 할 수 있다. 한국은 첨단 순항미사일 현무-3이 한국 대통령이 선택할 수 있는 최고의 공격무기가 되도록 하는 등 재래식 군사력 증강을 가속화해야 한다. 또한 한국은 북한 미사일을 무력화할 수 있는 레이저 기술을 구매하거나 개발해야 한다. 그러나 이 모든 조치들은 자체 핵무기 보유가 전제되지 않으면 무의미한 것이다. 한국 정부는 즉시 독자적인 핵 능력 보유의 타당성을 연구하는 국가 위원회를 구성하여야 한다. 또한 한국 정부는 미국 핵억지력과의 연관성을 탐색 및 형성하고 일본, 인도, 미국과 함께 태평양 동맹 조약 기구(Pacific Alliance Treaty Organization, PATO)의 창립 멤버가 되어야 한다.

김정은이 갑자기 사망하거나 퇴임하더라도 북한이 핵 보유국으로 존속하는 한 한국은 국가주권 수호에 만전을 기해야 한다. 핵 능력은 국가 주권의 궁극적인 상징이다. 핵확산금지조약(NPT)의 탈퇴와 이에 따른 국제 제재와 같은 후속 보복 조처는 독립적인 핵 능력을 획득하는 데 따르는 비용으로 간주 되어야 한다. 실제로 NPT는 조약 당사자국인 한국의 핵 능력을 차단하는 반면, 북한의 장점을 강화시켜 역내 불안정에 일조하고 있다. 한국의 핵 보유가 반드시 현재의 한미동맹 훼손을 전제하지 않는다. 오히려 이는 미국 정책당국자들로 하여금 주한 미군의 수를 줄일 수 있도록 함으로써 기존의 확장억제 장치를 강화하는 역할을 할 수 있다.

북한의 핵 능력이 고도화되고 핵무기 보유량이 늘어날 수록 미국의 확장억제력에 대한 신뢰성은 약화될 것이다. 그러므로 한국은 자주적인 핵 능력 보유 방안을 철저히 검토하여야 한다. 미국의 핵우산이 세계 안보의 핵심이라는 개념은 이제 구식이 되었으며, 지금의 현실과 다가올 미래에 맞도록 업데이트해야 한다. 가장 단순하게 요약하여 말하면, 미국과 북한은 핵무기를 보유하고 있지만 한국은 가지고 있지 않다는 것이다. 한반도에서 분쟁이 발생 하면 재래식 전쟁이 될 가능성이 높으며 한국은 재래식 무기로 싸울 수 밖에 없다. 만약 미국과 한국 둘 다 핵무기를 보유하고 있다는 시나리오에서는 핵억지가 존재하기에 전쟁가능성이 감소한다. 만약 핵억지가 실패한다고 하면 미국과 한국이 핵무기를 보유하고 있기에 북한과 직접 핵전쟁을 치를 수 있다. 위험하고도 근시안적인 상상이지만 만약 미국이 오늘 당장 핵우산을 접는다면, 북핵을 억지하기 위해서 한국의 핵무기 보유는 더 절실한 문제일 수 밖에 없다.

트럼프 대통령은 '공정한' 동맹관계 관련 격렬한 불만을 토로했다.[64] 이에 맞장구 치듯이, 2020년 1월 16일 미국의 폼페이오(Mike Pompeo) 미 국무장관과 에스퍼(Mark Esper) 국방장관은 유례없는 공동 기고문을 통해 한국은 부양가족처럼 굴지 말고 진정한 동맹국으로 나서야 한다고 주장했다.[65] 좋다! 그렇다면 한국은 그렇게 한다 하자. 즉, 한국은 나름의 방식으로 대가를 치를 것이다. 그리고 미국 역시 변화해야 한다. 현 주한미군사령관이 쓰고 있는 모자 3개(주한미군, 유엔사령부, 한미연합사령부)는 한일 양국을 총괄하는 단일 미군 사령관으로 대체 할 수 있을 것이다. 한국이 핵무기를 보유한다면 한국 영토에서 미군이 완전 철수 할 필요는 없지만 물리적 주둔 규모는 축소될 수 있다. 미국인도태평양사령부(USINDOPACOM)를 하와이에서 괌으로 이전할 수 있다. 이런 움직임은 미국이 '실제로' 및 '공정한' 동맹을 재건하기 위해 노력하고 있다는 강력한 신호가 될 것이다. 이렇듯 언제나 호혜성은 일방 아닌 양방향이다.

한·미·일 3국은 한국과 일본의 핵 능력이 미국의 핵억지력에 결합시키는 협상을 할 수 있다. 한국과 일본의 핵무장은 더 이상 금기시되어서는 안 된다. 미국의 핵비확산 목표는 중국과 북한의 핵 발전 속도에 비추어 볼 때 시대에 매우 뒤떨어져 있다. 냉전 시기의 최정점에 만들어진 비확산 정책을 명분으로 한국과 일본의 핵 무기 개발을 만류하는 것은 현실적이지도 않고 바람직하지도 않다. 한미동맹과 미일동맹이 한국과 일본의 핵 보유화와 양립할 수 없을 것이라는 생각은 버려야 한다. 한·미·일 3국은 개정된 새 조약에 서명할 수 있는 것이다. 동맹은 외교의 목적이 아니라 도구이며, 이 논리는 한국과 일본뿐만 아니라 미국에도 적용된다.

일본은 자국의 문제에 대해 스스로 결정을 내릴 수 있다. 그러나 일본은 동아시아 지역에서 미국의 정책조정을 예상하고 한국과 협력하는 것이 이득이다. 역사의 기억은 종종 고통스럽다. 그러나 일본에 대해서 '거부'라는 정서적인 전략보다는 중국과 북한의 위협이 중요성 면에서 훨씬 더 크다. 한국과 일본은 자연스러운 동맹이 되어야 한다. 역사가 길을 막도록 내버려 두어서는 안 된다. 정치인들은 정치적 편의성을 초월하여 변형시킴으로써 역사를 만든다. 한·미·일 3국의 군사동맹은 중국과 북한에 대한 효과적인 균형추가 될 것이다. 앞으로 세 나라의 지도자들은 문재인, 아베, 트럼프(2020년 3월 기준)가 없는 미래를 생각을 할 수 있어야 하고 반드시 그렇게 해야만 한다.

사실 트럼프식 미국내 포퓰리즘이 촉발한 힘들이 약 70년 전에 시작된 외교정책 관련 미국의 회의주의에 많은 영향을 미쳤다. 이제 미국은 국제 안보를 구축하는 새로운 방식을 모색해야 한다. 미국은 한국과 일본의 핵무장 구상을 포함한 새롭고 확장된 동맹 관계를 구축해야 한다. 이러한 정책은 북한의 정권 교체와 한반도 통일에 대한 관심이 미국 내 관심의 우선순위에서 밀려나고, 사실상 배제되는 상황에서도 확장억제에 대한 미국의 약속을 뒷받침할 것이다. 시간이 지남에 따라 이런 정책은 북한 정권 교체를 위한 여건 조성에 기여할 수 있다. 그러나 그때까지는 북한의 정권교체 정책은 보류하고 한국의 독자적인 핵 능력을 구축해야 한다.

미국은 2060년에도 여전히 가장 강력하고 가공할 국가로 남을 것이다. 그러나 미국이 핵무장한 한국과 일본이라는 두 국가와 의미 있는 동맹관계를 맺지 못한다면 미국은 더 이상 필수불가결한 국가로 존재할 수 없을 것이다. 돌이켜보면 냉전은 인류 역사에서 매우 비정상적인 현상이었다. 그 냉전 역사의 주요한 특징 중 하나는 각 국가가 오로지 자국의 편협한 국익 증진을 목표로 다른 국가들과 타협을 모색하는 것이었다. AI와 빅 데이터의 시대에도 불구하고 우리는 지금 미국의 중심 세계 질서 이전, 과거 냉전시대 이전으로 돌아가고 있다.

이제 여러 국가들이 앞장서서 미국과 함께 그 공동의 역사를 만드는데 함께 해야 할 때가 왔다. 한국과 일본은 이 역사적 과제 달성을 위하여 반드시 필요한 국가들이다. 북한의 비핵화는 실패했다. 설령 비핵화 달성을 위한 무력을 사용한다면, 이 또한 역시 전쟁이 끝나기도 전에 실패할 것이다. 왜냐하면 이러한 무력 사용은 정치적으로도 전혀 적절하지 않을뿐더러 군사적으로도 너무 위험하기 때문이다. 비확산 목표 자체는 찬사 받아 마땅하지만, 북핵과 중국의 핵 현대화 추세에 비추어 볼 때 이 목표는 무용지물과 다름이 없다. 이제 '비핵화'는 지우고, '억지력'이란 개념으로 바꿔야 한다. 미국의 확장억제는 한국과 일본의 핵무기 그리고 태평양 동맹 조약 기구와 결합될 경우에만 중국과 북핵을 억지할 수 있을 것이다. 또한 이는 확장억제력을 새로운 차원으로 발전시킬 것이다. 그러한 합의는 실제로 새로운 국제 질서를 예고한다. 아주 예사롭지 않은 시기가 도래했다. 이러한 때에는 비범하고 담대한 발상의 전환이 필요하다. 사고(思考)와 정책 측면에서 극적인 변화를 이끌어 내기 위하여 고민하고 토론을 시작 때, 바로 지금이다.

옹호와 진실*

2021년 3월, 국제법경제리뷰(International Review of Law and Economics)라는 저널에 게재될 하버드 로스쿨의 마크 램지어(John Mark Ramseyer) 교수가 쓴 ≪태평양 전쟁에서 성매매 계약(Contracting for Sex in the Pacific War)≫ 논문이 큰 파장을 불러 일으키고 있다.[66] 우리는 이에 대해 감정적으로 접근 할 필요가 없다. 오히려 이성과 논리로 차갑게 비판해야 한다. 그의 논문은 수정주의라는 이름을 앞세운 역사적 부정주의이다.

램지어의 조악한 논리의 문제점은 변호사들이 흔히들 말하는 '사실 그대로(ipso facto)'의 주장 – "내 주장은 내가 그렇게 말함으로써 증명된다" – 이다. 그가 작성한 논문의 출처나 증거 자료를 찾기는 힘들다.

입수한 그의 논문을 살펴보면 그는 '일본 사업가와 계약 문제'를 말한다. 그 계약이 무엇인지 찾을 수 없다. '인센티브 기반의 임금 계약'이라고 주장하는데 이 역시 증거가 없다. 섹션 2.2.2에서 "전시중 성관계에 대해 더 높은 가격을 협상한 매춘부들"이라고 말한다. 그러나 증거가 없다. '계약의 역학'이라는 게임이론을 분석 해야한다고 한다. 하지만 그는 분석을 하지 않았을 뿐만 아니라 게임이론의 기본도 모르고 있다. 존 폰 노이만(John von Neumann)과 존 내쉬(John F. Nash)가 무덤을 파고 나올 일이다. 그나마 다행인건 그는 논문 섹션 2.2.1에서 "선불금이 (위안소)여성들에게 얼마나 자주 지급되었는지 자세히 설명하는 출처를 알지 못한다"고 인정한다. 그리고 학문에서 사용하지 않는 표현인 '아마도(probably)'와 '해야한다(should have)'를 논문 곳곳에 쓰고 있다.

그는 대부분 일본 자료를 인용하였고 공신력 있는 한국자료나 미연합군이 일본을 제2차 세계대전에서 항복 시켰을 때 압수했던 문서들을 인용하지 않았

---

* 본고는 2021년 2월 19일 세르모국제연구소에 게재된 글 입니다.

다. 동북아역사재단에서 국내외 일본군 위안부 관계 공문서를 모아 발간한『일본군 '위안부' 자료 목록집(Ⅰ~Ⅳ)』4권을 살펴본 기록도 없다. 위안부 연구에 대해 필수적인 자료인 미군의 ≪Research Report No. 120: Amenities in the Japanese Armed Forces≫에 대한 언급 역시 없다. 호사카 유지 교수의 연구 역시 있을 턱이 없다. 그의 논문에 이러한 데이터와 1차 자료들이 없다면 구술 자료들이라도 참고하길 바랬다. 하지만 램지어가 언급한 오직 단 한 명의 여성인 문옥주. 그녀의 증언은 신빙성이 부족하다.

사실 그 무엇보다 램지어 논문의 치명적인 결함은 가정이다. 그는 한국인들이 일본 관리들과 그들의 당을 대표하여 협상할 수 있는 힘과 레버리지 그리고 지략을 가진 자주적이고 독립적인 일원이었다고 가정한다. 이는 당시 한국인들이 일본인과 동등 했음을 의미한다. 그렇다면 이 강력하고 실제 계약서를 쓸 수 있었던 한국인들은 누구였고 그 계약 조건은 무엇이었나? 역시 출처나 증거는 없고 또 없다.

역사적 사실은 이렇다. 식민지 기간 동안 일본은 한국의 문화와 관습을 지우려 했고 이에 더 나아가 창씨개명(創氏改名)까지 강요했다. 이런 상황에서 '약하고 천한 한국 여성들이 전능하신 대일본 제국의 군인들 뿐만 아니라 기회주의적인 한국 남성을 상대로 돈을 벌기 위해 매춘부로서 그들의 몸값을 협상할 수 있는 힘을 가졌다'고 램지어는 가정한다. 이렇게 지적으로나 상식적으로 말도 안되는 가정을 일본 눈치를 보며 아부하는 듯이 자랑스럽게 내미는 태도는 비웃음을 살 수 밖에 없다.

그의 논문은 학문이 아니다. 마치 '유대인들이 부헨발트와 아우슈비츠 수용소의 죄수들의 이빨에서 추출한 금을 얻기 위해 그들과 동등한 나치의 상대방과 협상했다'고 주장하는 나치의 선전과 비슷하다. 그의 논문은 역사가 아니다. 한나 아렌트(Hannah Arendt)가 말한 악의 평범화로 인한 전쟁범죄의 백지화이다. 이것은 의식적으로, 열광적으로 그리고 다운플레이를 통해 성매매라는 정당성을 부여한 뒤 일본의 직접적이고 침해적인 성매매를 부정하는 것이다. 그의 논문은 수정주의라는 이름을 앞세운 역사적 부정주의이다.

에드윈 레이샤워(Edwin Reischauer), 앨버트 크레이그(Albert Craig), 카

터 에커트(Carter Eckert), 아키라 이리예(Akira Iriye)는 아시아, 그중에서도 일본분야의 훌륭하고 인정받는 하버드대학교의 학자들이다. 이런 우수한 선상에 지금의 마크 램지어가 서있다. 램지어는 계약법의 렌즈를 통해 역사를 분석한다. 왜 법학 교수가 역사를 쓰고 있는가? 변호사의 어원은 라틴어 옹호론자(advocatus)들로 변론을 위해 고용된 사람이지 사학자처럼 역사적 사실을 객관적으로 평가하도록 훈련 받지 않는다. 램지어가 법대교수로서 변호사처럼 일본 견해를 옹호하는 것은 그의 권리이다. 하지만 칸나에의 한니발처럼, 학문이라는 경기장에서 검투사와 같이 그를 파괴하는 것은 나의 권리이다. 그게 사학자의 임무다.

핵 억지력, 선택의 순간*

2021년 1월 미국전략사령부(STRATCOM) 찰스 리처드(Charles A. Richard) 사령관은 미 방위언론사협회 인터뷰에서 핵 능력을 보유한 적대 세력인 두 국가의 전망에 대해 언급했다.[67] 두 국가는 러시아와 중국이다. 한 달 뒤 리처드 사령관은 미 해군연구소가 발행하는 잡지 '프로시딩스'에 칼럼을 기고했다. 그는 러시아와 중국이 미국의 국익을 훼손하기 위해 핵 사용을 고려할 것이라고 우려하며 "재래식 전쟁의 패배가 그들의 국가나 체제를 위협할 것이라고 러시아나 중국이 인식한다면 지역적 위기가 핵무기 사용을 촉발하는 전쟁으로 급속하게 확대될 수 있다"고 경고했다. 이어 "결과적으로 미군은 주요 가정을 '핵 사용은 불가능하다'에서 '(이제) 핵 사용은 현실적으로 가능하다'로 전환해야 한다"고 주장했다.[68]

필자는 이 문장을 제대로 읽었는지 세 번이나 확인해야 했다. 20여년 동안 군사전략, 핵 억지력에 몰두했던 전문가로서 이 문장들이 어떤 심각한 의미를 갖고 있는지 너무 잘 인식하고 있기에 며칠 동안 잠을 이루지 못했다.

리처드 사령관이 핵무기 사용을 고려한다는 것은 핵 억지 전략의 실패를 사실상 인정하는 것이다. 냉정한 핵 억지 철학이 이제는 핵무기를 사용할 수 있는 감정적인 전쟁 언어로 바뀌고 있다. 이것은 냉전이 최고조에 달했을 때 미국이 전통적 전쟁의 개념을 핵전쟁에 적용했던 것과 비슷한 맥락이다. 대군사력 전략(counterforce strategy) 개념으로 적의 군대를 핵으로 파괴시키고, 상쇄전략(countervailing strategy) 개념으로 핵전쟁을 이긴다는 의미다. 대표적인 예가 케네디 행정부의 단일통합작전계획 62(Single Integrated Operational Plan-62)다.

---

* 본고는 2021년 3월 8일, 국민일보 한반도포커스에 게재된 글 입니다.

한국의 존립은 핵 억지 전략의 성공 여부에 달려 있기에 이런 전략적 사고의 전환은 매우 우려스럽다. 일반적 인식과 달리 핵무기는 억지를 생성하기 위해 존재하는 것이 아니다. 오히려 정반대로 억지력은 핵무기를 감당하기 위해 존재한다. 핵 억지력의 존재 이유는 핵전쟁을 피하기 위해서다. 억지력은 본질적으로 역설적 전략이다. 사용하지 않을 무기를 만들고 만약 사용하게 되면 억지 전략은 사라지게 된다.

한반도의 전쟁 상황은 생각만 해도 끔찍하지만 핵전쟁은 더더욱 상상하는 것으로도 공포 그 자체다. 재래식 전쟁에서는 승자와 패자가 있다. 그러나 핵전쟁에서는 승자가 없고 오로지 패자만 있다. 미국의 최고 전략핵사령관이 핵무기 사용을 고려하고 있다면 한국은 이제 독자적 핵무기 생산능력의 실현 가능성에 대해 진지하게 원칙적인 방식을 따져봐야 할 때다. 정치적 실행 의지가 그런 프로젝트를 시작하는 데 필수 요소지만 외교정책 및 기술 전문가들의 전략적 사고와 계획이 선행돼야 한다. 그 첫 단계로 핵확산금지조약(NPT)과 개정된 한미원자력협정 등 주요 조약의 의무와 예산을 충분히 고려해 핵 연료주기 등을 자체적으로 완벽히 연구·습득할 수 있는가를 분석하는 타당성조사에 착수하는 것이 급선무다. 핵 지휘통제 시스템, 작전 독트린, 표적 획득 시스템, 안전하고 보안이 철저한 저장시설, 핵 기술자와 보안 인력에 대한 교육 등에 대한 타당성조사도 포함돼야 한다. 이는 대통령이 정확한 정보를 바탕으로 결정할 수 있는 옵션을 제공한다.

불행하게도 우리는 억지력이 없다. 상대방이 감당해야 할 가공할 핵무기가 없기 때문이다. 대한민국은 독립적 억지력을 세워 사용하지 않을 핵무기를 만들 필요성이 있다. 핵무기를 만들기로 결정한다 해도 진정한 핵무기 프로그램을 구축하는 것은 그야말로 단기간에 완성할 수 없는 방대하고 정교한 작업이다. 바로 지금이 그 시작을 검토할 때다.

독이 든 성배[*]

중국이라는 문제가 있다. 필자는 지역적으로 다양하고 특색 있는 중국 음식을 즐긴다. 또한 중국인 개개인들과 깊은 우정을 나누고 있다. 그러나 중국 공산당정부는 단호히 반대한다. 지금 중국은 역사를 다시 쓰고 있다. 윤동주 시인을 조선족이라 하고 김치, 한복, 판소리의 원조가 중국임을 주장한다.[69] 중국은 한반도 문화를 슬그머니 차지하려는 것을 넘어 아예 그들의 역사로 편입시키려 하고 있다. 오래된 프로젝트 중 하나였던 동북공정을 이제는 세계공정으로 확대해가고 있다.

중국이 역사를 다시 쓰려는 이유는 근대화 과정에서 겪었던 쓰라린 패배와 수모에서 기인한 역사적 열등감이 그 기저에 깔려 있다. 어떤 국가든지 역사와 문화에 대한 자신감이 있으면 열린 자세를 갖게 되는 법이다. 중국의 이런 편협한 소행은 매우 미성숙하지만 결코 무시할 수 없다. 국제관계에서는 군사, 무기, 외교, 경제보다 그전에 보이지 않는 전략적인 움직임이 있다. 그것이 바로 문화다. 우리는 단순히 반박하는 차원을 뛰어넘어 몇 배 더 강력하게 응징해야 한다.

현재 중국은 두려운 것이 없는 듯 행동하고 있다. 밑바탕에는 군사적 자신감이 깔려 있다. 1987년 미국과 소련이 체결한 중거리핵전력(INF) 조약을 통해 양국은 사정거리 500~5,500km의 미사일 개발을 금지했다.[70] 중국은 그 조약의 허점을 이용하여 현재 상당한 양의 중거리 미사일을 개발, 보유하고 있다.

최근 몇 년간 중국은 군비를 급격하게 확장하고 있다. 남중국해에 군사적 목적을 위한 인공섬을 조성해 군사 시설들을 설치하였고, 대만과 맞닿아 있는 중국의 해안 지역에 대량의 미사일을 배치하였다. 2021년 2월 중국 국방부는

---

[*] 본고는 2021년 4월 5일, 국민일보 한반도포커스에 게재된 글 입니다.

중간단계 탄도탄 요격미사일실험을 실시하였다고 발표했지만 사실상 이 실험의 실체는 위성공격무기 실험으로 본다.[71]

이러한 중국의 모든 행동은 미국이 강조하고 있는 규칙기반질서에 대한 강력한 도전이다. 최근 애틀랜틱 카운슬에서 발간한 ≪더 긴 전문(The Longer Telegram)≫에 따르면 중국 정치국 안에는 여러 계파가 있음을 가정한다. 미국이 그중 친서방 라인을 잘 설득하면 중국을 다시 자유주의 국제 질서 안으로 편입시킬 수 있을 것이라 주장한다.[72] 이는 단지 미국의 희망 사항일 뿐이다. 중국은 중국식 세계 재편을 시도하고 있다. 그러나 넘치는 자신감과 지나친 교만함은 결국 치명적인 실수를 낳게 된다는 것이 역사의 교훈이다. 문화적 오만함과 역사의 왜곡, 단기간의 군비 확장 이 세 가지의 조합은 독이 든 성배라는 것을 명심하여야 한다.

1974년 4월 10일, 유엔 6차 특별회의 연설에서 한 명의 지도자가 이렇게 말했다.

> "만일 어느 날 중국이 색깔을 바꿔 초강대국이 되어, 세계를 지배하고, 다른 나라를 괴롭히고, 다른 나라를 침략하고 착취한다면, 전 세계인들은 중국을 '사회제국주의'라고 반드시 비판하여야 한다. 그리고 그들은 중국의 본색을 만천하에 드러나게 하여 반대하고 맞서야 하며, 중국 인민들과 함께 타도하여야 한다."[73]

그의 이름은 덩샤오핑(Deng Xiaoping)이다. 불행하게도 그의 경고가 서서히 운명이 되고 있다. 작금의 시진핑과 중국 공산당 지도부들은 덩샤오핑이 경고한 바로 그런 패권 국가의 길로 달려가고 있다. 47년 전 덩샤오핑의 경고는 그때도 맞고, 지금도 맞다.

모든 눈물은 똑같다[*]

'진실은 상대적이고 역사적 상황에 따라 변한다.' 이것은 진보 이데올로기의 핵심이다. 조 바이든 미국 대통령은 2021년 2월 CNN이 주최한 타운홀 미팅에서 중국 위구르 대학살에 대한 질문에 "문화적으로 각 나라와 그 지도자들이 따라야 하는 각기 다른 규범이 있다"고 답했다.[74] 단순한 말실수가 아니었다. 그의 발언은 분명하고 명료했다. '문화적 차이'라는 명분으로 인권문제를 제기하지 않겠다는 의미였다.

그의 발언에 대해 많은 전문가들이 거칠게 비난을 할 것으로 예상했지만 깊은 침묵만이 드리워졌다. 국제관계에서 현실주의 모자를 쓰고 바라볼 때 바이든 발언은 나름 일리가 있다. 원칙과 보편적 가치는 때때로 현실에 의해 제약 받을 수는 있다. 여러 문제가 복잡하게 얽힌 세상에서 인권과 전략적 고려라는 이분법적 사고보다는 그 사이에서 균형을 찾아야 하는 것이 바로 현실주의 관점이다. 하지만 그 모자는 어색하고 불편하다. 여기에서는 인간이라는 단어가 들어설 자리가 없기 때문이다. 국제정치의 작동원리는 각국의 끊임없는 국익 추구, 그 자체라고 배웠다.

첨단산업에 중요한 희토류를 확보하기 위해서는 언제든지 인권이라는 이슈는 잠시 제쳐 놓아도 되는 것인 양 암묵적인 동의가 있다. 콩고민주공화국에는 코발트가, 볼리비아에는 리튬이 세계 최대로 매장돼 있다.[75][76] 이 두 물질은 컴퓨터와 스마트폰, 전기차 등의 핵심 부품인 리튬이온전지의 필수 원료다. 그런데 누가 이런 물질을 채굴하는가? 전기차에서 스마트폰을 통해 우리가 영상을 볼 수 있도록 하기 위해 5~6살밖에 되지 않은 콩고의 어린이들이 작고 가느다란 손가락을 사용해 그 치명적인 물질을 채굴한다. 안타깝게도 많은 수의 콩고

---

[*] 본고는 2021년 5월 3일, 국민일보 한반도포커스에 게재된 글 입니다.

어린아이들은 리튬과 코발트 채굴 중에 발생한 치명적인 독성을 들이마시다가 발병한 질병으로 사망하고 있다.[77]

혹자는 콩고의 어린아이들이 이러한 강제노동조차 없으면 굶어 죽을 것이라고 합리화하며 애써 외면한다. 하지만 이런 주장 역시 불편하다. 콩고와 볼리비아뿐만 아니라 북한, 미얀마, 발루치스탄은 선진국의 전략물자에 필요한 희귀 광물을 풍부하게 보유하고 있다. 이 모든 국가에 대해 인권문제는 가끔 정치적 이슈로 제기만 될 뿐 왜 준수해야 할 가치로 강요되지는 못하고 있는가?

이에 대해 현실주의적 세계관은 '상황에 따라 다르다(it depends)'고 답한다. 그러나 '인권'이라는 단어에 '상황에 따라 다르다'라는 단서가 추가되면 그것은 무의미한 수사에 불과한 것이다. 북한 인권문제도 "상황에 따라 다르다"고 넘어가면 그만인가? 우리는 비핵화라는 지상 목표를 위해서는 북한 인권문제를 외면해도 되는 것인가? 이 문제에 대해 오늘 침묵한다면 내일도 침묵할 것이다. 누군가는 그 침묵을 도덕적 중립이라고 한다. 그러나 1986년 노벨평화상을 받은 엘리 위젤(Elie Wiesel)은 "도덕적 중립은 피해자가 아니라 억압자를 도울 뿐 억압받는 사람들에게는 결코 도움이 되지 못한다"고 했다.

김정은 체제의 폭정과 탄압에 대해 북한 인권문제를 제기하는 것은 마치 계란을 벽에 던지는 것으로 헛수고를 거듭하는 것처럼 보인다. 계란이 벽을 결코 부수지 못한다는 것을 알지만 그 벽을 더럽히기 위해서라도 계란은 계속해서 던져야 한다. 물론 이 게임에서 승리할 가능성은 매우 낮다. 그러나 필자는 레닌과 함께 이기는 것보다 소크라테스와 같이 지는 것에 더 의미를 둔다. 진보주의가 주장하는 '상대적' 원칙과 바이든이 말하는 '다른 규범'은 착각이다. 상황에 따라 달라져야 하는 진실은 존재하지 않는다. 진실은 보편적이다. 언제나 그래왔고, 앞으로도 그럴 것이다. 모든 눈물은 똑같기 때문이다.

공허한 자들의 빈말*

    2021년 5월 21일 진행된 한·미 정상회담은 외교안보 측면에서 미사일지침 종료 성과를 제외하면 실망스럽다. 한·미 공동성명은 대북정책에서 '정교하고 실용적인 집근법(calibrated and practical approach)'을 상소했다.[78] 이는 '전략적 모호성'과 '균형외교'라는 문재인정부의 애매모호한 정책과 그 궤를 같이하고 있을 뿐이다.
    많은 사람들은 미국 대북정책이 정권에 따라 바뀐다고 주장한다. 하지만 사실은 그렇지 않다. 일방적으로 북한 제재를 완화하거나 비핵화를 철회한 미국 대통령은 단 한 명도 없었다. 정권에 따라 전술과 강조하는 부분들은 미세한 차이가 있지만 실무진에서 형성된 정책 일관성은 유지되고 있다. 문제는 그 일관성이란 것이 지속적으로 잘못된 방향을 향하고 있다는 것이다. 그것은 바로 인사 탓이다.
    조 바이든 대통령은 공동기자회견에서 성 김(Sung Kim) 국무부 차관보 대행을 대북특별대표로 임명했다. 인사가 정책 그 자체라는 측면에서 볼 때 바이든 정부의 대북정책 기조는 오바마 정부의 복사판이 될 가능성이 농후하다. 크리스토퍼 힐(Christopher Hill)을 멘토로 둔 성 김은 2008년 영변 원자로 냉각탑 폭파를 지켜본 뒤 '북한 비핵화를 위한 중대한 진전'이라고 자화자찬했다.[79] 하지만 그 당시 핵 전문가들은 그것은 실질적으로 원자로 운영에 미치는 영향이 없기에 비핵화에 아무런 의미가 없다는 것을 이미 알고 있었다. 그럼에도 불구하고 당시 미국 내 비둘기파들은 그 사건을 북한의 비핵화 신호로 여겼던 것이다.
    성 김 대북특사는 앞으로 토니 블링컨(Tony Blinken) 국무장관에게 직접 보

---

* 본고는 2021년 5월 31일, 국민일보 한반도포커스에 게재된 글 입니다.

고하겠지만 실질적인 영향력을 갖기 위해서는 반드시 내부의 주요 핵심 인물들과 협업하고 조율해야 한다. 그중 한 명이 미국 백악관 국가안보보좌관인 제이크 설리번(Jake Sullivan)이다. 설리번은 힐러리 클린턴(Hillary Clinton)의 측근으로 녹색혁명 지지를 거부했을 뿐만 아니라 오히려 이란핵합의(JCPOA) 당시 대가로 현금 지불 방안에 찬성했다. 또한 2016년 미 대선에서 트럼프와 러시아가 공모했다며 트럼프 임기 4년 내내 음모론를 주장하기도 했다.[80] 또 다른 한 명은 웬디 셔먼(Wendy Sherman) 국무부 부장관이다. 그녀는 북한, 이란, 시리아, 아프가니스탄 관련 '유화 정책'에 대하여 이제까지 단 한번도 반대해 본 적이 없었다.

마지막으로 '아시아 차르'인 커트 캠벨(Kurt Campbell). 미국 정부에서 대표적으로 과대평가된, 매우 얄팍한 사람 중 한 명이다. 그는 중국 공산당, 그리고 바이든 대통령의 아들 헌터 바이든과 친밀한 관계로 이해충돌을 겪고 있을 뿐만 아니라 아부의 대가다.[81] T.S. 엘리엇은 제1차 세계대전 후 실력 없는 사람들을 "형태 없는 형체, 색 없는 음영, 마비된 힘, 동작 없는 몸짓"의 공허한 군상으로 묘사했다.[82] 현재 바이든 정부의 대북담당 멤버들이 그렇다.

문재인정부의 치명적인 문제점 중 하나는 바로 유화적인 사고방식이다. 북한뿐 아니라 중국에 대해서도 마찬가지다. 처칠이 말한 "유화주의자는 악어가 마지막에는 자신을 잡아먹을 것을 기대하며 악어에게 먹이를 주는 사람이다"라는 것을 명심해야 한다.

유화정책 추종자들은 주로 행동보다는 포장된 말에 의지한다. 하지만 거친 국제사회에서 국익을 위해 일해야 하는 외교안보 인사들은 때로는 단호하고 강경해야 한다.

얼마 전 테오도로 록신(Teodoro Locsin Jr.) 필리핀 외무장관은 중국을 향해 "꺼져 버려!(GET THE FUCK OUT)"라며 원색적으로 비난한 바 있다.[83] 한국에 록신처럼 대담한 외교부 장관이 있었으면 어떨까 생각한다. 물론 공허한 사람들의 빈말이라도 가끔은 위안이 되기도 한다. 하지만 이들의 의미 없는 텅 빈 말들은 지금의 대한민국 안보에 그저 위협일 뿐이다.

바로 군인이다*

노르망디 상륙작전은 제2차 세계대전에서 미군을 포함한 연합군의 승리를 견인한 결정적인 계기가 됐다. 미국은 이 작전을 감행한 6월 6일을 국경일로 정해 기념한다. 역대 미국 대통령들과 주요 인사들은 이날 열리는 기념식에 참석해 감동적인 추모 연설을 통해 그 '역사적 승리'와 아울러 이를 위해 산화한 군인들을 기억하는 전통을 가지고 있다. 그중 1984년 로널드 레이건 전 대통령의 '푸앙트 뒤 오크(Pointe du Hoc)' 연설문은 희생된 군인들을 기리는 가장 아름답고 감동적인 연설문으로 남아 있다. 스티븐 스필버그(Steven Spielberg)는 '라이언 일병 구하기' 영화를 통해 노르망디 해안가에서 벌어진 전투의 처참함과 야만성, 용맹함을 영화 초반 24분간 보여주며 노르망디 작전을 대중의 뇌리 속에 깊이 각인시켰다.

하지만 올해 미국 조 바이든 대통령은 이 중요한 기념일 관련 어떠한 기념사나 추모의 언급도 없었다. 해리스(Kamala Harris) 부통령 또한 이에 대한 특별한 언급 없이 미국의 메모리얼데이 휴일을 앞두고 '긴 주말을 즐기라'는 트위터를 남겨 대중의 뭇매를 맞았다.[84] 당일이 돼서야 트위터에 노르망디 작전에 대한 짧은 추모의 글을 남겼을 뿐이다.

공교롭게도 한국의 6월은 호국보훈의 달로 지정돼 국가를 위해 헌신하고 희생한 순국선열과 호국영령을 추모하고 기억하고 있다. 하지만 6월 6일 현충일과 6·25전쟁 당일 언론 보도들은 하나같이 기념사 내용과 과거 비극적 전쟁 상흔에 대한 단편적인 사건들을 형식적으로 나열할 뿐이었다.

요즈음 한국 사회 분위기는 군대와 군인들의 역할을 너무나 경시하고 있다. 대중은 방탄소년단이나 축구 국가대표팀 선수들의 이름을 줄줄이 외우고 있지

---

* 본고는 2021년 6월 28일, 국민일보 한반도포커스에 게재된 글 입니다.

만 천안함에서 희생된 46명의 군인 이름을 어느 누구 1명이라도 제대로 기억하고 있을까? 우리는 국가의 이름과 국민의 자격으로 그들의 노고와 헌신을 기억하고 지속적으로 감사와 경의를 표현해야 한다. 이를 기념일로 지정한 진짜 이유가 여기에 있다. 민주주의는 국가와 정부를 분리한다. 하지만 군인은 언제나 국가를 대표한다. 이는 절대 변하지 않고 변해서도 안 된다.

분명한 역설은 전쟁 준비 태세의 날카로움이 현재 우리가 누리고 있는 자유와 여유로움을 보장하고 있다는 것이다. 조지 오웰(George Orwell)은 "국민이 그럼에도 편히 잘 수 있는 것은 국민을 해치려는 자들을 응징하기 위해 거친 사내들이 감내하고 있는 만반의 준비 태세 덕분이다"라고 말했다.[85] 하지만 이 말보다 더 아름다운 글이 있다.

> 우리가 신앙의 자유를 누리게 해준 자는 성직자가 아니라 군인이다.
> 우리가 언론의 자유를 누리게 해준 자는 기자가 아니라 군인이다.
> 우리가 표현의 자유를 누리게 해준 자는 시인이 아니라 군인이다.
> 우리가 시위할 자유를 누리게 해준 자는 학생운동가가 아니라 군인이다.
> 우리가 공정한 재판을 받을 권리를 누리게 해준 자는 변호사가 아니라 군인이다.
> 우리가 투표할 권리를 누리게 해준 자는 정치인이 아니라 군인이다.
> 국기에 경례하고, 국기를 받들어 봉사하고, 시신을 넣은 관이 국기로 덮이고,
> 시위자가 국기를 태울 자유를 누리도록 해주는 자는 군인이다.[86]

미국 육군 퇴역군인 찰스 M 프라빈스(Charles M. Province)의 ≪바로 군인이다(It is the soldier)≫라는 글이다. 이 긴 글은 전체적으로 인용할 만한 가치가 있다.

기업가, 학자, 지식인, 언론인, 의사, 엔지니어들과 AI, 핀테크, 4차 산업혁명, 가상화폐, 애플리케이션, 사이버 기술 또한 우리 사회에서 매우 중요하다. 하지만 군인이 없다면 그 어떠한 것도 가능하지 않다. 나라를 지키기 위해 희생하고 헌신한 사람을 존중하지 않는 국가는 반드시 실패할 수밖에 없다.

반격의 시작*

　지난 몇 년 동안 중국과 세계 각지의 그 추종 세력은 2049년까지 중국이 미국을 제치고 세계 경제 1위 자리를 차지할 것이라는 서사를 퍼뜨려 왔다. 그러나 이제 중국 관련 이 거짓된 서사에 대한 미국의 반격 움직임이 본격적으로 시작됐음을 보여주는 의미 있는 확실한 징후들이 나타나고 있다.
　미 공군은 2021년 7월 말 '퍼시픽 아이언 2021 작전' 실행 과정에서 괌과 티니언섬에 레이더에 잘 잡히지 않는 F-22 랩터를 무려 25대나 투입한다. 미국은 중국이 현재 보유한 전체 5세대 전투기보다 더 많은 수의 5세대 전투기를 언제든지 예고 없이 대거 투입할 수 있다는 메시지를 중국에 보낸 것이다. 지난 6월 미 국방부는 로드리고 두테르테(Rodrigo Duterte) 필리핀 대통령이 방문군협정(VFA) 종료를 6개월 더 연장한 것을 적극 환영했다.[87] 1998년 필리핀과 미국 사이에 체결된 군사협정인 VFA는 미군 차량과 장비가 필리핀 영토에 드나드는 것을 가능하게 한다. VFA는 1951년 미국과 필리핀이 체결한 상호방위조약 제4조의 핵심으로 중국의 남중국해 장악 시도에 대한 억지력을 제공하고 있다. 이는 두테르테 이후의 필리핀 정권도 중국의 침략에 대해 미국 최전선 방어의 필수적인 부분이 될 수 있다는 것을 의미한다.
　바로 여기, 지리학적인 횡포가 있다. 필리핀의 수빅만은 루손해협을 통제하는 데 매우 중요한 전략적 해군기지다. 루손해협은 필리핀해와 남중국해를 연결하는 대만과 루손섬 사이의 해협이다. 루손을 지배하는 자가 남중국해에서 서태평양으로 들어가는 진입로인 바시해협을 지배하게 된다. 이것은 일본 오키나와 남부에 위치한 전략적으로 중요한 국제 수로인 미야코해협의 통제에 영향을 미치게 된다. 결국 이렇게 연결된 해상 항로에 대한 접근은 주요 무역, 군

---

*　본고는 2021년 7월 26일, 국민일보 한반도포커스에 게재된 글 입니다.

사 전략에 막대한 영향을 끼치게 된다. '제1도련선'인 바로 이곳이 미국과 중국의 패권 다툼을 위한 잠재적 제1 충돌 지점이기도 하다. 뿐만 아니라 많은 통신 케이블이 루손해협을 통과한다. 이러한 케이블은 중국 홍콩 대만 일본 및 한국에 중요한 데이터 서비스를 제공한다. 대다수 사람은 인터넷망의 중심을 위성과 기지국이라고 생각하지만 사실 가장 중요한 구성 요소는 대륙 간 모든 데이터 및 커뮤니케이션 트래픽의 95% 이상을 전송하는 380개의 해저 케이블이다. 제이미 포고 제독(Adm. James Foggo)은 "수중 케이블은 우리의 중요한 인프라의 일부이며 세계 경제에 필수적"이라고 말했다.[88] 미국은 세계은행이 주도한 태평양 미크로네시아 통신케이블 부설 사업 프로젝트를 중국이 참여한다는 이유로 반대했으며 결국 해당 사업은 백지화됐다. 해당 프로젝트는 미국 정부가 주로 사용하는 한트루-1(HANTRU-1)과 연결을 계획했었다. 하지만 이 케이블은 상당한 군사 자산을 보유한 미국 영토인 괌을 지나고 있기에 미국 입장에서 상당히 민감한 사항이었다.[89]

최근 문제인 대통령은 디지털 생활의 모든 측면에 필수적인 반도체를 만드는 기계를 생산하는 네덜란드의 ASML 회사와 전략적 파트너십을 강화했다. 기본적으로 네덜란드가 장비를 만들고 한국이 이를 통해 반도체를 생산한다. 바이든 행정부는 전 트럼프 행정부의 기조를 이어받아 네덜란드 정부에 중국에 ASML 장비를 팔지 말라고 압박하고 있다. 그리고 미국은 북대서양조약기구(NATO)의 주요 회원국인 네덜란드와 비NATO 주요 동맹국인 한국과의 관계를 이용해 중국이 이 중요한 장비와 반도체를 사용하는 것을 적극적으로 저지하려 하고 있다.

첨단 무기 개발과 같은 군사적인 하드웨어는 언제나 중요하다. 그러나 향후 한국의 외교안보전략에 있어서 반도체 역시 대한민국의 새로운 '전략무기'가 될 것이다.

사이버 외교관을 찾습니다*

아돌프 히틀러(Adolf Hitler)의 악명 높은 이력서에 추가해야 할 진실이 하나 더 있다. 그것은 바로 '프로파간다(propaganda)'라는 단어에 대한 오염이다.

사실 이 단어의 기원은 종교적 맥락에서 유래했다. '프로파간다'는 '전파'를 의미하는 라틴어 'propagare'에 그 뿌리를 두고 있다. 1622년 교황 그레고리 15세는 가톨릭 선교활동을 촉진시키기 위해 '신앙의 전파를 위한 신성한 연합(Congregatio de Propaganda Fide)'을 설립했다. 즉, 천주교의 철학을 '전파'한다는 것이다. 하지만 히틀러로 인해 '선전'이란 단어는 거짓과 선동이라는 부정적인 이미지로 변형됐다.

국제정치에서 국가를 대변하는 선전을 공공외교라고 불렀다. 이제는 세월의 흐름에 따라 소프트파워라고 불린다. 비록 쓰이는 단어는 바뀌었지만 그 의미에는 변함이 없다. 그리고 트위터, 페이스북과 같은 SNS는 공공외교의 새로운 '선전' 도구가 되었다.

21세기 공공외교는 영어로 그 영향력을 펼치는 전쟁이다. 신임 주미 중국대사 친강(秦剛)은 워싱턴으로 부임하기 전 SNS에 중국 공산당 초기 중앙 당사 앞에서 찍은 사진과 깔끔한 영어로 부임 소감을 밝혔다. 그리고 그는 미국에 도착한 뒤 2주간의 격리를 마치고 첫 공식 일정 후 올린 트위터에서 "합리적이고 안정적이며 관리 가능하고 건설적인 중·미 관계를 위해 미국 동료들과 계속 대화하고 소통할 것"이라며 외교적이며 상냥한 어조로 말했다.[90] 뿐만 아니라 그는 SNS를 이용하여 스미스소니언 박물관에 축하 메시지, 도쿄올림픽과 미국 팀에 대한 찬사를 아낌없이 보냈다.

테오도로 록신 필리핀 외무장관은 자국을 위해 영어를 사용하면서 SNS를

---

* 본고는 2021년 8월 23일, 국민일보 한반도포커스에 게재된 글 입니다.

다방면으로 활용하고 있다. 그는 우디 앨런(Woody Allen), 그리스 철학자와 독일 철학을 언급하며 트위터를 한다. 또한 그는 미국 제약회사의 실수로 필리핀 백신 수급에 차질을 빚자 트위터에 다음과 같이 썼다.

> "나는 우리 국민과 외교단을 위해 3만개의 모더나를 약속받았다. 도대체 어디로 갔는지 모르지만 부끄러움과 분노를 말로 표현할 수 없다. 아무도 우리 국민을 위험에 빠뜨릴 수 없다. 아무도." [91]

모더나는 그 후 신속하게 필리핀에 백신 배송을 처리했다. 뿐만 아니라 록신은 필리핀의 외교 정책 철학을 정확하고도 거칠게 설명했다.

> "내 나라를 건들면, 난 너를 '조질' 것이다." [92]

강하지 않은 국력을 가진 모국을 위하여 작은 남자이지만, 그는 자신의 무게를 넘어 강력한 의지와 투지를 보여준다.

SNS를 통한 외교는 우리가 생각하는 그 이상 강력하다. 하지만 한국의 SNS 외교는 필리핀보다 영향력이 약하다. 모든 지표에서 한국이 필리핀보다 앞서 있는데 왜 이 분야는 우리가 뒤처져 있어야 하는가.

얼마 전 북한 김영철 통전부장은 대한민국을 향해 "잘못된 선택으로 스스로 얼마나 엄청난 안보 위기에 다가가고 있는지 시시각각으로 느끼게 해줄 것"이라고 했다. 만약 이승만 대통령이 SNS 외교를 했다면 얼마나 강력한 대응을 했을까. 그는 미국 프린스턴에서 배운 학식과 국제관계에 대한 혜안을 바탕으로 유창한 영어를 통해 대한민국의 국익을 위하여 적극적으로 옹호하는 트위터를 했을 것이다.

이제 대한민국 정부에도 사이버 외교관 팀을 구성해야 할 때다. 문제 발생 즉시 SNS를 이용하여 촌철살인의 한마디로 대한민국 국익을 대변하고 영어와 수사(rhetoric)를 통해 국제사회를 설득할 수 있는 인재들로 구성된 팀 말이다. 이러한 SNS 외교를 통해 그동안 오염됐던 '프로파간다'라는 단어도 사이버 외교의 본래 의미로 복원되는 길이 될 것이다.

아프간 철군 사태를 통해 본 미국 리더십의 위기: 바이든 대통령의 직무유기*

20년 전, 하늘에서 사람이 추락했다. 2001년 9월 11일, 흠잡을 데 없이 차려입은 남성이 연기가 피어오르는 세계 무역 센터(World Trade Center)에서 떨어지던 장면을 우리는 기억하고 있다. 그로부터 20년 후, 아프가니스탄 카불에서 어린 소년 두 명이 하늘에서 떨어졌다. 이륙하는 C-17 수송기 바퀴에 매달려 있다 추락한 것이다. 재앙의 시작과 끝.

그러나 이번 재앙은 피할 수 있었다.

'아무도 뒤에 남기지 않는다' 이것이 미국의 신조다. 미군이 한국전쟁에 참전한 전사자의 유골을 지금까지도 찾고 있는 이유다.

베트남전쟁 영웅 할 무어(Harold G. Moore) 중령의 말은 이러한 미국 정신의 근간을 잘 보여준다.

> "여러분을 무사히 데려오겠다는 약속은 해줄 수 없습니다. 하지만 사랑하는 가족과 전지전능한 하나님 앞에 이것만은 맹세할 수 있습니다. 우리가 전투에 투입되면 여러분이 가는 길에 앞서 내가 맨 먼저 적진을 밟을 것이고 또한 맨 마지막에 적진에서 나올 것이며 단 한 명도 내 뒤에 남겨두지 않을 것입니다. 우린 살아서든 죽어서든 다 같이 고국으로 돌아갈 겁니다." [93]

바이든 대통령은 이런 미국의 신조를 따르지 않았다. 그가 아프가니스탄 철군을 결정한 이유는 간단하다. 바로 전쟁을 끝낸 대통령으로 기억되기를 바라서가 아닐까. 그것뿐이다. 생명과 명예 그리고 미국에 대한 신뢰보다는 후대에

---

* 본고는 2021년 10월 6일 세르모국제연구소에 게재된 글 입니다.

남을 그의 레거시(legacy), 즉 유산(遺産)만을 고려했다.

바이든 대통령의 잘못된 외교적 판단은 이번이 처음이 아니다. 조지 W 부시와 오바마 대통령 정부에 몸담았던 로버트 게이츠(Robert Gates) 국방장관은 2014년에 『의무: 전장에 선 장관의 회고록』을 냈다. 여기에서 그는 이렇게 썼다.

> "바이든은 지난 40년간 거의 모든 주요한 외교 정책과 국가 안보 사안에서 틀렸다." [94]

월남 원조 반대 전력

8월 19일, 피터 웨너(Peter Wehner)는 아틀란틱 잡지에 바이든 대통령의 과거 언행을 다음과 같이 정리하였다.

> "1975년 베트남전쟁 당시 바이든은 남베트남 정부에 미국이 원조를 하는 걸 반대했다. 1991년 바이든은 걸프전에 반대했다. 2003년 바이든은 이라크전쟁을 지지했지만, 시간이 흐른 뒤 자신의 의회 표결을 후회한다고 밝혔다. 2007년 그는 조지 W 부시 대통령의 새로운 반군 전략과 이라크 주둔 병력 증강을 '비극적인 실수'라며 반대했다. 2011년 12월, 대통령이었던 오바마와 바이든 부통령은 이라크에 주둔하는 미군 병력을 대폭 축소했다." [95]

국익과 도덕성

바이든은 기자회견에서 아프간에서의 철수를 가장한 참담한 대피에 대해 미국의 '중요한 국익'을 호소하며 마치 자신이 옳은 판단을 한 현실주의자인 것처럼 의기양양하게 말했다. [96]

'국익 우선'은 국제정치학자 한스 모겐소(Hans Morgenthau)가 1949년 발표한 동명의 논문 ≪국익 우선(The Primacy of the National Interest)≫에서 강조한 개념이다. 모겐소는 이 개념을 미국의 외교 정책에서 그가 법률주의, 도덕주의, 감상주의로 특징지었던 것을 개선하기 위해 필요한 시정조치로 제시하였다. 그는 외교 정책에는 오직 권력을 향한 포석을 수행하는 냉철한 시각이 필

요하다고 주장했다.[97]

그러나 미국의 외교 정책에는 또 다른 강력한 전통이 있다. 보편적 도덕성이다. 미국 예외주의를 세계에 접목시키려는 전통적인 도덕적 기류는 여전히 강력한 힘을 발휘하고 있다. 매사추세츠만의 최초의 주지사였던 존 윈스럽(John Winthrop)이 말한 '언덕 위의 빛나는 도시(A Shining City upon a Hill)'라는 문구는 미국 대통령의 핏줄 속에 흐르고 있다.[98] 이 두 전통의 충돌과 혼합(융화)은 미국의 외교 정책에 영향을 미치고 있다. 미국은 권력 관계를 계산하지만 도덕적 가치에도 신경을 쓴다는 뜻이다.

미국인 52%, '바이든 사퇴해야'

미국인들의 도덕적 기류는 '바이든이 아프가니스탄을 어떻게 다루었는가?'에 대한 반응에서 뚜렷이 나타난다. 여론조사 기관 라스무센이 지난 8월 30일부터 31일까지 1000명을 대상으로 실시한 설문조사를 보면, 응답자의 52%가 '바이든이 아프가니스탄 정책에 책임지고 사퇴해야 한다'고 답했다. 39%는 사퇴에 동의하지 않았다. 참고로 이 여론조사의 표본을 보면 민주당 지지자들이 14% 더 많았다.[99]

시간이 갈수록 아프가니스탄 관련 뉴스는 신문 1면에서 밀려나고 있다. 이 여론조사가 포착한 사람들의 생각도 변할 수 있다. 그러나 결과 자체는 여전히 주목할 만하다. 응답자의 60%가 '바이든이 사임하지 않을 경우(물론 사임하지 않는다) 탄핵해야 한다'고 답했다. 라스무센은 린지 그레이엄 상원의원의 말을 인용해 응답자들에게 그와 동의하는지 질문했다. 그레이엄 의원은 이렇게 말했다.

> "바이든은 우리와 함께 싸운 수천 명의 아프간인들을 버렸고, 탈레반에 굴복한 8월 31일 대피 시한까지 일부 미국 국민을 버리게 될 것이기에 탄핵되어야 마땅하다."[100]

백악관에서 흘러나오는 말들을 보면 그런 기류가 두드러지게 나타난다. 폴리티코(Politico)에 따르면 한 백악관 관계자는 "탈레반이 아프간 내에서 권력을 공고히 하고 사형 집행을 하는 동안 미국인들의 발이 묶이게 내버려 두기로 한 대통령의 결정에 망연자실했다"며 "나는 미국인들을 그곳에 남겨둔 결정에 대해 완전히 경악하고, 말 그대로 공포에 떨었다"고 말했다. 또한 "수천 명의 미국인 인질 구출 작전인 비전투원 후송 작전(NEO)은 실패할 수 없는 임무임에도 불구하고 실패했다"며 비난했다. 또 다른 관계자는 "미국인들이 아프가니스탄에 버려진다면 이 임무가 완수되지 않을 것"이라고 말했다.[101] 이런 관계자들의 우려는 바이든이 철군을 강력히 옹호했던 바로 그날 나왔다.

아프간 작전은 나토의 작전

도덕적인 면은 일단 접어두자. 냉철한 전략적 계산 측면에서 보면 어떨까. 아프가니스탄 철수는 미국의 일방적인 작전이 아닌 북대서양조약기구(NATO) 차원의 작전이었다.

선데이 타임스에 따르면 바이든의 기자회견을 지켜본 영국의 한 관료는 바이든을 '완전히 미쳤다'고 표현하며 '두달리(doolally, 정신을 잃다)'라고 묘사했다.[102] 텔레그래프는 "영국 의회가 '재앙적'이며 '부끄러운 일'이라고 바이든을 규탄하며 전례 없는 질책을 했다"고 보도했다. 영국의 여러 의원은 좌우를 막론하고 "바이든 대통령이 우리와 다른 모든 사람을 불에 집어 던졌다"고 하며, "그가 '아프간 군이 전투 의지를 갖고 있지 않다'고 비판한 것은 부도덕한 일"이라고 비난했다.[103]

한미동맹도 재점검해야

독일의 아르민 라셰트(Armin Laschet) 집권 기민당(CDU) 대표는 바이든에 대해 "나토가 창설된 이래 겪은 최악의 실패"라고 가혹하게 비난했다. 프랑크-발터 슈타인마이어(Frank-Walter Steinmeier) 독일 대통령은 "카불 공항에 떠오른 절망의 이미지는 서구의 수치"라 덧붙였다.[104]

크렉 위트록(Craig Whitlock)이 쓴 『아프가니스탄 페이퍼(The Afghan Papers: A Secret History of the War)』는 아프가니스탄 실패에 대한 책임이 미국 민주당과 공화당 양쪽 모두에 있다는 걸 보여준다.[105] 그러나 터무니없는 방식으로 철수를 결정한 건 결국 바이든 대통령이었다.

　이 실패에 대한 유일한 책임은 바이든, 그에게만 있다고 봐야 한다. 다른 어떤 미국 대통령도 바이든과 같은 결정은 하지 않았을 것이다. 정치 경력 40년 동안의 그릇되고 비참한 판단은 이해할 수 없는 바그람 공군기지의 포기와 카불의 혼란 속에서 절정에 달했다. 바이든은 동정과 회개 대신 자신이 내린 모든 결정이 '비범한 성공'이었다며 도전적이고 오만하게 스스로를 평가했다.

　바이든이 NATO를 하나로 묶지 못한다면 신뢰만으로 맺어진 한미동맹, 미일동맹은 어떻게 제대로 관리할 수 있겠는가. 한국과 일본은 국제관계에서 미국의 '패권국으로부터의 퇴보'라는 전략적 시사점을 통해 미국을 어느 정도까지 의지할 수 있는지 한 번쯤 생각해봐야 한다. 대한민국은 현 미국 행정부를 맡고 있는 조 바이든 대통령, 카멀라 해리스 부통령, 토니 블링컨 국무장관, 로이드 오스틴 국방장관, 마크 밀리 합참의장의 아프간 문제와 같은 비참한 직무유기 사태에 대비해야 한다. 아마도 2024년 미국의 차기 정부는 이러한 상황을 반전시킬 수 있을 것이다. 하지만 우리는 그때까지 기다릴 수 있는 시간이 없다.

탈레반의 시간

　바이든의 대통령 임기는 3년 정도 남았다. 체력 저하를 감안한다면 바이든은 그 임기를 채우지 못할 수도 있다. 만약 그런 상황이 발생하면 그 뒤를 이을 부대통령인 해리스의 업무대행 결과가 더 나쁠 수도 있다. 해리스의 안보 보좌관은 미국 국무부 산하 외교연구원 소장이었던 낸시 맥엘다우니(Nancy McEldowney)이다. 맥엘다우니는 주불가리아 대사, 주터키, 아제르바이잔 공사대리 등을 역임했다. 클린턴 행정부에선 국가안전보장회의(NSC) 유럽 담당 국장, 유럽·유라시아 담당 차관보였다. 이 경력을 봐도 알 수 있듯 맥엘다우니는 유럽 전문가일 뿐이다. 북한, 중국, 동아시아에 대해선 아무것도 알지 못한다.

　탈레반은 미국인들을 이런 말로 조롱해왔다.

　"당신들은 시계를 갖고 있지만 우리에게는 시간이 있다."[106]

　2021년 8월 29일, 바이든 대통령은 도버 공군기지에서 아프가니스탄 카불

공항 자폭테러로 숨진 13명의 미군 유해가 도착하기를 기다리며 거듭 시계를 들여다봤다. 이 상황을 표현하기에 이보다 더 적절하고 비극적인 말이 있을까.

이제 탈레반의 시간이 시작됐다. 음악을 금지하고, 여성에게 성노예를 강요하고, 마수드 장군의 후예들의 20년간의 희생을 뒤엎고, 아라비아에 코란이 출현한 7세기의 야만적인 법령을 부활시킬 모든 시간을 탈레반은 갖게 될 거다. 샤리아(Sharia)는 아랍어로 직역하면 '올바른 길'이라는 뜻이다. 앞으로 국제사회는 탈레반이 그 '길(path)' 위를 통한 행진 결과에 직면해야 할 것이다. 그런 의미에서 바이든 대통령의 철군 결정은 수치스럽고, 불명예스럽고, 경멸스럽다.

필자는 2001년 9·11테러로 4명의 동료를 잃었다. 바이든 대통령은 그 죽음에 책임이 있는 자들을 다시 복귀시켰다. 바이든 대통령의 레거시(legacy, 유산)로 우리는 무엇을 기억하게 될까. 거기에 패배와 배신 그리고 거짓말 이 세 단어가 포함될까 우려된다.

스냅백은 없다*

2021년 9월 한 달 동안 북한은 네 차례 미사일 시험발사를 강행했다. 장거리 순항미사일, 철도기동 탄도미사일, 극초음속 미사일이라고 주장하는 '화성 8형', 지대공미사일.

정의용 외교부 장관은 특히 북한의 순항미사일 시험발사에 대해 "유엔 안보리 결의 위반은 아니므로 도발이 아니다"라고 거듭 강조했다. 하지만 북한이 쏘아 올린 것은 한국과 일본 전역의 목표물을 핵탄두나 재래식 탄두로 타격할 수 있는 지상 공격 순항미사일이다. 그것은 미사일 방어 레이더에 잡히지 않게 비행하도록 설계돼 매우 위협적이다. 북한은 "발사된 미사일들은 설정된 타원 및 8자 형 궤도를 따라 7,580초를 비행해 1,500km 계선의 표적을 명중했다"고 자랑했다.[107] 만약 그 주장이 사실이라면 이는 비행 기동성(in-flight maneuverability)과 종말유도(terminal guidance) 기술을 이미 북한이 보유하고 있다는 의미다.

그러나 문재인 대통령은 이러한 북한의 위협에 대하여 지난 유엔총회 연설에서 한마디도 언급하지 않았다. 대신 그는 현 상태에서 사실상 무의미한 종전선언을 제안했고, 그의 참모는 꺼져가는 남북 간 대화의 불씨를 되살리기 위하여 교묘한 방안을 언급했다. 북한의 합의 위반 시 제재를 복원하는 '스냅백'을 할 수 있다며, 북한 제재 완화 주장이 바로 그것이다.[108]

그러나 제재 조치를 완화했다가 언제 스냅백을 실행한 적이 있었던가. 2008년, 조지 W 부시가 북한을 테러지원국 명단에서 제외했을 때 경험이 부족한 당시 버락 오바마 상원의원은 언제든 북한에 스냅백 제재를 가할 수 있다고 주장했다.[109] 하지만 북한의 네 번의 핵실험이 있은 후에도 스냅백은 없었다.

스냅백은 손가락을 '탁' 튕기면 바로 작동하는 것이 아니다. 그러므로 국제사회가 언제든지 스냅백을 할 수 있다고 생각하는 것은 제재 시스템이 어떻게

---

* 본고는 2021년 10월 18일, 국민일보 한반도포커스에 게재된 글 입니다.

작동하는지 전혀 모르는 무지의 소치다. 제재는 수년간의 법 집행 조사, 정보 제공자의 양성, 제재 대상 기관의 분류(designation packages), 대배심 절차, 기소, 플리바게닝, 벌금 협상 등을 통해 만들어진 결과물이다.

물론 제재의 중단은 90일 이내에 제재를 다시 가할 여지를 남기기는 한다. 하지만 그마저도 지난한 외교적 협상 과정을 거쳐야 한다. 일단 제재 완화 후 제재를 재개하기 위해서는 관련한 모든 조건을 다시 협상해야 하는 등 매우 복잡한 문제를 감수해야 한다. 즉, 스냅백은 생각하는 만큼 빠르고 간단하지 않다. 따라서 북한과의 대화를 위한 제재 완화는 굉장히 어리석은 일이다.

제재 시스템에 대한 이해 부족과 아울러 문재인 대통령의 BTS 유엔 특별대사 임명은 대한민국 외교의 중량감(gravitas)과 전문성을 격하하는 결과를 낳았다. 사랑과 희망의 단어로 세상을 바꿀 것이라고 생각하는 아이돌이 시도 때도 없이 무력 시위를 감행하는 위협자들의 생각에 어떤 영향을 미칠 수 있을까. 만약 문 대통령이 유엔 연설에서 뻔한 종전선언 대신 차라리 칸트(Immanuel Kant)의 '영구 평화론(*Perpetual peace*)'에 나오는 평화연맹(*foedus pacificum*)과 같은 청사진을 제안했다면 오히려 외교적 품격이라도 과시했을 것이다. 그러나 그런 일은 결코 없었다.

고린도서 13장 11절은 이렇게 충고한다.

> "내가 어린아이였을 때는 어린아이같이 말하고 어린아이같이 이해하며, 어린아이같이 생각하였으나, 어른이 되고 나서는 어린아이의 일들을 버렸노라."

문재인정부는 이제 미온적이고 유화적인 태도 버리고 북한에 대한 환상에서 벗어나야 한다. 대한민국은 세계 8번째 SLBM을 보유한 국가로서 이제 그 위상에 걸맞은 외교를 펼쳐야 할 때이다.

악마는 디테일에 있다*

　2021년 9월 15일, 미국 영국 호주는 '오커스(AUKUS)'라는 새로운 삼자 안보협력 체제를 구축했고, 미국은 호주에 핵 추진 잠수함 기술 지원 계획을 밝혔다. 미국이 1958년 영국에 핵 잠수함 기술을 전수한 이후 호주는 미국으로부터 관련 기술을 전수받는 첫 국가가 됐다.
　오커스의 결정에 영감을 받은 것인지 일부 국내 전문가들은 잠수함 프로그램에 대한 고농축우라늄(HEU) 제한 해제를 주장한다. 그리고 대다수 외교 전문가들마저 우리도 무턱대고 핵 잠수함을 만들어야 한다며 목소리를 높이고 있다. 하지만 이러한 주장들은 국제조약과 국제법을 제대로 조사하거나 연구도 하지 않았다는 방증이나 다름없다. 우리는 보다 논리적으로 세밀하게 접근해야 한다. 핵심은 그 세부 사항에 있다.
　민감한 핵 기술과 능력을 다른 국가들과 공유한다는 것은 결코 그렇게 단순하지 않으며 복잡한 법적인 문제들이 도처에 깔려 있다. 핵확산금지조약(NPT)에 서명한 호주가 NPT를 준수하면서 어떻게 핵 추진 잠수함을 확보할 수 있다는 것일까? 국제원자력기구(IAEA) 안전조치협정(INFCIRC/153)의 제14조에 답이 있다. 규정은 다음과 같다.

　　　"국가가 이 협정에 따른 안전조치의 대상이 되는 핵물질을 이 협정에 따른 안전조치의 적용을 요하지 아니하는 핵 활동에 이용하기 위한 재량을 가지고자 의도하는 경우에는, 다음의 절차가 적용된다. (a) 국가는 다음 사항을 명백히 해 그 활동을 기구에 통고한다. (i) 핵물질의 비금지 군사적 활동에의 이용은 그 물질이 평화적 핵 활동에만

---
* 본고는 2021년 11월 15일, 국민일보 한반도포커스에 게재된 글 입니다.

이용될 것이라는 … 약속과는 모순되지 아니한다. (ii) 안전조치의 비적용 기간 그 핵물질은 핵무기 또는 기타 핵폭발 장치의 생산에 이용되지 아니한다."[110]

이를 요약하자면 이 안전조치협정의 핵심은 민감한 핵물질을 핵무기로 전용하지 않는다는 것이다. 즉, 핵연료는 평화로운 핵 잠수함에는 사용될 수 있다. 왜냐하면 핵 잠수함은 핵무기가 아니기 때문이다.

아직 이 조항을 단 한 번이라도 활용한 국가는 없었다. 오래전 이탈리아와 네덜란드가 핵 관련 해군 기술에 관심을 갖고 있을 당시 해당 문서 초안에 언급된 적이 있을 뿐이다. 따라서 제14조는 처음 작성된 이후 거의 휴면 상태로 남아 있었다. 대한민국은 당연히 핵 잠수함을 개발하고 보유하기 위해 이 조항을 언급하며 활용할 수가 있다.

또한 제14조는 원자력공급국그룹(Nuclear Suppliers Group, NSG)에 관한 한국의 의무와 일치해야 한다. 원자력공급국그룹의 지침 INFCIRC/254는 국가의 농축 기술 이전 목적이 평화적인 경우에만 타국으로의 이전을 허용토록 권장하고 있다. INFCIRC/254의 '민감한 수출에 대한 특별 통제' 섹션에는 "농축·재처리 설비, 장비 및 기술이 평화적 목적으로만 사용되는 것을 확인하기 위해 잠재적 수혜국과 협의하며, 기타 제반 사항에 대해서도 신중히 고려한다"라고 규정돼 있다.[111]

우리는 이 조약의 허점을 이용해 비확산 체제하에서 핵 잠수함 개발을 요구할 수 있다. 이러한 군사적 투자는 NPT와 NSG 의무에 충실하고 우리의 안보를 위한 순수한 목적이며 평화적인 활동임을 주장해야 한다. 필자가 줄곧 주장해온 바와 같이, 한국 정부는 독립적인 핵 개발이라는 장기적인 목표를 설정하고 단기 목표로 이 조약의 모호성을 이용해서 핵 잠수함 개발부터 추진할 수 있다. 이러한 정책 결정은 시기적으로 현 정부에는 한계가 있기에 대한민국의 국익과 안보를 위해 차기 정부의 최우선 국정 과제로 논의돼야 한다.

軍, 그들은 그들답게*

요즘 한국 사회에서 군대를 비판하는 목소리가 크다. 군대에서 발생하는 학대를 다루는 영화, 입대한 아들의 군 처우에 대해 지휘관을 질책하는 기사, 군인들의 인권 보호를 위한 목소리 등등 말이다.

필자는 얼마 전 지금의 군 내부 분위기를 적나라하게 보여주는 어느 한 기사를 읽었다. 그 기사에서 인용한 어느 일선 대대장의 비통한 말 한마디가 아직 머릿속을 어지럽게 맴돌고 있다. 그것은 다름 아닌 "민원과 문책이 두려워 제대로 된 훈련도 할 수가 없다"는 장탄식이었다.[112] 현재 군대 내에서 발생하는 부실 급식, 성 비위 등과 같은 문제들 그 자체를 옹호하자는 것이 결코 아니다. 다만 이러한 문제를 해결한다는 명목하에 군 본연의 모습을 약화시켜서는 안 된다는 것이다.

사실 이와 비슷한 상황은 미국에서도 벌어지고 있다. 미 국방장관 로이드 오스틴(Lloyd Austin)은 미군을 향해 "군은 지키고자 하는 국가 미국의 사회 변화를 적극 반영해야 한다"고 했다. 그는 미군이 변화를 '절대적으로 포용'하기 위해서 '더 노력해야 한다'고 주장했다.[113]

그러나 이것은 옳지 않다. 군대는 자신이 지켜야 할 일반 사회와 같은 모습이 되어선 안 된다. 군대가 잘하는 것이 있다면 젊고 평범한 남성을 징집해 원래의 모습을 부수고 애국심 넘치는 용감한 군인으로 거듭나게 하는 것이다. 군대에서는 기풍과 용기, 의무, 명예와 같은 군인 정신을 심어준다. 이러한 것은 자유롭고 민주적인 사회의 가치들에 반하는 것처럼 보인다. 하지만 군대는 바로 그렇게 하는 곳이며 그렇게 해야만 한다.

1957년 새뮤얼 헌팅턴(Samuel Huntington)은 저서 『군인과 국가(The

---

* 본고는 2021년 12월 13일, 국민일보 한반도포커스에 게재된 글 입니다.

Soldier and the State)』에서 "군인과 정치인 사이의 긴장은 각자 가지고 있는 전문성의 본질적인 차이에 바탕을 두고 있다"고 썼다. 그는 군인 정신이 보수적이고 현실적이면서 인간의 본성에 대해 매우 비관적이라고 묘사했다. 바람직한 민군 관계의 모델로 '객관적 문민 통제(objective civilian control)'를 제시하며, 명확하게 정의된 군사 영역 내에서 군이 자율성을 충분히 유지할 수 있도록 해야 한다고 주장했다.[114]

군대는 보통의 사회와는 다른 별개의 사회로서, 때로는 일반 사회의 상식과 충돌되더라도 군만의 독특한 가치와 일하는 방식을 유지해야 한다. 간단히 말해서 군대는 일반 사회의 작동 방식과 너무 비슷해서는 안 된다는 것이다. 군의 기풍은 일반 사회의 자유롭고 부드러우며 관용적이고 여성스러운 덕목과는 달라야 한다. 병사들이 바람에 나부끼는 가을 낙엽 같은 존재가 돼선 안 된다. 고대 로마의 정치가 키케로는 '의무에 관하여'에서 그리스 단어 '안드레아(Andreia)'를 강조했다. 이 단어는 바로 강인함(Fortitude), 남자다움을 의미한다.

군인은 창의 끝이다. 그리고 그 끝은 끊임없이 날카롭게 유지돼야 한다. 군인들은 교실에 앉아 성인지 교육을 받는 것보다 훈련장에서 지쳐서 쓰러질 정도의 훈련을 해야 한다. 지휘관은 현장에서 그의 부하들을 절대적으로 통제해야 하고, 군대에서 손가락을 다친 병사 아버지가 지휘관에게 항의한다고 해서 그 지휘관의 권위를 훼손해선 안 된다.

문민 통제는 민주주의에서 중요한 원칙이다. 그러나 군대는 그 자체가 군대이어야 한다. 군대의 목적과 임무는 전장에서의 승리다. 다른 모든 것은 부차적이다. 프리드리히 니체(Friedrich Nietzsche)는 『권력에의 의지(The Will to Power)』에서 "인간에 대한 저주는, 인간의 타락이 아닌 인간을 나약하게 만드는 것"이라고 했다. 군의 고유 영역을 인정하자. 이것은 군인들이 일반 사회를 파괴하고자 호시탐탐 노리는 적들의 공격을 막아내는 마지막 '선(line)'이 될 것이다. 군대가 그 선을 지킬 수 있도록 언제나 지지해야 하는 것이 바로 우리 국민의 역할이다.

2048년, 발칙한 상상*

매해 연초마다 각 분야의 많은 전문가들은 국제정치 예측과 전망을 쏟아낸다. 이런 전문가들의 예상은 오늘을 살아가고 있는 우리에게 미래를 대비하여 참고할 중요한 시사점을 제공하고 있는 것이 사실이다. 필자는 오늘만큼은 이상주의자가 되어 조금 더 멀리 있는 미래를 상상해 보려 한다.

상상력을 제대로 발휘한다면 현실을 예상할 수도 있다. 사실상 거의 모든 전문가들은 소련의 붕괴에 대하여 예측은커녕 상상조차 하지 못했다. 단, 두 명만 제외하고 말이다. 마르크스주의자였던 두 독일인. 한 명은 서독의 시인 한스 마그누스 엔첸스베르거였고, 또 다른 한 명은 동독의 철학자 루돌프 바로였다. 특히 바로가 예측한 소련 붕괴의 정확성은 소름 끼칠 정도로 맞아떨어졌다. 그만큼 상상하는 것은 중요하다.

대한민국이 건국 100주년 기념식을 맞이한 2048년 8월 15일, 그날은 어떤 모습일지 상상해 본다. 그때쯤이면 필자의 육체는 이미 땅속에 묻혀 있겠지만, 영혼은 세계 이곳저곳을 아무 제약 없이 돌아다니며 더욱더 역동적으로 변화하고 있는 세상을 바라보고 있을 것이다. 사랑하는 대한민국은 다음과 같이 변해 있지 않을까 기대한다.

바야흐로 2048년. 북한이라는 존재는 역사의 쓰레기통 속으로 흔적도 없이 사라졌다. 김정은은 이미 심장마비로 사망했고, 그의 여동생인 김여정의 통치는 불과 1년도 채 되지 않아 반란군의 충격으로 종식됐다.

북한이 붕괴되는 과정에서 중국은 사태를 수수방관했다. 오히려 중국은 미국, 일본과 함께 대한민국의 흡수통일을 인정하는 자세를 취했다. 중국은 경제발전을 위한 에너지 확대 전략의 일환으로 150개의 대규모 신규 원자로 건설을

---

* 본고는 2022년 1월 10일, 국민일보 한반도포커스에 게재된 글 입니다.

완료했는데, 이는 과거 26년 동안 전 세계가 건설한 것보다 더 많다. 반면에 중국은 경제적으로 미국을 따라잡는 데 철저히 실패했다. 결국 중국 공산당은 당명을 중국 인민당으로 바꿨다.

지금 내 눈에는 막강한 경제력과 군사력을 갖춘 민주주의 통일 대한민국이 보인다. 1인당 국민소득은 10만 달러를 돌파했다. 통일 대한민국은 핵무기를 보유하고, 핵이 없는 일본은 통일 대한민국과의 군사동맹을 지속적으로 요구했다. 그 결과 통일 대한민국은 일본에 핵우산을 제공해주고 있다. 미군이 한국과 일본에서 모두 철수함에 따라 한·미 방위조약은 진정한 의미에서의 한·미·일 공동방어전략으로 수정됐다. 통일 대한민국은 독일, 일본, 인도, 브라질과 함께 텐아이스(Ten Eyes)의 필수적인 중심 국가가 됐다. 현무-10은 세계 최고의 순항미사일로 미국의 토마호크를 완벽하게 대체했다. 국가정보원은 최고 수준의 수집, 분석, 작전 능력을 갖춘 막강한 정보기관으로 거듭났다.

한국의 소프트 파워는 세계를 지배하고, 막강한 소셜미디어 영향력을 행사하고 있다. 통일 대한민국의 외교 정책의 원칙과 전략은 최고의 전략가와 실천가들로 구성된 전략 연구 그룹에 의해 만들어지고 있다. 그들의 상상력은 대담할 뿐만 아니라 실행력 또한 매우 선도적이다.

이제 국제사회에서 통일 대한민국에 대한 명성은 드높다. 그들은 통일 대한민국을 "이보다 더 좋은 친구는 없다. 그리고 이보다 더 나쁜 적도 없다"라고 찬사와 질시의 감정을 뒤섞어 평가한다. 한니발은 "길을 찾을 수 없다면, 길을 만들라"고 했다. 이 한니발의 조언이 향후 대한민국 모든 대통령의 마음가짐이 돼야 한다. 바로 그것이 위대한 대한민국 100주년에 이르는 길이다. 좋은 꿈이 있다면, 반면에 지독한 악몽도 있는 법. 아, 이제는 괴롭지만 2048년 대한민국이 맞닥칠 최악의 상황에 대해서도 고민해 봐야겠다.

2048년, 끔찍한 악몽*

필자는 지난 칼럼(국민일보 한반도포커스, 2022년 1월 10일)에서 2048년 대한민국의 희망적인 비전을 상상했다. 하지만 악몽도 존재하며 이 역시 상상력이 필요하다. 디스토피아적 상상은 그 자체만으로도 고통스럽다. 하지만 때로는 그 고통이 혼란스러운 마음을 정화시켜 주기도 한다.

베르길리우스(Publius Vergilius Maro)의 서사시 『아이네이스(Aeneid)』의 첫 문장은 '무기와 사내를 노래한다(arma virumque cano)'로 시작한다. 인간의 고뇌는 무기(힘)와 삶의 다른 위태로운 요소들의 투쟁임을 표현하고 있다. 2048년 한반도에서 이와 같은 고뇌는 계속되고 있다.

쇠퇴를 거듭한 미국은 지금 2차 내전이 발발할 위기에 놓여있고, 민주주의의 핵심인 적법절차 원칙을 삭제한 제54차 수정헌법마저 통과되었다. 다수의 횡포로 운영되는 미국사회에서 이제 소수의 목소리를 찾아보기 힘들어졌고, 심각한 재정난으로 국제적 주도권을 사실상 상실하고야 말았다.

중국은 3,500개의 핵탄두를 보유함으로서 미국과 핵무기 균형에 임박했고, 한(漢) 민족주의가 맹위를 떨치면서 그렇게 원했던 대만을 마침내 정복했다. 중국, 사우디아라비아, 아랍에미리트(UAE)는 전기 운송 체제를 기반으로 과거 OPEC과 같은 새로운 카르텔을 결성했다. 이와 아울러 중국은 미국의 소형 공격용 드론인 스위치블레이드의 핵심적이고 민감한 기술들을 빼내어, 심지어 역설계한 자체 군사용 드론 제작에 성공하였다.

일본은 20세기 초 제국주의의 슬로건이었던 '대동아공영권'을 다시 완벽하게 부활시켰다. 일본, 영국, 호주는 한국을 일본의 영향력 아래 두는 3국 방위동맹을 맺었다.

---

* 본고는 2022년 1월 10일에 작성한 미발표 글입니다.

대한민국은 과거 선진국의 영광이 무색하리만큼 초라한 신세로 전락하였다. 미국은 한국을 이제 더 이상 신뢰할 수 없는 동맹국으로 간주해 한미동맹을 파기했다. 한국의 대북정책은 오직 허울뿐인 '제재'정책만을 고수하고 있을 뿐, 외교정책 엘리트들은 충동적이고 원칙 없는 안보정책 공방만 벌이다 결국 자주적 핵 능력 획득기회 조차 완전히 잃고 말았다.

국내정치는 좌우를 막론하고 포퓰리스트들이 득세하고 있다. 중소기업, 자영업자들이 제대로 커나갈 수 있는 환경을 조성하기는 커녕 오히려 섣불리 재벌을 해체를 시도하다가 한국의 경제는 오히려 피폐해졌다. 더욱이 평등과 정의라는 명분으로 국민 대부분의 경제 수준이 하향 평준화되었고, 구조적 불공정이 일상이 되었다. '피해의식'과 '당연한 권리'의 문화가 성취의 문화를 철저히 잠식하고 말았다. 2020년 출산율 0.837명을 기점으로 한국은 급격한 인구감소 국가가 되었다. 정부가 국민 삶의 너무 많은 측면에 개입하고자 함에 따라 무정부 상태와 유토피아 사이에서 갈피를 잡지 못하고 있다.

대기권 재진입 기술을 완벽하게 터득한 북한은 다탄두 각개목표설정 재돌입 비행체(MIRV) 기술뿐 만 아니라 영국, 프랑스, 브라질에 버금가는 수소폭탄를 비축하고 있다. 한국은 북한 김정은이 시시때때로 휘두르는 미사일과 핵무기의 실질적인 위협에 굴복하여 막대한 경제적 조공을 지불하고 있다. 거듭된 국방 예산 삭감과 훈련 축소로 말미암아 한국의 국방력은 북한에 비해 형편없이 약화되었다.

부정적으로 생각하는 것은 쉽다. 폴리아나식 관점을 비판하고 매니키이즘의 관점으로 세상을 관조하는 것이 오히려 현실적인 관점으로 세상을 살아가는 것이라며 소위 '힙(hip)'하게 보이기까지 한다. 하지만 진정한 현실주의자는 상상하는 것을 실현시키기 위해 현상을 있는 그대로 냉정하게 바라본다.

대한민국은 국내외적으로 어려운 과제를 안고 있다. 그 어려운 과제를 제대로 해결하려면 현실을 객관적이고 냉철하게 바라보는 지도자가 절대적으로 필요하다. 2022년 2월부터 오는 2048년 8월 15일까지 대한민국 대통령의 임무는 세계 정치의 스킬라와 카리브디스 사이에서, 그리고 국내의 복잡하고 어려운 여러가지 사안에 대해서 국가라는 거대한 배가 안전하게 항해 할 수 있도록 잘 조종하는 것이다. 알버트 카뮈(Albert Camus)는 "미래에 대한 진정한 관용은 현재의 모든 것에 몰입하는 것이다"고 했다. 그의 말이 맞다. 대한민국에서 이러한 악몽이 절대 펼쳐지지 않도록 현재와 미래의 대통령은 존재하는 국내외적 현안 해결에 자신의 모든 것을 바치겠다는 각오를 항상 다져야 하겠다.

힘의 상관관계*

북한이 2022년 1월 30일 중거리탄도미사일(IRBM)을 발사했다. 새해 들어 7번째 무력시위다. 북한이 지금 이 같은 행동을 재개한 이유는 무엇일까? 바로 '힘의 상관관계(correlation of forces)'가 북한에 유리한 방향으로 변화하고 있다는 것을 계산한 결과다. 이 개념은 마르크스가 혁명이론에서 처음 언급했고, 레닌이 1917년 러시아 혁명에 적용했으며, 1970년대 소련은 국제관계에서 자신의 대외관계를 규정하는 핵심적인 이론적 틀로 발전시켰다. 북한은 이 개념을 렌즈로 삼아 세계의 권력관계를 바라보고 있다.

북한에 그 첫 번째 '유리한 방향'은 한국이다. 북한은 이러한 군사적 도발이 앞으로 다가올 대통령 선거에 영향을 미칠 수 있다는 것을 또렷이 알고 있다. 만약 보수 후보가 당선된다면 상식선으로 볼 때 북한에 불리해 보일 수 있다. 하지만 역설적이게도 이러한 도발을 통해 북한이 한국 사회에 여전히 강력한 영향력을 행사할 수 있음을 또렷하게 보여주는 증거가 된다. 뿐만 아니라 앞으로 한국에 그 어떤 정권이 들어서든지 관계없이 국제무대의 협상 테이블에서 한국을 배제시키려는 목적이다.

두 번째 '유리한 방향'은 매끄럽지 않은 한·미 관계다. 이런 북한의 도발은 현 정부에서 한·미 관계의 균열을 더욱 증폭시키는 방향으로 전개하도록 한다. 미국은 2022년 1월 두 차례에 걸쳐 일본, 영국 등 다른 나라들과 함께 북한 미사일 발사를 규탄하는 공동성명을 발표했다. 그러나 두 차례 모두 직접 당사국인 한국은 불참했다. 한국 정부는 북한의 미사일 발사에 대해 직접적으로 규탄하는 발언 대신 1월 5일에는 '우려', 11일과 14일에는 '강한 유감' 그리고 17일 '매우 유감' 정도의 표현을 냈을 뿐이었다. 그럼 이 다음 행해질 북한의 도발에

---

* 본고는 2022년 2월 7일, 국민일보 한반도포커스에 게재된 글 입니다.

는 '참으로, 진심으로 유감'이라고 발표할 것인가? 이러한 정부의 대응은 미국으로 하여금 동맹국인 한국에 대한 신뢰를 약화시키게 한다.

세 번째 '유리한 방향'은 북한을 둘러싸고 있는 국가의 현재 상황이다. 중국은 베이징올림픽, 러시아는 우크라이나 사태로 북한 문제는 우선순위에 밀려나 있다. 특히 북한의 도발은 중국에 대한 레버리지를 높이게 한다. 만약 북한이 올림픽 기간에 또 다른 미사일 실험을 한다면 북한은 이제 중국조차도 통제할 수 없는 독립적인 나라라는 이미지를 세계에 각인시키게 된다. 더불어 김정은의 정치적 위상도 더욱 강화될 것이다.

마지막 '유리한 방향'은 나약한 미국 대통령이다. 김정은은 조 바이든을 시험하고 있다. 아프가니스탄에서의 끔찍한 철수작전 실패와 우크라이나 상황에 대한 형편없는 대응에서 볼 수 있듯이 바이든의 국제사회 관리 능력 부족은 김정은으로 하여금 현 상황을 더욱 대담하게 악용하도록 만들고 있다.

2018년 김정은은 중거리 및 대륙간탄도미사일(ICBM) 발사 관련 모라토리엄을 선언했지만 지난 시험발사를 통해 이를 파기했다. 이제 북한은 대기권 재진입 기술만이 남은 ICBM 시험발사를 눈앞에 두고 있다. 만약 이 시험발사가 성공하게 된다면 북한은 미국 본토를 정확히 타격할 수 있는 완벽한 미사일 기술을 보유하게 된다. 이를 통해 북한은 사실상 직접적으로 미국에 대한 억지력을 갖게 되는 것이다. 만약 이런 상황이 발생한다면 미국은 한미상호방위조약뿐만 아니라 제2차 세계대전 이후에 갖고 있던 동아시아에 대한 안보정책, 특히 그중 핵심인 확장억제에 대한 계산이 달라지게 된다. 냉전시대에 미국의 핵반격을 의심했던 프랑스의 샤를 드골 대통령이 한반도를 바라보며 스스로 질문을 한다. '과연 미국이 서울을 보호하기 위해 워싱턴을 희생할 수 있을까?' 그의 답은, '모르겠다(Je ne sais pas)'이다.

무기와 사내를 노래하다*

역사는 복잡하다. 단순히 선과 악이라는 이분법으로 역사를 바라본다면 접근방식은 간단하겠지만, 이를 통하여 역사적 교훈을 얻기는 매우 어렵다.

러시아가 크림반도를 군사력으로 강제 병합한 지 8년이 되는 해, 지난 2022년 2월 24일 블라디미르 푸틴 대통령은 우크라이나 '재침공'에 나섰다. 지금까지 언론을 통해 전해지고 있는 이야기들은 몹시 단편적이고 불확실하다.

우크라이나 남단의 즈미니섬, 13명의 우크라이나 국경수비대원들은 항복을 요구하는 러시아 전함에 "꺼져라" 외치며 저항했고 결국 모두 전사했다는 보도로 전세계에 깊은 인상을 남겼다. 처음 며칠 동안, 이 보도는 우크라이나 저항정신의 상징처럼 연일 보도되었다. 특히 젤렌스키 우크라이나 대통령은 전사한 국경수비대원들을 국가 영웅이라고 선전했다. 하지만 사실은 그들이 러시아 군에 항복했으며 살아 있는 것으로 밝혀졌다.[115]

우크라이나의 미그-29기 조종사가 6대의 러시아 군용 항공기를 격추했다며 '키이우의 유령'으로 불린다는 실체 없는 소문이 나돌았다. 그것이 사실이라면 얼마나 좋았을까. 하지만 이는 밈(meme)이고 심리전일 뿐이었다.[116] 헬멧을 쓰고 군용 벙커를 순찰하는 도전적이고 용감한 젤렌스키의 모습! 이것은 사실 2014년 군사훈련 때 찍은 사진이다. 러시아가 유대인 학살 추모시설 '바비야르'를 폭격했다며 젤렌스키를 포함한 세계 지도자들은 격렬하게 성토하며 비난의 수위를 높였다. 그러나 이 기념관은 손상되지 않는 멀쩡한 상태를 유지하고 있다.[117]

이 모든 확실하지 않는 정보들이 세계인들의 눈과 귀를 장악하고 있다. 매번 시도 때도 없이 받아보는 속보와 양측의 조작성 이야기들, 그 뒤에 숨어 있

---

* 본고는 2022년 3월 29일 세르모국제연구소에 게재된 글 입니다.

는 진실은 무엇일까? 현재 상황에 대한 막연한 추측보다 무엇이 우크라이나 전쟁이라는 비극을 초래한 것인지 분석하고 이해하는 것이 더 현명하지 않을까 감히 생각한다.

이를 위해서 동서 냉전이 사실상 막을 내린 31년 전, 1990년으로 돌아가야 한다. 1990년 2월, 냉전의 출발점이자 종착역이었던 독일의 운명이 한창 논의되고 있었다. 독일 통일 관련 가장 중요한 협상의 본질은 '과연 소련이 NATO 확장 중단이라는 대가로 독일의 통일 받아들일 수 있을까?'였다.

1990년 2월 9일, 미하일 고르바초프 사무총장, 예두아르트 셰바르드나제(Eduard Shevardnadze) 소련 외무장관, 제임스 베이커(James Baker) 미국 국무장관이 크렘린궁에서 2시간 동안 회담을 가졌다. 베이커 미 국무장관은 러시아에게 직설적이고 명확하게 다음과 같이 말했다.

> "우리는 동유럽 국가에 대한 소련의 확신이 필요하다는 것을 이해한다. 그러므로 나토의 일원인 독일에 미군을 배치하더라도, 나토 관할권(jurisdiction)은 동쪽으로 1인치도 확장하지 않겠다." [118]

이것이 그 유명한 베이커의 '1인치' 발언이다.

그럼 왜 소련은 나토의 확장에 대해 민감하게 반응하였던 것일까? 나토 초대 사무총장을 지낸 이스메이경(Lord Ismay)은 "러시아를 막고 미국을 끌어들이고 독일을 억제하는 것"이 나토의 목표라 했다. 이러한 관점에서 협상이 타결될 수 있는 실마리가 보였다. 마침내 고르바초프는 통일된 독일을 미국과 나토가 통제하되, 더 이상 동유럽 국가들을 나토에 편입시키지 않는다는 조건으로 독일 통일을 받아 들이게 된다. 그 당시 회의록을 살펴보면 그 어떠한 애매함도 없다. 우크라이나는 이 회담의 협상 어젠다에 올라가 있지도 않았다.

베이커의 '1인치 발언'은 보는 관점에 따라 냉전 종식의 첫 단추를 잘못 끼운 원죄 일수도 있고, 러시아가 독일의 통일을 승인하게 한 진정한 약속 일수도 있다. 그러나 원죄이자 진정한 약속이 될 수는 없다. 4년 후인 1994년, 미국 빌 클린턴 대통령, 앨 고어(Al Gore) 부통령, 스트로브 탤벗(Strobe Talbott) 백악관 러시아 전담 보좌관은 부다페스트 각서를 체결하였다. 이는 미국과 영국이 우크라이나가 핵무기를 포기한 대가로 그들의 안전보장을 약속한 것이다. 우크라이나는 이 각서를 믿고 당시 보유하고 있었던 1,900여개의 핵탄두를 모두 러시아로 반출했다.

베이커의 '1인치' 발언이 진정한 약속이었다면 부다페스트 각서는 가장 노골적인 위반이었다. 그러나 만약 베이커의 발언이 원죄였다면 클린턴의 이 같은 행위는 베이커의 그 원죄를 씻어주는 계기가 되었다. 현재 벌어지고 있는 우크라이나 사태에서 나토를 1인치도 움직이지 않고 우크라이나를 지킨다는 것은 모순이다. 우크라이나가 나토 회원국이 아닌데 우크라이나의 방어를 약속하는 것은 나토의 확장과 다를 바 없다.

부다페스트 각서 체결 후 3년 후, 봉쇄 정책을 고안한 조지 케넌(George Cannon)은 러시아의 극심한 경제적, 사회적 혼란기를 이용한 클린턴 행정부의 대러시아 정책을 가차없이 질책 했다. 1997년 2월 5일, 캐넌은 뉴욕타임즈에 다음과 같이 기고했다.

> "러시아 사람들은 나토의 확장이 적대적인 의도가 전혀 없다는 미국의 호언장담을 쉽게 받아들이지 않는다. 러시아 사람들은 그들의 국가적 위신과 안보에 부정적인 영향을 받는다고 확신할 것이다"

라고 썼다. 그리고 그는 불길한 경고로 마무리 했다.

> "나토의 확장은 탈냉전 시대 전체를 통틀어 미국의 외교안보정책 중 가장 치명적인 오류가 될 것이다." [119]

그로부터 몇 달 후인 1997년 6월 26일, 프레드 이클(Fred Ikle), 샘 넌(Sam Nunn), 로버트 맥나마라 등 미국 각계각층의 러시아 전문가와 핵 전문가들이 클린턴에게 나토 확장에 반대하는 서신을 보냈다.[120] 특히 그 서한에 서명한 사람 중에는 NSC-68의 저자이자 존 제이 이후 미국 역사상 가장 영향력 있는 고문이었던 폴 니츠(Paul Nitze)도 포함되어 있었다. 안타깝게도 클린턴은 냉전 기간 동안 미국 외교 정책을 담당했던 유능한 전문가들의 이러한 경고와 의견을 철저히 무시하였다.

1999년 6월, 미국은 슬로보단 밀로세비치(Slobodan Milosevic)가 자행한 코소보의 알바니아계 무슬림을 죽이는 '인종청소'를 막기 위해 '인도적 차원'에서 최초로 나토 연합군 작전에 참여했다. 78일 간의 공습으로 코소보의 독립을 얻어낸 미국과 나토에 대해 모두들 찬사를 보냈지만, 유일하게 단 한 명만이 우려를 표했다. 그는 국제법 학자인 루스 웨지우드(Ruth Wedgwood)였다. 그녀는 코소보 사태에 대해 미국이 유엔헌장 제2조에 명시된 국가주권과 영토주권을 위반한 선례를 남긴 것은 향후 커다란 분쟁 소지를 야기할 것이라고 경고하였다. 당시 러시아 총리로 임명된 푸틴은 이런 역사적 선례를 꼼꼼히 기록하고 기억해 두었다. 푸틴은 우크라이나 침공을 정당화 하는 근거로 미국이 코소보에 개입한 것을 언급하며 다음과 같이 말했다. "코소보와 무엇이 다르다는 것인가?" [121] 역사는 절대 사라지지 않는다.

2022년 현재 미 CIA 수장인 윌리엄 번즈(William Burns)는 1995년 러시아 주재 미국 대사관에서 정치 참사관 시절 다음과 같은 메모를 남겼다.

> "초기 나토 확대에 대한 적대감은 이곳(러시아) 국내 정치 스펙트럼 전반에 걸쳐 널리 감지되고 있다"

또한 번스는 2008년 콘돌리자 라이스(Condoleezza Rice) 미 국무장관에게 보낸 메모에서 우크라이나의 나토 가입에 대한 러시아의 반대를 재차 강조했다.

> "2년 반이 넘는 기간 동안 러시아 주요 인사들과의 대화에서 - 크렘린 궁 내부 어두운 곳의 거친 사람들부터(knuckle-draggers) 푸틴에 대하여 매우 비판적인 진보 지식인들까지- 우크라이나의 나토 가입은 러시아의 국익에 대한 직접적인 위협이라는 관점 이외의 시각을 가진 사람들은 전혀 찾아볼 수 없었다."

이에 덧붙여 "우크라이나의 나토 가입은 푸틴과 러시아 엘리트들에게 보내는 가장 강력한 레드라인"이라고 경고 했다.[122]

2014년 3월 5일, 헨리 키신저는 워싱턴 포스트에 기고한 글에 "서방국가들은 러시아에게 우크라이나가 결코 단순한 외국이 될 수 없다는 것을 이해해야 한다"라고 썼다. 이 견해는 우크라이나 상황이 단지 러시아 집권층에만 국한된 것이 아니라는 점을 재차 강조하고 있다. "알렉산드르 솔제니친과 조지프 브로드스키와 같은 유명한 반체제 인사들조차 우크라이나는 러시아 역사의 한 부문일 뿐만이 아니라 실제로 러시아의 불가분의 일부라고 주장했다"라고 했다. 키신저는 비관적인 어조로 다음과 같은 결론을 내렸다.

> "(러시아와 우크라이나의 문제에 대해) 앞서 언급한 요소나 이와 유사한 방안을 기반으로 한 그 어떠한 해결책이 강구되지 않을 경우, (러시아와 우크라이나의) 대립으로 향하는 움직임은 더욱 가속화될 것이다. 그 때는 곧 올 것이다."[123]

지금 이 경고는 현실이 되었다. 아무 이유 없이 헨리 키신저를 외교의 거장이라고 말하지 않는다.

시카고 대학의 존 미어샤이머(John Mearsheimer) 교수는 2014년 포린 어페어스에 기고한 글에 "미국과 유럽 동맹국들은 이 위기(크림반도 사태)에 대한 큰 책임이 있다. 이 사태의 근본적인 문제는 우크라이나를 러시아의 궤도에서 벗어나 서방에 통합하려는 나토의 확대에 있다"라고 했다. 미어샤이머의 현실주의에 동의하든, 그의 개인적인 의견으로 치부하든 간에 그의 국제 정치학적 통찰력만은 부인할 수 없다.[124]

이러한 수 많은 전문가들의 경고와 의견이 수 년 동안 지속되어 왔지만 국제사회는 어떻게 대처했기에 이 단계까지 오게 되었나? 도대체 우크라이나에는 무엇이 있다는 것인가? 그 핵심을 알기 위해서는 지정학적 접근방법으로 이야기를 시작해야 한다. 지도를 보면서 말이다.

우크라이나는 러시아와 유럽연합(EU)이라는 두 강대국 사이에 위치하고 있다. 즉, 우크라이나는 완충국가(buffer)이다. 하지만 우크라이나 자체만으로 접근하면 안된다. 현재 많은 전문가들이 고려하지 못하는 두 지역이 있다. 바로 수바우키 회랑과 칼리닌 그라드이다.

수바우키 회랑은 폴란드와 리투아니아의 국경을 이루는 65km 길이의 이 회랑이다. 이 지역은 나토의 군사개입 시 러시아에 대하여 직접적이고 즉각적인 영향을 미치는 전력적 요충지이다. 이 회랑의 서쪽은 러시아의 역외 영토인 칼리닌그라드와 맞닿아있다. 벨기에 영토 절반 정도의 면적인 칼리닌그라드는 독일 영토였지만 제2차 세계대전 후, 포츠담 회담을 통해 소련에 합병된 지역이다. 특히 이 지역은 러시아에서 유일하게 얼음이 없는 항구이기도 하다.

수바우키 회랑에는 2개의 주요 간선도로와 1개의 철도 밖에 없다. 하지만 만약 러시아가 이 회랑을 장악한다면 발트 3국에 대한 나토의 지원은 원천적으로 차단된다. 이곳이 바로 나토의 아킬레스 건이다. 2022년 2월 27일 벨라루스의 헌법 개정안이 통과된 이후, 만약 러시아의 핵무기를 벨라루스가 반입하기로 결정한다면 유럽과 나토의 지정학 전략 지도는 급변하게 된다. 이에 비하면 1980년대 소련의 SS-20 배치에 맞선 미국의 퍼싱-II 배치 갈등마저 단순히 아이들의 소꿉놀이쯤으로 비춰질 수 있다.

러시아는 이 모든 상황을 알고 있다. NATO 역시 알고 있다. 물론 미국도 알고 있다. 모든 군사 작전 전문가들도 이것을 알고 있다. 하지만 그 누구도 이에 대해 공개적으로 이야기하려 하지 않는다. 그들은 우크라이나 분쟁이 러시아와 나토의 실제 군사적 대결로 전이될 가능성이 있기에 이에 대해 말하는 것을 꺼리고 있다. 최근에 이 '어두운 비밀'을 넘어 핵 전쟁에 대한 수사(rhetoric)마저 푸틴의 발언을 통해 노골적으로 나오기 시작했다.

푸틴은 지난 2022년 2월 24일 "다른 국가들에게 경고한다. 러시아를 방해하지 말라. 어떠한 방해에 대하여 신속한 반응을 할 것이다. 그 대응은 이전 역사에서도 찾아 볼 수 없을 것이다. 관련한 모든 결정은 내려졌다. 내 말을 듣는 것이 좋을 것"[125]이라며 협박성 경고를 했다. 그가 말한 핵 위협을 이해하기 위해 언어학자의 도움까지 필요치 않다. 미 국방부는 혹시나 모를 오해나 오인을 피하기 위해 당초 예정됐던 미니트맨 ICBM 시험발사 결정을 보류했다. 이는 어찌 보면 다행스러운 결정일 수 있다.

그러나 현실은 낙관적이거나 불확실성 해소와는 거리가 멀다. 당연히 푸틴을 비난 할 수 있다. 러시아에 고강도 제재도 할 수 있다. 그러나 부인할 수 없는 것은 러시아가 단일 국가 중 가장 많은 핵탄두를 보유하고 있다는 사실이다. 존 메케인(John McCain) 전 상원의원은 러시아를 "이탈리아(경제수준) 정도 밖에 안되는 그저 핵무기 보유한 주유소 수준"이라고 얕잡아 보았다.[126] 하지만 러시아의 그 엄청난 핵무기 비축량과 기술을 견줄 수 있는 나라는 오직 미국 밖에 없다. 즉, 러시아는 '우리 모두가 우크라이나인이다'라는 슬로건이나 국제사회의 제재로 쉽게 제압할 수 없는 막강한 핵 전력 강대국이라는 것이다.

러시아에 대한 제재는 단순히 무기일 뿐, 전략적 정책이 될 수 없다. 그러면 의미 있는 정책은 무엇인가? 1936년에 체결된 몽트뢰 협약 21조에 따라 터키와 긴밀히 협약하여 다르다넬과 보스포루스 해협을 봉쇄하는 것인가?[127] 러시아와 핵전쟁 위험이 있는 우크라이나 상공에 비행금지구역 지정인가? 아니면 2022년 2월 23일 전의 상황으로 되돌리는 것인가? 아니면 전쟁 이후 분할된 우크라이나의 서방국가로의 흡수인가? 명확한 답은 찾기 어렵다.

분명한 것은 이러한 상황에서도 미국과 유럽은 서로 다른 긴급한 국제적인 현안의 관리 차원에서라도 여전히 러시아가 필요하다는 점이다. 특히 이란 핵 합의 복원 협상에서 러시아의 직접적이고 적극적인 지원과 협조는 필수적이다. 뿐만 아니라 여전히 북한 비핵화 정책, 특히 기존 대북 제재들의 효과적인 실행을 위해 러시아의 역할은 중요하다.

러시아는 비료의 주 원료인 질산암모늄의 세계 최대 생산국이다.[128] 또한 러시아와 우크라이나는 곡물의 주요 수출국이며 이들의 밀 수출량은 전 세계 밀 거래량의 약 3분의 1을 차지한다.[129] 식량은 전쟁에서 무기 다음으로 중요한 전략적 가치를 지닌다. 이미 미국은 코로나 여파로 심각한 내부 공급망 문제가 발생했고 이로 인해 인플레이션의 영향을 받고 있다. 하지만 우크라이나 사태로 인해 고공으로 치솟고 있는 기름값은 식품 가격 상승을 가속화하며 현재 바이든 행정부에 대한 미국인들의 인내심을 꺾는 도화선이 될 수도 있다.

푸틴이 우크라이나 점령에 성공한다면 미국의 군사 태세에 상당히 복잡한 영향을 미칠 것이다. 심지어 러시아가 우크라이나를 직접적으로 통제하지 않더라도 말이다. 인실릭과 아비아노를 포함하여 유럽에 곳곳에 배치된 핵탄두는 푸틴이 벨라루스에 핵무기를 배치할지 여부에 따라 재고 되거나 재편될 가능성이 높다. 만약 우크라이나가 러시아에 편입되어 사라지거나 사실상 중립국이 된다면 미국과 나토, 특히 나토의 최전선국가인 폴란드, 리투아니아, 라트비아 및 에스토니아 등은 자국의 군사전략을 변경할 것이다.

이러한 변화는 결국 동아시아와 대만 해협에 대한 미국의 방어태세에 영향을 미치게 될 것이다. 자원, 시간, 그리고 정치적 관심은 결코 무한대로 존재하지 않기 때문이다.

최근 미국 해병대는 자국 정치 노선의 영향을 크게 받는 한국과 일본의 동맹기지에 대해 '의존하기 보다는 신속한 원정군 투입'을 골자로 하는 역외축소전략(offshore retrenchment strategy)을 수립했다.[130] 이는 한국 정부에 함축된 의미가 크다. 만약 억지력이 실패하여 전쟁이 발발한 경우 주한미군이 주둔하고 인계철선이 있다면 미국은 즉각적으로 한국을 방어할 수 있다. 하지만 주한미군이나 인계철선이 없다면 한국은 미국의 지원이 도착하기 전까지 스스로 방어해야 한다. 현실적으로 미국이 우리를 지원하기까지 과연 우리가 몇일 정도 버틸 수 있을까?

상상하기도 싫지만 한국이 미국의 핵우산 아래 숨어있다 할지라도 미국이 중요한 순간 한국을 지켜주지 못할 가능성 역시 대비해야 한다. 만약 자체적으로 핵무장을 한다면 우리는 국제적인 비난과 제재를 감당할 준비가 되어 있을까? 이런 비난과 재제라는 비용보다 국가 안보라는 효익이 훨씬 더 크다면 우리는 지금부터 핵무기 프로그램 구축을 검토해야 한다.

필자는 적들이 내는 위협적인 소음보다 동맹국들의 무서운 침묵을 걱정한다. 대한민국을 온전하게 유지하려는 이러한 노력에서 우리를 도와줄 수 있는, 없어서는 안될 단 한 국가의 행동만을 보고 있다. 한국에서 끔찍한 전쟁이 일어나면 미국은 침묵할 것인가? 아니면 크게 떠들 것인가? 피할 것인가? 아니면 같이 싸울 것인가?

베르길리우스의 서사시 『아이네이스(Aeneid)』의 첫 문장은 '무기와 사내를 노래한다(arma virumque cano)'이다. 이 서사시는 인간 고뇌의 원인은 무기(힘)와 삶의 다른 위태로운 요소들 사이의 투쟁이라고 표현하고 있다. 현재 벌어지고 있는 우크라이나 사태는 인간과 인간이 가지고 있는 무기(힘) 투쟁, 이야기의 연속선상에 있다. 3,000년 전이나 지금이나 인간은 비극적이게도 힘을 통한 투쟁으로 갈등을 해소하려는 어리석음과 그 한계를 반복하고 있다. 결국 진실은 언제나 같은 이야기이기 때문이다.

기획자의 변(辨)

저자가 글을 썼다며 읽어보라고 건네 주었을 때마다 무언가로부터 압도되는 감정을 느꼈다. 한번 검토해보라는 글이었지만, 문장에서 엄청난 기운이 몰려왔다. 핵, 북한, 전략, 국력, 국제 관계 그리고 한 발 너 나아가 직선적이고 노골적인 표현들.

비록 영어로 쓴 초고였지만 한국 언론에서 다루지 않았고, 다른 연구물에서 찾아볼 수 없었던 새로운 시각 … 많은 레퍼런스를 지닌 글. 읽는 시간보다 그 의미를 알고자 공부하는 시간이 수 배는 걸렸던 글. 그리고 섬세하면서도 강한 단어들로 글은 채워져 있었다.

저자의 글이 신선하고 통찰력있기에 영어로 작성되었더라도 사람들이 직접 찾아서 단어를 찾아보며 읽어볼 것 이라는 다소 안일한 생각을 갖고 있었다. 그러나 첫 허들이 영어이기에 많은 사람들이 접근하는데 큰 장애물이였음을 뒤늦게 깨닫게 되었다.

과거에 저자의 글을 몇 차례 전문 번역가에게 맡겨도 보았지만, 저자의 의도와 뉘앙스를 제대로 살린 번역가는 찾아보기 어려웠다. 물론 많은 돈을 들이면 더 좋은 번역가를 찾을 수 있었겠지만 현실적인 제약이 뒤따랐다.

고육지책으로나마 가장 근거리에서 저자의 생각을 가장 잘 알고, 읽을 수 있는 사람. 비록 정치외교를 전공하지 않았고, 미국에서 교육을 받지 않은 직원들이 커다란 부담감과 압박감으로 주요 글들을 번역하기 시작했다. 부족한 번역 후 에디팅을 도와주신 감사한 분도 계셨다.

이 책에 실린 저자의 모든 영문 글들이 한국어로 번역 된 것은 아니다. 하지만 대한민국 국민들, 특히 지도자, 정책입안자들이 꼭 읽어야 하는 글들은 필수로 영문 번역 하였다. 역으로 국문으로 언론에 발표된 중앙일보 익그클루시브,

국민일보 한반도포커스의 경우 저자가 처음으로 썼던 영어 원문 역시 이 책에 함께 수록하였다.

저자의 철학과 지식은 이 글에 모두 담겨있지는 않지만 이 책을 통해, 이 책의 제목처럼 지도자들이 선택 그 이상을 너머 대한민국을 위해 올바른 판단을 할 수있길 소망한다.

송구스럽지만 거친 번역에 대해 독자들께서 너른 이해를 바란다.

세르모그룹 전략운영실장

참고문헌

1. 박승준, "중국 네티즌 일깨운 한 대학의 졸업식 연설", 주간조선, 2018년 7월 6일. http://weekly.chosun.com/news/articleView.html?idxno=13216

2. Donald J. Trump (@realDonaldTrump), Twitter, May 6, 2019. Reuters Staff, "Factbox: Tariff wars - duties imposed by Trump and U.S. trading partners," *Reuters*, May 14, 2019. https://www.reuters.com/article/us-usa-trade-tariffs-factbox-idUSKCN1SJ1ZJ

3. Donald Trump, "Message to the Congress on Securing the Information and Communications Technology and Services Supply Chain," The White House, May 15, 2019. https://www.presidency.ucsb.edu/documents/message-the-congress-securing-the-information-and-communications-technology-and-services

4. Martin Matishak , "Bipartisan bill seeks to toughen Trump approach on China," *Politico*, January 4, 2019. https://www.politico.com/story/2019/01/04/bipartisan-bill-trump-approach-china-1060974

5. "Donald Trump says 'Tariff King' India Wants Trade eal with US Primarily to Keep Him 'Happy,'" The Statesman, October 2, 2018. https://www.thestatesman.com/world/donald-trump-says-tariff-king-india-wants-trade-deal-us-primarily-keep-happy-1502691908.html. 장용승, "폭주하는 트럼프…" 관세왕 인도 · 불공정 브라질 나와라", 매일경제, 2018년 10월 2일. https://www.mk.co.kr/news/world/view/2018/10/615426/

6. "Interview: Steve Hilton Interviews Donald Trump," *Fox News*, The Next Revolution, May 19, 2019. https://www.youtube.com/watch?v=H9ys30khGM8

7. Ronald Reagan, "Remarks on East-West Relations at the Brandenburg Gate in West Berlin, Germany," June 12, 1987. https://www.presidency.ucsb.edu/documents/remarks-east-west-relations-the-brandenburg-gate-west-berlin

8. 해당 이미지는 다음을 참고하면 된다. "Saudi Arabia. September 17, 2019. Imagery released September 15, 2019." *Alamy*. https://www.alamy.com/saudi-arabia-17th-sep-2019-imagery-released-15th-sep-2019-the-damage-caused-by-a-drone-attack-on-saudi-aramcos-kuirais-oil-field-in-buqyaq-saudi-arabia-can-be-seen-in-this-image-released-by-the-us-government-and-

digitalglobe-on-september-15-2019-the-attack-on-this-and-saudi-aramcos-abaqaiq-oil-processing-facility-has-halted-oil-production-of-57-million-barrels-of-crude-oil-per-day-photo-via-us-governmentdigitalglobeupi-credit-upialamy-live-news-image274651252.html

9   Jennifer Agiesta, "CNN Poll: Support for Impeaching Trump Rises Among Independents and Republicans," *CNN*, September 30, 2019. https://edition.cnn.com/2019/09/30/politics/cnn-poll-impeachment-ukraine/index.html

10   Monica Alba, "Trump, RNC combine for $125 million raised in third quarter," *CNBC News*, October 1, 2019. https://www.nbcnews.com/politics/meet-the-press/blog/meet-press-blog-latest-news-analysis-data-driving-political-discussion-n988541/ncrd1061041#blogHeader

11   Alex Ward, "Read the Transcript of Trump's Call with Ukraine's President," *Vox News*, September 25, 2019. https://www.vox.com/2019/9/25/20883325/transcript-trump-ukraine-president-impeachment

12   Politico Staff, "Read the Trump-Ukraine Whistleblower Complaint," *Politico*, September 26, 2019. https://www.politico.com/news/2019/09/26/read-the-trump-ukraine-whistleblower-complaint-002239

13   "Foreign Affairs Issue Launch with Former Vice President Joe Biden," *Council on Foreign Relations*, January 23, 2018. https://www.cfr.org/event/foreign-affairs-issue-launch-former-vice-president-joe-biden

14   Paul Craig Roberts, "Sworn Statement of Ukraine Prosecutor General Viktor Shokin that He Was Forced out of Office by US VP Joe Biden," *TheAltWorld*, September 27, 2019. http://thealtworld.com/paul_craig_roberts/sworn-statement-of-ukraine-prosecutor-general-viktor-shokin-that-he-was-forced-out-of-office-by-us-vp-joe-biden

15   Alex Ward, *op.cit.*

16   Politico, *op.cit.*

17   Council on Foreign Relations, *op.cit.*

18   John Solomon, "These Once-Secret Memos Cast Doubt on Joe Biden's Ukraine story," *The Hill*, September 26, 2019. Sworn statement of former Ukraine Prosecutor General Viktor Shokin. https://www.scribd.com/document/427618359/Shokin-Statement

19   *Ibid.*

20   Pamela Falk, "Nikki Haley says North Korean Regime 'Will Be Utterly

Destroyed' if War Comes," *CBS News*, November 30, 2017. https://www.cbsnews.com/news/north-korea-regime-destroyed-if-war-comes-nikki-haley-united-nations-ambassador/

21   Cited in Stephen Jinwoo Kim, *Master of Manipulation: Syngman Rhee and the Seoul-Washington Alliance, 1953-1960* (Seoul: Yonsei University Press, 2001).

22   Michelle Ye Hee Lee, "North Korea Nuclear Test May Have Been Twice as Strong as First Thought," *Washington Post*, September 13, 2017. https://www.washingtonpost.com/world/north-korea-nuclear-test-maybe-have-been-twice-as-strong-as-first-thought/2017/09/13/19b026d8-985b-11e7-a527-3573bd073e02_story.html

23   Scott Stump, "'It's Deja Vu All Over Again': 27 of Yogi Berra's Most Memorable 'Yogi-isms,'" *Today*, September 23, 2015. https://www.today.com/news/its-deja-vu-all-over-again-27-yogi-berras-most-t45781

24   James Felkerson, "$29,000,000,000,000: A detailed Look at The Fed's Bailout by Funding Facility and Recipient," *Levy Economics Institute of Bard College Working Paper* 698 (2011).

25   Politico Staff, "Full Text: Donald Trump 2016 RNC Draft Speech Transcript," *Politico*, July 21, 2016. https://www.politico.com/story/2016/07/full-transcript-donald-trump-nomination-acceptance-speech-at-rnc-225974

26   Quoted in Barry Popik, "All Politics is Local," June 13, 2009. https://www.barrypopik.com/index.php/new_york_city/entry/all_politics_is_local/

27   J. D. Vance, *Hillbilly Elegy: A Memoir of a Family and Culture in Crisis* (New York: Harper, 2016).

28   Salena Zito, "Taking Trump Seriously, Not Literally," *The Atlantic*, September 23, 2016.

29   위의 글.

30   Christopher Hitchens, *God Is Not Great: How Religion Poisons Everything* (New York: Atlantic Books, 2007), p. 258.

31   Donald Trump, "Remarks by President Trump at the Economic Club," *The White House*, November 12, 2019. https://trumpwhitehouse.archives.gov/briefings-statements/remarks-president-trump-economic-club-new-york-new-york-ny/

32   "Job Openings and Labor Turnover Survey Highlights January 2019," *U.S. Department of Labor, Bureau of Labor Statistics*, March 15, 2019. https://www.bls.gov/jlt/jlt_labstatgraphs_jan2019.pdf

33 "Labor Force Statistics from the Current Population Survey," *U.S. Department of Labor, Bureau of Labor Statistics*. https://www.bls.gov/cps/cpsaat01.htm.

34 "Unemployment Insurance Weekly Claims," *U.S. Department of Labor, News Release*, September 6, 2018. https://www.dol.gov/sites/dolgov/files/OPA/newsreleases/ui-claims/20181422.pdf

35 "Unemployment Rate Unchanged at 3.6 percent in May 2019," *U.S. Department of Labor, Bureau of Labor Statistics*. https://www.bls.gov/opub/ted/2019/unemployment-rate-unchanged-at-3-point-6-percent-in-may-2019.htm

36 Erica York, "The Benefits of Cutting the Corporate Income Tax Rate," *Fiscal Fact*, No. 606, *The Tax Foundation*. https://files.taxfoundation.org/20180813165516/The-Benefits-of-Cutting-the-Corporate-Income-Tax_FF606.pdf?_gl=1*g9twb4*_ga*MTg5MzY4NzU3OS4xNjYzMDQwNDU0*_ga_FP7KWDV08V*MTY2MzA0MDQ1NS4xLjAuMTY2MzA0MDQ1NS42MC4wLjA.

37 Javier Blas, "The U.S. Just Became a Net Oil Exporter for the First Time in 75 Years," *Bloomberg*, December 7, 2018. https://www.bloomberg.com/news/articles/2018-12-06/u-s-becomes-a-net-oil-exporter-for-the-first-time-in-75-years

38 Marquette Law School Poll, "New Marquette Law School Poll Finds Shifts in Wisconsin Public Opinion Favorable to President Trump on Impeachment and Presidential election Preferences," *News Release*, November 20, 2019. https://law.marquette.edu/poll/wp-content/uploads/2019/11/MLSP55PressRelease.pdf

39 Relevant dates were selected from Morgan Chalfant, "Timeline: Trump, Ukraine and impeachment," *The Hill*, October 28, 2019. https://thehill.com/policy/national-security/467590-timeline-trump-ukraine-and-impeachment/

40 Adam Taylor, "Amid Trump Impeachment Drama, Ukrainians Ponder a Putin meeting," *Washington Post*, November 14, 2019. https://www.washingtonpost.com/world/2019/11/14/amid-trump-impeachment-drama-ukrainians-ponder-putin-meeting/

41 Simon Shuster, "'I Don't Trust Anyone at All,' Ukrainian President Volodymyr Zelensky Speaks Out on Trump, Putin and a Divided Europe," *Time*, December 2, 2019. https://time.com/5742108/ukraine-zelensky-interview-trump-putin-europe/

42 Reuters Staff, "Obama Tells Russia's Medvedev More Flexibility After Election,"

43 *Reuters*, March 26, 2012. https://www.reuters.com/article/us-nuclear-summit-obama-medvedev-idUSBRE82P0JI20120326

43 Charlie Spiering, "Flashback: President Barack Obama Fired All George W. Bush-Appointed Ambassadors in 2008," *Breitbart*, November 15, 2019. https://www.breitbart.com/politics/2019/11/15/flashback-president-barack-obama-fired-all-george-w-bush-appointed-ambassadors-in-2008/

44 "November National Poll: Support for Impeachment Declines: Biden and Sanders Lead Democratic Primary," *Emerson Polling*, November 2019. https://emersonpolling.reportablenews.com/pr/november-national-poll-support-for-impcachment-declines-biden-and-sanders-lead-democratic-primary

45 Glenn Thrush, "Trump's Blistering Speech at CPAC Follows Bannon's Blueprint," *New York Times*, February 24, 2017. https://www.nytimes.com/2017/02/24/us/politics/trump-conservative-political-action-conference-speech.html

46 Zeke Miller, "Trump Campaign to Report $30 Million Haul," *NBC Boston*, April 14, 2019. https://www.nbcboston.com/news/politics/trump-campaign-report-30-million/141582/

47 Quoted in Salena Zito, *The Great Revolt: Inside the Populist Coalition Reshaping American Politics* (New York: Crown Forum, 2018).

48 David Foster Wallace, Commencement Address, Kenyon College, May 21, 2005.

49 Quoted in Tim Weiner, "Robert S. McNamara, Architect of a Futile War, Dies at 93," *New York Times*, July 6, 2009. For his overall philosophy, see his article, The Military Role of Nuclear Weapons: Perceptions and Misperceptions," *Foreign Affairs*, Fall 1983.

50 Kenneth Waltz, "The Spread of Nuclear Weapons: More May Better," *Adelphi Papers*, Number 171 (London: International Institute for Strategic Studies, 1981).

51 Quoted in Robert W. Tucker, "The Nuclear Debate," *Foreign Affairs*, Fall 1984.

52 (나토 헌장 제5조) 나토의 한 동맹국에 대한 공격은 모든 동맹국에 대한 공격으로 간주되며, 만약 이러한 무력 공격이 일어난다면, 개인 또는 집단적 자위권을 행사하여 나토 각 회원국은 집단적 또는 독자적으로 공격받는 국가를 돕는다.

53 Eric Hoffer, *The True Believer: Thoughts on the Nature of Mass Movements* (New York: Perennial, 2002).

54 José Ortega y Gasset, *The Revolt of the Masses* (New York: Norton, 1993).

55 Keith B. Payne, "Nuclear Deterrence in A New Age: Comparative Strategy," *Comparative Strategy*, February 16, 2018, p.1.

56 "Nuclear Posture Review 2018," *U.S. Department of Defense*, February 2018.

57 위의 글.

58 "Essentials of Post-Cold War Deterrence," *STRATCOM*, 1995. https://www.nukestrat.com/us/stratcom/SAGessentials.PDF

59 위의 글.

60 위의 글, p.4

61 Sinéad Baker, "The Most Powerful Countries on Earth, Ranked," *Insider*, March 2, 2019. https://www.businessinsider.com/most-powerful-countries-ranked-us-news-and-world-report-2019-2#10-south-korea-16

62 보도자료, "2017회계년도 세입.세출 마감 결과," 기획재정부, 2018년 2월 9일. https://www.moef.go.kr/nw/nes/detailNesDtaView.do?searchBbsId1=MOSFBBS_000000000028&searchNttId1=MOSF_000000000015609&menuNo=4010100

63 "Fourth Quarter Fiscal Year 2018 Earnings," *Walmart*, February 20, 2018, p.1. https://corporate.walmart.com/media-library/document/management-commentary/_proxyDocument?id=00000161-b0bf-de73-af67-b2fffe5d0000

64 Donald Trump, "Remarks by President Trump to the 72nd Session of the United Nations General Assembly," *The White House*, September 19, 2017. https://2017-2021-translations.state.gov/2017/09/19/remarks-by-president-trump-to-the-72nd-session-of-the-united-nations-general-assembly/index.html

65 Michael R. Pompeo and Mark T. Esper, "South Korea Is an Ally, Not a Dependent," *Wall Street Journal*, January 16, 2020.

66 J. Mark Ramseyer, "Contracting for Sex in the Pacific War," *International Review of Law and Economics*, Volume 65 (March 2021).

67 Admiral Charles Richard, "Interview with the Defense Writers Group," *U.S. Strategic Command*, January. 8, 2021. https://www.stratcom.mil/Media/Speeches/Article/2466803/interview-with-the-defense-writers-group/

68 Charles Richard, "U. S. Navy. "Forging 21st-Century Strategic Deterrence," *US Naval Institute Proceedings*, Vol. 147, No. 2, 2021.

69 최민우, ""운동주는 중국인" "김치도 중국 것" 도 넘은 왜곡", 국민일보, 2020년 12월 30일. http://news.kmib.co.kr/article/view.asp?arcid=0015375146&code=61131111

70 Daryl Kimball, "The Intermediate-Range Nuclear Forces (INF) Treaty at a Glance," *The Arms Control Association*, August 2019. https://www.armscontrol.org/factsheets/INFtreaty.

71 "China Conducts Successful Land-Based Mid-Course Missile Interception Test," *CGTN*, February 5, 2021. https://news.cgtn.com/news/2021-02-04/China-successfully-conducts-missile-interception-test-XCaJvPO7EQ/index.html

72 ANONYMOUS, "The Longer Telegram: Toward A New American China Strategy," *Atlantic Council*, 2021. https://www.atlanticcouncil.org/wp-content/uploads/2021/01/The-Longer-Telegram-Toward-A-New-American-China-Strategy.pdf

73 Deng Xiaoping, "Speech at the Special Session of the UN General Assembly," April 10, 1974. https://www.marxists.org/reference/archive/deng-xiaoping/1974/04/10.htm.

74 "CNN Presidential Town Hall With Joe Biden," *CNN*, February 16, 2021. https://transcripts.cnn.com/show/se/date/2021-02-16/segment/01

75 "Reserves of Cobalt Worldwide in 2021, by country," *Statista*, 2021. https://www.statista.com/statistics/264930/global-cobalt-reserves/

76 Diego Ore, "Set to Build Large Lithium Plant in Uyuni," *Reuters*, October 1, 2009. https://www.reuters.com/article/bolivia-lithium-idUKN3021269020090930

77 "Democratic Republic of Congo: 'This is What We Die For': Human Rights Abuses in the Democratic Republic of the Congo Power the Global Trade in Cobalt," *Amnesty International*, January 19, 2016. https://www.amnesty.org/en/documents/afr62/3183/2016/en/

78 "U.S.-ROK Leaders' Joint Statement," *The White House*, May 21, 2021. https://www.whitehouse.gov/briefing-room/statements-releases/2021/05/21/u-s-rok-leaders-joint-statement/

79 "N. Korea Destroys Nuclear Reactor Tower," *CNN*, June 27, 2008. https://edition.cnn.com/2008/WORLD/asiapcf/06/27/northkorea.explosion/index.html

80 "Statement from Jake Sullivan on New Report Exposing Trump's Secret Line of Communication to Russia," *The American Presidency Project*, October 31, 2016. https://www.presidency.ucsb.edu/documents/statement-from-jake-sullivan-new-report-exposing-trumps-secret-line-communication-russia

81 Dale Hurd, "Is Biden in Deep with Beijing? Why Chinese Leaders Believe They Can Push Him Around,'" *CBN News*, March 11, 2021. https://www1.cbn.com/cbnnews/world/2021/march/is-biden-in-deep-with-beijing-why-chinese-leaders-believe-they-can-push-him-around

82 T. S. Eliot, "The Hollow Men," *The Complete Poems and Plays* (London: Faber and Faber. 2004), p. 81

83 Teddy Locsin Jr. (@teddyboylocsin), "GET THE FUCK OUT," *Twitter*, May 3, 2021.

84 Kamala Harris (@VP), "Enjoy the long weekend." *Twitter*, May 29, 2021.

85 George Orwell, *Brainy Quote*. https://www.brainyquote.com/quotes/george_orwell_159448

86 Charles M. Province, *U.S. Army*, 2005. http://www.pattonhq.com/koreamemorial.html

87 Idrees Ali and Karen Lema, "Philippines Again Suspends Scrapping of Troop Pact with U.S. amid China Dispute," *Reuters*, June 15, 2021. https://www.reuters.com/world/asia-pacific/philippines-suspends-decision-scrap-troop-pact-with-united-states-2021-06-14/

88 James Stavridis, "Opinion: China a Threat to Underwater Data Cables," *The Post and Courier*, April 10, 2019. https://www.postandcourier.com/opinion/commentary/opinion-china-a-threat-to-underwater-data-cables/article_4c87d528-5bd3-11e9-bcb0-6b4aa8ed0fd9.html

89 Jonathan Barrett and Yew Lun Tian, "Pacific Undersea Cable Project Sinks after U.S. Warns against Chinese Bid," *Reuters*, June 18, 2021. https://www.reuters.com/world/asia-pacific/exclusive-pacific-undersea-cable-project-sinks-after-us-warns-against-chinese-2021-06-18/

90 Qin Gang (@AmbQinGang)," Thank you DeputySecState Wendy Sherman for meeting with me StateDept on my 1st day out of self-quarantine. Look forward to continuing dialogue and communication with American colleagues for a rational, stable, manageable & constructive China-US relationship." *Twitter*, August 13, 2021.

91 Teddy Locsin Jr. (@teddyboylocsin), "I was promised 30,000 Moderna for my people and the diplomatic corps. My people who are frontliners. I don't know where the f**k that went, but words cannot express my embarrassment and anger. No one endangers my people. No one" *Twitter*, August 1, 2021.

92 위의 자료, "F**k my country I'll f@@k yours." *Twitter*, August 9, 2021.

93 "We Were Soldiers," Paramount Pictures, 2001. https://atloa.org/ltc-hal-moore-and-the-battle-of-the-ia-drang-valley-14-16-november-1965/

94 Quoted in Robert Gates, *Duty: Memoirs of a Secretary at War* (New York: Vintage, 2015).

95 Peter Wehner, "Biden's Long Trail of Betrayals," *The Atlantic*, August 19, 2021.

96 Joe Biden, "Remarks by President Biden on the End of the War in Afghanistan," *The White House*, August 31, 2021. https://www.whitehouse.gov/briefing-room/speeches-remarks/2021/08/31/remarks-by-president-biden-on-the-end-of-the-war-in-afghanistan/

97 Hans J. Morgenthau, "National Interest and Moral Principles in Foreign Policy: The Primacy of the National Interest," *American Scholar*, No. 18., 1949.

98 Ronald Reagan, "Farewell Address to the Nation," *Ronald Reagan Presidential Library and Museum*, January 11, 1989. https://www.reaganlibrary.gov/archives/speech/farewell-address-nation

99 "52% of Voters Think Biden Should Resign Over Afghanistan Withdrawal," *Rasmussen Reports*, September 1, 2021. https://www.rasmussenreports.com/public_content/politics/biden_administration/52_of_voters_think_biden_should_resign_over_afghanistan_withdrawal

100 위의 글. 또한 Lexi Lonas, "Lindsey Graham: 'I think Joe Biden deserves to be impeached,'" *The Hill*, August 25, 2021. https://thehill.com/homenews/senate/569351-lindsey-graham-i-think-joe-biden-deserves-to-be-impeached/ 참고.

101 Alex Thompson and Christopher Cadelago, "Biden Tries to Shift Blame on Afghanistan," *Politico*, August 31, 2021.

102 Tim Shipman and Josh Glancy, "The 2-trillion Afghan Shambles," *Sunday Times*, August 22, 2021. https://www.thetimes.co.uk/article/the-2-trillion-afghani-shambles-58sdwt3t7]

103 Ben Riley-Smith, "Parliament Holds Joe Biden in Contempt over Afghanistan," *The Telegraph*, August 18, 2021.

104 Quoted in Vijeta Uniyal, "Germany Calls Biden's Afghanistan Pull-Out the 'Biggest Debacle' for NATO," *Legal Insurrection*, August 18, 2021.

105 Craig Whitlock, *The Afghanistan Papers: A Secret History of the War* (New York: Simon and Schuster, 2021).

106 Sami Yousafzai, "10 Years of Afghan War: How the Taliban Go On," *Newsweek*, October 2, 2011. https://www.newsweek.com/10-years-afghan-war-how-taliban-go-68223

107 Samantha Beech, Jake Kwon and Oren Liebermann, "North Korea Says It Fired New Long-Range Cruise Missiles, according to State Media," *CNN*, September 13, 2021. https://edition.cnn.com/2021/09/12/asia/north-korea-missile-launch-new-intl/index.html

108 "A Conversation with Foreign Minister Chung Eui-yong of the Republic of Korea," *Council on Foreign Relations*, September 22 2021. https://www.cfr.org/event/conversation-foreign-minister-chung-eui-yong-republic-korea

109 "Statement of Senator Barack Obama on the North Korean Declaration," *New York Times*, June 26, 2008. https://www.nytimes.com/2008/06/26/world/americas/26iht-26nuclear-obama.14017843.html

110 "The Structure and Content of Agreements between the Agency and States Required in Connection with the Treaty on the Non-Proliferation of Nuclear Weapons," INFCIRC/153, *IAEA*, 1972. https://www.iaea.org/publica tions/documents/infcircs/structure-and-content-agreements-between-agency-and-statesrequired-connection-treaty-non-proliferation-nuclear-weapons

111 "Guidelines for Nuclear Transfers," INFCIRC/254/Rev.11/Part 1, *IAEA*. http://www.iaea.org/Publications/Documents/Infcircs/2012/infcirc254r11p1.pdf

112 원선우, "MZ세대 병사 등쌀에… 軍 대대장 잘 보살펴라"" 조선일보, 2021년 9월 20일. https://www.chosun.com/politics/diplomacy-defense/2021/09/02/PZSNGQYT3NEK3IU6GJ72HRYAKQ/

113 Morgan Phillips, "Cotton Presses Defense Secretary on 'anti-American Indoctrination' as Austin Defends Diversity Push," *Fox News*, June 10 2021. https://www.foxnews.com/politics/cotton-defense-secretary-anti-american-indoctrination-austin-diversity

114 Samuel P. Huntington, *The Soldier and the State: The Theory and Politics of Civil-Military Relations* (Cambridge: Harvard University Press, 1957).

115 Camille Gijs, "The 'go fuck yourself' Ukrainian soldiers on Snake Island are

alive, Navy says," *Politico*, February 28, 2022. https://www.politico.eu/article/ukrainian-soldiers-on-snake-island-are-alive-navy-says/

116 Thomas Novelly, "Ukraine's Fighter Ace 'Ghost of Kyiv' May Be a Myth, But It's Lethal as War Morale," Military.com, March 2, 2022. https://www.military.com/daily-news/2022/03/02/ukraines-fighter-ace-ghost-of-kyiv-may-be-myth-its-lethal-war-morale.html

117 Joseph Watson "Babi Yar Holocaust Memorial "Unscathed" According to Israeli Journalist," *Summit News*, 3 March, 2022. https://summit.news/2022/03/03/babi-yar-holocaust-memorial-unscathed-according-to-israeli-journalist/

118 Record of Conversation between Mikhail Gorbachev and James Baker, Kremlin, February 9, 1990. For the full array of primary documents, see https://nsarchive.gwu.edu/briefing-book/russia-programs/2017-12-12/nato-expansion-what-gorbachev-heard-western-leaders-early

119 George F. Kennan, "A Fateful Error," *New York Times*, February 5, 1997.

120 "Letter to the President, 'Opposition to NATO Expansion,'" June 26, 1997. https://www.armscontrol.org/act/1997-06/arms-control-today/opposition-nato-expansion

121 "Putin: "How is it different from Kosovo?", *B92*, February 22, 2022. https://www.b92.net/eng/news/world.php?nav_id=113110

122 Cited in *Congressional Record*, Volume 168, Number 27, February 10, 2022. https://www.govinfo.gov/content/pkg/CREC-2022-02-10/html/CREC-2022-02-10-pt1-PgS632-2.htm

123 Henry Kissinger, "To Settle the Ukraine Crisis, Start at the End," *Washington Post*, March 5, 2014.

124 John Mearsheimer, "Why the Ukraine Crisis is the West's Fault," *Foreign Affairs*, September-October 2014.

125 "Transcript: Vladimir Putin's Televised Address on Ukraine," *Bloomberg*, February 24, 2022.

126 Brett Logiurato, "John McCain: Russia is a 'Gas Station Masquerading as a Country,'" *Business Insider*, March 16, 2014. https://www.businessinsider.in/john-mccain-russia-is-a-gas-station-masquerading-as-a-country/articleshow/32154817.cms

127 Article 21 states, "Should Turkey consider herself to be threatened with imminent danger of war she shall have the right to apply the provisions of Article

20 of the present Convention" *1936 CONVENTION REGARDING THE REGIME OF THE STRAITS, Adopted in Montreux, Switzerland on 20 July 1936.* https://cil.nus.edu.sg/wp-content/uploads/formidable/18/1936-Convention-Regarding-the-Regime-of-the-Straits.pdf

128 "Ammonium Nitrate Production by Country, 2021" *Knoema.* https://knoema.com/atlas/topics/Agriculture/Fertilizers-Production-Quantity-in-Nutrients/Ammonium-nitrate-production

129 Hanna Duggal and Mohammed Haddad, "Infographic: Russia, Ukraine and the Global Wheat Supply," *Al Jazeera*, February 17, 2022. https://www.aljazeera.com/news/2022/2/17/infographic-russia-ukraine-and-the-global-wheat-supply-interactive

130 Gen. David H. Berger, U.S. Marine Corps, "Preparing for the Future: Marine Corps Support to Joint Operations in Contested Littorals," *Military Review*, April 2021.

김진우 박사

김진우 박사는 영어 교육 컨설팅 회사 세르모그룹(SERMO Group)의 대표이며, 비영리 싱크탱크 세르모국제연구소 소장이다. 현재 서강대 국제대학원 겸임교수로서 한미관계, 국가정보, 미국 외교안보정책, 국제기구 관련 강의를 하고 있다.

그는 미국 정부의 정책, 군사, 정보기관에서 근무하며 중국, 북한, 파키스탄, 이란, 전략적 핵 억지력, 대량살상무기에 대한 업무를 담당했다. 해군분석센터 작전분석그룹에서 군사작전 및 동아시아 담당 분석관으로 재직하였고, 미 로렌스 리버모어 국립연구소에서 선임분석관으로 정책, 군사, 정보 관련 업무를 담당하였다. 또한 미 전략사령부(STRATCOM)와 NATO의 핵 억지력 및 타격작전에 대해 자문역할을 수행하였고, 미 국무부 검증·준수·이행국 총괄 선임고문으로 재직했다. 미 국무부에 합류하기 이전, 미 국방부 산하 총괄평가국(Office of Net Assessment) 국장이었던 Andrew Marshall의 특별 보좌관을 역임했다.

김진우 박사는 미 조지타운대학교에서 역사·외교학사(History and Diplomacy), 하버드대학교에서 외교안보(International Affairs and Security) 석사, 예일 대학교에서 역사학(History) 박사학위를 취득하였다.

김진우 박사 트위터 주소 @jinwookimsays

스킬라와 카리브디스 그 너머: 국가경영의 예술
(BEYOND SCYLLA AND CHARYBDIS: THE ART OF STATECRAFT)

초판 1쇄 발행 2022년 11월 1일

지 은 이   김진우 (STEPHEN JINWOO KIM)
발 행 처   세르모그룹
펴 낸 이   김진우
주   소   서울특별시 강남구 언주로134길 6, 202호-B340
출판등록   제2022-000242호
전   화   02-701-5335
이 메 일   office@sermo.co.kr
홈페이지   www.sermo.co.kr

ISBN 979-11-980277-0-2(04340)
ISBN 979-11-980277-9-5(04340) (세트)
값 25,000원

ⓒ 김진우, 2022
이 책은 저작권법에 의해 보호를 받는 저작물이므로 저자와 출판사의 허락 없이 내용의 일부를 인용하거나 발췌하는 것을 금합니다.

BEYOND SCYLLA AND CHARYBDIS

THE ART OF STATECRAFT

SELECTED WRITINGS
OF
STEPHEN JINWOO KIM

Foreword

My first encounter with Dr. Kim Jinwoo, came at Yale University in the fall of 1994. The exact details of where I met him fail me now, but I can assure you we weren't exactly holding academic hands at the Sterling Memorial library. Though he was a Korean-American who had immigrated to the United States at a young age while in elementary school, I mistook him for an international student due to his fluency in Korean. He was a doctoral student in history, specifically modern Western history, and his English was superb. I remember several Korean students who were indebted to him for his linguistical assistance in their academic endeavors. Such was his fluency.

He was also a friend who could hold his liquor, and an excellent athlete, particularly in tennis and golf. We socialized often and I got to know him well. But there was something fundamental that "prevented" me from becoming truly intimate with Dr. Kim. This intellectually brilliant and learned fellow was not only an ardent Republican, but also an arch conservative, a stance I found befuddling as a liberal. There was no one like him – a young man in his 20s who held a Ph.D. in the field of history as a strident conservative in an Ivy League university. I cannot fathom anyone today that can replicate him. No one has done so. Whenever a group of people would engage in contentious debates with Dr. Kim, he would frequently pose the following question: "Why does everyone mistakenly assume that smart people are always leftists?" It was more than a disagreement disguised as sarcasm. It was an iron fist wrapped in a velvet glove.

In 1996, I returned to Korea. Our usual contacts were few and far between. But in 2003, Dr. Kim came to Korea on a business trip. Through drinks to smooth our reacquaintance, we inevitably stumbled upon a heated argument about the war in Iraq. He asked me, "What do you know about nuclear weapons and war? How can one talk about American policy after reading a few books by Noam Chomsky, a linguist who is not even a political scientist?" I didn't know then, but looking back on it now, it is clear that Dr. Kim was already deeply involved in nuclear-related work for the U.S. government. I have reunited with him since his return to Korea and have kept in close touch for the past 3 years. To be sure, even today, I have never once heard Dr. Kim mention anything about his work for the American government from 2000 henceforth. His mouth remains sealed even as I suspect he has engaged in very sensitive work. I can only imagine the type and amount of secrets he harbors within the confines of that mind. But I can decipher some of his thinking and work, albeit fragmentarily, through his newspaper columns, articles, and papers. For full disclosure, I have just been an ordinary office worker and never set foot in the political arena. But I retain a critical interest in politics, finding refuge in the adage that "even God and beast cannot be free from politics."

I want to deposit a few words after digesting the contents of this collection of his writings. First, I am deeply concerned that his eloquent and exquisite English cannot be properly, accurately, and clearly translated into proper Korean. I wonder if the Korean translation can do justice to the intricacies of nuclear jargon, events, and characters in international political history as set forth in his writings. One of the key arguments in this book is Dr. Kim's development of the logic of linking the nuclear weapons of South Korea and Japan to the strengthening of the U.S.' extended nuclear deterrence against China and North Korea. Even if one takes issue with his political proclivities and insistence on the necessity of an independent nuclear arsenal, his logic is tight and rigorous even in the eyes of non-nuclear and apolitical observers such as myself. I am especially appreciative that he never conflates or distorts objective facts with his personal opinions. It is a pity, perhaps a tragedy, that a *bona fide* expert in nuclear strategy such as Dr. Kim stands outside public forums on the North Korean problem and other strategic nuclear issues. Such a reality is a national loss for the Republic of Korea. I hope the publication of this book reverses that reality.

King Lear's soliloquy resurfaces in my mind, but this time paraphrased as a parody: "Who in this land can properly address what nuclear (nuclear weapons) means for the Republic of Korea?" Is South Korea's nuclear capability a guarantor of peace on the Korean Peninsula or a self-afflicted delusion? While we seek a more definitive answer, the aspiration to such understanding can be satiated by this collection of writing. The Korean translation may be wooden. But the English is impeccable. It is worth reading Dr. Kim Jinwoo's writings in its totality.

Jeong Bon KIM
General Director
Soorim Cultural Foundation

Preface

I am a Catholic and catholic.

That is, I was taught at an early age to be "universal" in outlook and thinking. But that didn't mean anything goes.

Non possumus is a Latin phrase that translates as "we cannot." *Non possumus* is a religious phrase originating from the story of the martyrs of Abitinae when Diocletian prohibited Christians from celebrating the Eucharist on Sunday. The full context of the phrase is *Sine dominico non possumus* – 'we cannot live without Sunday.' That is, some things are not acceptable. In the context of modern narcissism, it means that I stand against the fashionable intellectual consensus. I cannot concede to or concur with a hollow or unchecked herd-mentality.

I cannot exist without text. The 'texts' we write descend from the Latin *'texere,'* to 'weave,' because we weave and thread our words just as we weave our cloth. Heraclitus said "we cannot step even once in the same river." That is apropos to words as well. Same text, new eyes. But someone has to engage in the arduous labor of putting down the words in the first place and then, do it again when a different context provides information that evokes a deeper understanding.

During my tenure in the U.S. government, I worked on a myriad of classified projects. Though my briefings, in-depth analysis, and one-page memos were judged superior by my superiors, they were relegated to obscurity, never to see the light of day. From that time till today, I do not have a scholastic thesis under my name for obvious reasons. After I returned to Seoul in 2016, I had little under my name except my book on Rhee Syngman. With the indefatigable encouragement of Clara, Frances, and Jungbon Kim, I reluctantly decided to put pen to paper. I wrote on everything from Afghanistan, to nuclear weapons, to Ukraine.

I was guided by three overarching themes. The first was the perennial dilemma that statesmen faced – how to guide the ship of state through the perilous waters of international relations. The default position is the metaphor of navigating between Scylla and Charybdis. I wanted to go beyond that false choice, in the belief that great leaders, political or non-political, could and must see beyond the temporal dilemmas to seek more lasting arrangements.

The second theme has to do with a style grounded in integrity. I have a reputation of being blunt. I wear that reputation proudly – it is my robe of greatest familiarity. I can write floridly. But I prefer the direct approach. Thus explains my preference for primary sources and raw criticism. I don't mince words. I abhor *blandior*. I refuse to be ruled by political winds. On this – my best thinking, advice, and counsel – I refuse to compromise, accommodate, or moderate, no matter how many times so many have pushed me to do so.

The last guiding light is the Roman poet Juvenal who coined the term, *Quis custodiet ipsos custodes*? It is literally translated as "Who will guard the guards themselves?" In the contemporary iteration, it is "Who will watch the watchmen?" The watchmen of our age are the opinion leaders, the scholars, the police, the prosecutors, the bureaucrats, and finally, the politicians – the establishment writ large. They have an inordinate influence over the thoughts and lives of normal individuals. But who watches over them? Who corrects them? Who scourges them? Who holds them accountable? This problem of controlling the actions of persons in positions of power was discussed by Plato in *The Republic*. I appointed myself to serve in that role through my writing.

I wrote to offer my small contribution to the rich diversity of opinions that enable the pursuit of truth. John Stuart Mill in *On Liberty* was cogent: "Protection, therefore against the tyranny of the magistrate is not enough…

There needs to be protection also against the tyranny of the prevailing opinion and feeling." Government censorship is dangerous but social conformity is more tyrannous – in any social context, in any nation.

I understand I am in a tiny minority. But I take refuge in the knowledge that well-organized minorities have always and everywhere prevailed over disorganized majorities, be it aristocracies, monarchies, theocracies, oligarchies, ancient democracies and republics, or modern liberal democracies. And true leadership always emanates from that minority. Henry Kissinger laid out the 5 qualities of leadership: tellers of the hard truths; visionary; bold; capable of spending time alone in solitude, and lastly; not afraid of being controversial or divisive. I believe my writings showcase these traits.

I believe that every human being has the ability to reason. More than that, I believe men have a moral duty to think. I believe in conservatism, by which I mean, conserving the greatness of human rationality and accomplishments, and criticizing anything that detracts from that. I like Augustine more than Pelagius. I prefer Metternich over Wilson. I lean towards Milton over Lenin. Most of all, I believe in truth, rationality, and humanity, even if recorded history appears to vitiate that belief. Perhaps it is not belief, but faith. It is a faith I cling to with joy.

From prison, the Turkish poet Nazim Hikmet (1902-1963) penned, "A True Travel":

> The most magnificent poem hasn't been written yet.
> The most beautiful song hasn't been sung yet.
> The most glorious day hasn't been lived yet.
> The most immense sea hasn't been pioneered yet.
> The most prolonged travel hasn't been done yet.

The immortal dance hasn't been performed yet.
The most shining star hasn't been discovered yet.
When we don't know any more what we are supposed to do,
It's the time when we can truly do something.
When we don't know any more where we are supposed to go,
It's the start when the true travel has just begun.

Indeed.
My true travel has just begun.

Stephen Jinwoo KIM

Contents

Foreword 2

Preface 5

When Deterrence Fails 12

Taking a Punch 15

The Quest for Normalcy in East Asia 17

Is a Korean Peace Any Closer? 20

Talking to North Korea is a Risk Worth Taking 24

Bring a Long Spoon: The Korean Deal 30

Trump Huffs and Puffs, But Doesn't Bluff 35

From Berlin to Panmunjom 39

With High Accuracy and Sophistication:
The Abqaiq Strikes 41

Trump's Impeachment Brouhaha:
The Primacy of Primary Sources 43

Planning for the Failure of Deterrence 47

TRUMP 2020 – Part 1: Revisiting the Lessons of 2016 ... 51

TRUMP 2020 – Part 2: The Road to 2020 59

The Essence of Nuclear Deterrence 64

2060 East Asia: A Nuclear South Korea, a Nuclear Japan,
a Pacific Alliance Treaty Organization and the New
American Extended Deterrence 73

Contracting For Truth 87

Nuclear Deterrence: The Moment of Choice 90

The Holy Grail of Poison	93
All Tears are the Same	95
Empty Words of Hollow Men	97
It is the Soldier	99
Korea Must Make Its Moves Too	101
Position Available: Korea's Cyber Diplomats	103
American Dereliction of Duty	106
There is No Snapback	111
The Devil is in the Details	114
Let Them Be	116
August 15, 2048	118
The Nightmare	120
Correlation of Forces	122
Of Arms And Men In Ukraine	124
Source Notes	133

*The essays are arranged in chronological order.

When Deterrence Fails*

Si vis pacem, para bellum
Vegetius

Deterrence has failed on the Korean peninsula. Deterrence has failed to prevent North Korea from acquiring and developing nuclear weapons. Each and every day that passes, North Korea's nuclear power gains strength.

The word, deterrence, is derived from the Latin, *de* (away from) and *terrere* (to frighten). Deterrence works when the adversary perceives that the willpower and capabilities of its opponent are credible. Deterrence fails when that credibility erodes.

North Korea is not frightened by the Republic of Korea. It is time to reinstill that fear in the minds of North Korean decision makers.

The power to take away, the power to purchase, and the power to persuade may be appealing to the modern man. But the raw power to inflict violence (capability) and the willpower to carry it through (credibility) remain the *sine qua non* of national power. Words become that much more important in the service of power and the advancement of national interest, and in the intervening period in which massive power is absent. But words can never substitute for action and the deployment of hard, violent power. Building a formidable conventional capability and planning for warfighting are essential for the survivability of South Korea.

North Korea is a nuclear weapons state. South Korea is not.

Unless South Korea is prepared to pursue an independent nuclear capability, it must immediately launch a massive buildup of its conventional offensive capability. A rapid and vast augmentation of military power is

---

* This essay was written on September 1, 2016 but was not published.

recommended.

Specifically, the Republic of Korea should call for crash production of Hyunmoo-3c cruise missiles (with a 1,500km range and Terrain Contour Matching (TERCOM) and Digital Scene-Matching Area Correlation (DSMAC) capabilities) and the acceleration of new nuclear submarines to add to South Korea's 15 diesel submarines. For that, the ROK needs to negotiate with the U.S. to allow the limited production of highly enriched uranium (HEU) to power these nuclear submarines.

In a few years, North Korea will have a much more enhanced nuclear capability. The window of opportunity to nip this in the bud and buy Seoul a 20-year period to augment its military capability is narrowing. The time to strike is now. Missiles in the absence of ground launch pads are futile. The difficulty of locating and destroying mobile launchers should not dissuade against striking what we know. Currently, North Korea has two launch pads at Sohae and Tonghae. North Korea reportedly has one 2,000-ton Sinpo class submarine able to fire Submarine-Launched Ballistic Missiles (SLBMs).

The calculus of three targets (two missiles dedicated per target) dictates the employment of only six cruise missiles to destroy those targets. After preemptively taking out North Korea's launch capability, South Korea must be prepared to fight a war. In anticipation of the North's retaliation, South Korea needs to prepare to conduct extensive Suppression of Enemy Air Defense (SEAD) operations to pave the way for South Korean fighter jets to undertake a preponderant and decisive carpet bombing of amassed frontline North Korean artillery forces. Thereafter, South Korea can prepare for a more extensive campaign against key command and control targets, in a swift, covert, devastating strike. South Korea's Special Forces are incredibly capable and will be instrumental in the success of strikes against North Korean leadership targets.

The international condemnation that will bombard South Korea in the aftermath of such a preemptive strike must be borne in the name of national interest. The strike against Osirak and Al Kibar removed an existential threat and bought Tel Aviv and the international community precious time to contain the nuclear threat. Bombing Yongbyon would be counter-productive since North Korea already possesses nuclear weapons and also because of the potential radioactive fallout from such destruction. Bombing the three missile launch-related targets gives Seoul time to neutralize and set back North Korea's immediate nuclear threat. The time that would be afforded by such a strike would allow Seoul to shore up its offensive military capability while contemplating the complex decision to pursue an independent nuclear capability.

South Korea's national security cannot be contracted out to allies and cannot be held hostage by foes. Terminal High Altitude Area Defense (THAAD) deployment is welcome but South Korea needs a sharper and more powerful sword to accompany its new shield. The pursuit of a robust advanced conventional military capability and a preemptive military strike against three immediate, tangible and visible threats would serve the national interest in the face of a nuclear armed North Korea. And as such, would restore balance to the equation of deterrence. A nation worth its salt must be prepared to go to war to ensure its survival and advance its national interest.

Taking a Punch*

China has undertaken punitive economic retaliation for Seoul's decision to deploy Terminal High Altitude Area Defense (THAAD). The reactions across the political spectrum were predictable. The Left sought to placate China's concerns, mobilize resistance to the deployment, and underscore the plight of businesses affected. The Right defended the decision as a limited but crucial counter to the North Korean threat, pushed back against the excessive pro-China tilt of South Korean diplomacy, and called for strengthening the U.S.-ROK alliance.

The debate may never settle. But there is a silver lining to what appears to be a major blow to Seoul-Beijing relations and South Korean economic interests. If a middle power – South Korea – can bear down and demonstrate that it can take and withstand the hard punch thrown by a major power like China, then its national power and credibility will be greatly enhanced.

Boxing legend Rocky Marciano won 49 of 49 contests, with 43 knockouts. Standing 5 feet 11 inches and weighing on average 180 pounds, he was a modern middle weight who bested the heavyweights of his time. Many speak of his awesome punching power, but what is less often talked about, is his nearly "unhuman" ability to take a hard punch. One of his fellow competitors, Curtis "The Hatchet" Sheppard, recalled: "He could keep coming and with that chin and power, he couldn't be denied."[1]

The greatness of a boxer is measured by the ability to withstand punches and endure and overcome. It is the same with nations. Taking punches, refusing to go down, and getting back up demoralize the opponent. No matter how hard you are hit, you get right back up. That resiliency and tenacity is the source of national credibility. And in the final analysis, national credibility is what counts most in foreign policy. That is the ultimate

---
* This essay was written on July 4, 2017 but was not published.

source of national power.

Credible action not sweet words. As with individuals, it is action that matters more than words in the affairs of the nation.

South Korea has the guts to absorb the amateurish and feckless display of power from China. So bring on more boycotts and retaliation and sanctions. South Korea can take the punches. The government can assist the affected businesses in the name of national security. What matters more than material concerns is the dignity and pride of a nation. The Sword of Damocles hangs over the Republic of Korea as the North Korean nuclear threat looms larger by the day. But there is a glimmer of hope. Remember, Damocles' sword hangs over but does not fall. South Korea will get through this as well – with determination, magnanimity, and confidence.

The Quest for Normalcy in East Asia*

The current disruptions on the Korean peninsula can only be understood in the context of the shared desire of Japan, South Korea and China to return to normalcy.

The state of affairs in East Asia since 1945 has been defined by the presence of "abnormal" arrangements that have metastasized into today's volatile situation. How we deal with the Korean and Japanese desire to become normal nations is the key to understanding and shaping the future of East Asia.

Behind their push is a dissatisfaction at having to depend on another nation for defense. As Japan and South Korea see themselves, they are not whole, they are not complete, they are not one – they are not fully sovereign so long as they are not self-sufficient. Thanks to these deficiencies, South Korean and Japanesse nationalists have capitalized on an appeal to reinvigorate and resuscitate a powerful, potent, and romantic past.

The *bushido* doctrine in Japan and the *uri minjok* sentiment in Korea share an emphasis on ethnic and cultural unity, continuity, and tradition. It is a common, shared unitary ethos that can bind and overcome class divisions and regional differences, no mean feat in Asian societies. This ethos is more powerful than any electoral mandate. It is not a temporary political victory, but a permanent reflection of a nation's culture, history and tradition. What do mainstream political forces in South Korea and Japan (on both the Left and the Right) say when confronted by those compatriots who ask: "Are you against handling our own-matters as a truly sovereign nation?"

The Korean peninsula is far from normal. A unitary race and culture has been split in half since 1948. Both North and South claim to be the sole and

---

* This essay was published in *CapX* on August 10, 2017. The original essay has been edited for clarity and standardization of vocabulary.

legitimate government for all of the territory on the Korean peninsula. The U.S. retains operational control over South Korea's armed forces in times of war. Half a century after the Korean War, there is only an armistice - not a peace treaty.

The armistice was signed by the head of the United Nations command in Korea Mark Clark, Kim Il Sung, and Chinese military leader Peng Dehuai. Rhee Syngman, the President of South Korea, refused to sign for fear that it would undermine and delay Korean unification, but also because it would leave open the option of reunifying the nation under South Korean auspices. If any politician on the Left or the Right in South Korea taps into this dormant line of thinking, watch out. Such a move would constitute a crucial shift towards South Korea developing into a normal, fully sovereign country.

Neither is Japan a normal country. Constitutionally, it may not resort to the use of force. It cannot retain an offensive capability. History looms large in Japan's contemporary politics which has failed to put its past behind it by confronting and debating it (as in Germany). Unless Japan's Self-Defense Forces (SDF) can do what their name implies, and unless it can boast of a true Ministry of Defense or a true intelligence organization, it cannot become a normal nation.

To be sure, Japan is an economically advanced nation. And its SDF takes part in peace-keeping missions in Afghanistan and Iraq, supports NATO operations, and participates in war game exercises. But it cannot exercise the most rudimentary and fundamental aspect of sovereignty - the sovereign right to conduct a war. Such a situation cannot hold indefinitely.

China is a superpower, but like Korea and Japan, it isn't normal either. It may not have irredentist claims or extra-territorial ambitions, but China does not believe it is completely "normal" or whole. The job is unfinished. Hong Kong and Macau returned to the fold after decades of foreign rule. Taiwan is the last piece of the territorial puzzle.

Dig a bit deeper into the philosophical roots of China's economic dynamism, and you can see what makes the country tick. The more China develops economically, the likelihood of a rise in anti-foreign (not necessarily anti-Western) sentiment increases. During the Boxer Rebellion, the Chinese threw stones and wielded bamboo sticks. Buttressed by state capitalism, they now use sovereign wealth funds to acquire minerals and deposits all over the world, especially in Central Asia, Africa, and Latin America.

As internal grievances, fostered by domestic economic trouble, increase, Chinese political authorities will be tempted to redirect such pent-up socio-economic steam. The Chinese have an obsession with not feeling powerless. And rather than advancing a sense of individualistic freedom, the internet has boosted a sense of wounded national pride. This nationalism taps into past historical cultural denigration and envisions a future in which pride stems from China's superpower status. China also seeks to return to a full, complete, unified normal state. China believes it is only a matter of time before Taiwan returns to the fold.

History does not repeat but it does sometimes rhyme. It is worth recalling that the urge for normalcy was the driving force and appeal of nationalism in the 1930s. This desire to return to a purer, more wholesome, complete statehood and unified society undermined and de-legitimized the very foundations of pluralistic, diverse, and cosmopolitan Weimar Germany and Taisho Japan, and contributed to the rise of extreme nationalistic sentiments that had serious consequences for Europe, Asia, and the rest of the world.

The desire to return to normalcy will be the driving force in East Asian geopolitics for the foreseeable future. And it will determine the balance of power in the region for years to come.

Is a Korean Peace Any Closer?*

There she was. All 5 feet and 4 inches of her. Perky, yet self-effacing and plainly dressed, with no ostentatious display of materialistic adornments or personal embellishment, the South Korean media fawned over the comportment and appearance of the 30-year-old younger sister of Kim Jong-Un at the 2018 Pyeongchang Olympics.

There was little content in the message that Kim Yo-Jung carried to South Korea and the world. Yet, symbols and gestures matter as much as substance in international affairs. To wit, North Korea has invited South Korean President Moon Jae-In to Pyongyang. President Moon remains open to the invitation.

But what about the substantive questions behind these gestures: How significant are these gestures? Will the thaw continue? Is the "spirit of Pyeongchang" likely to have a lasting impact on the Korean peninsula and the world? Or will it be a harbinger of the ghost of Chamberlain's "peace in our time"?

Like the multiple stages of grief – denial, anger, bargaining, depression, and acceptance – unwinding conflict between nations also needs to pass through a series of stages. Contact, then thawing, then détente, then rapprochement, then normalization. No skipping allowed.

To be sure, thawing does not inevitably lead to rapprochement, even less to amicability. The residual liquid that accompanies the thawing must be cleaned up and managed. Managed well, could this thawing lead to an Entente Cordiale in East Asia? If managed ineptly, will it at least ease tensions between North and South?

There is no simple answer. The complexity is thanks to the untidy

---

* This essay was published in *CapX* on February 26, 2018. The original essay has been edited for clarity and standardization of vocabulary.

balance of power in East Asia. The bilateral security commitments between Washington and Seoul, and Washington and Tokyo are no less important because of the absence of a NATO-like Article 5 collective assurance of retaliation. But because they are bilateral, North Korea, along with China, can pry loose alliance ties. Strength lies in numbers – be it the composition of military force or the organization of allies.

The cohesion of the alliance between Washington and Seoul is linked to the credibility of America's extended nuclear deterrence. The recently released Nuclear Posture Review (NPR) anticipates the consideration of employing low-yield, highly precise nuclear warheads, and highly accurate cruise missiles for possible use in a conflict that may not necessitate the use of higher yield, less accurate warheads.

NPR proponents argue that high-yield weapons undermine the credibility of deterrence (primary and extended), and that lower yield, but more accurate weapons, enhance the credibility of extended deterrence. The political question of alliance credibility, posed by DeGaulle, and more colorfully paraphrased by President Trump in another context, remains difficult to deny: will the United States sacrifice New York for Paris? In the Korean context, will the U.S. sacrifice San Francisco for Seoul? Under the logic of the new NPR, the U.S. wants to avoid that dilemma by signaling to friend and foe alike that more layered lethal measures can offer more credible options. This posture obviates the need for a maximalist approach in Korea and buttresses the assurances of extended deterrence.

Critics argue that the NPR would encourage leaders to be less wary of using nuclear weapons in a conflict. They point out that employing lower yield weapons is tantamount to lowering the threshold for nuclear usage and claim that nuclear war has to be so appalling and unthinkable that any consideration of usage has to be extirpated from the minds of decision makers. Accordingly, allies such as South Korea and Japan would be further alienated and alarmed if the employment of nuclear weapons became a much more likely consideration. After all, any nuclear exchange between the United States and North Korea will take place on allied territory. This would exacerbate allies' concerns about the fear of war, thus degrading rather than enhancing extended deterrence.

Whichever side one takes, the debate over the NPR is a debate about the integrity and credibility of Washington's defense commitments in Korea. So how do the allies view such postures? That depends on where they are on the political spectrum.

South Korea is a testbed for Washington's defense commitments. This is where the rubber meets the road, where theories and concepts of deterrence come face to face with political and military reality. And the reality on the ground is, again, complicated. While deterrence is a simple and clear formula, it requires a complex calculus. Deterrence works when both intention and capacity are credibly believed – simultaneously.

The steady but relentless build-up of military assets around and surrounding Korea remains unabated. Defense Secretary James Mattis undoubtedly adheres to the motto of the Roman general Vegetius – if you want peace, prepare for war. Mattis has operational combat experience. He knows war and how to fight one and win. That adds credibility to the intention, capacity, and commitment of the United States to denuclearize North Korea. Japan adheres to the hardline approach, while China continues to try to split the difference.

Meanwhile, the euphoria of hosting another Olympics is widespread throughout South Korea. The consequential pride is genuine and growing. But despite media excess, the quiet majority of South Korean society is deeply ambivalent, if not downright hostile, to what they perceive as North Korea's hijacking of Seoul's spotlight. Government officials or university professors might be positive. But ask a taxi driver or restaurant worker and they wonder why the North Korean interlopers are given more attention and coverage.

It was *South* Korea that hosted the games. The younger generation that has never known poverty, nor the destitution and despair of the Korean War, is baffled by the obsequiousness of North Korean-sympathizing citizens and belittles the unctuousness of government officials.

Moreover, many in the South Korean foreign policy establishment carelessly toss around the term, "Korea passing." Actually, this is a misnomer. What they mean to say is that they feel Korea is being bypassed. But if that is the case, then Seoul has no one but itself to blame. The South

Korean government is allowing itself to be bypassed in the name of dialogue and reconciliation. It is one thing to accommodate to compromise, to modify. It is another thing to bend over backwards so far that you fall over. That is what South Korea is doing.

It's not hard to imagine Kim Jong Un's happiness at South Korea's eagerness to negotiate. But Kim's happiness won't last long. If there is a formidable match for his unpredictability, President Trump qualifies in spades. The stereotypical view of Trump as an out-of-control madman is just that – a caricature. In fact, he is using unpredictability to gain leverage.

Many observers denigrate President Trump as a dealmaker. But you don't get very far in the construction business in New York by not knowing how to negotiate. There is a reason why North Korea would prefer to talk to the likes of the last negotiating team rather than a Donald Trump.

Whether the bilateral summit between Kim Jong Un and Moon Jae-In occurs or not, South Korea must steer between the Scylla of President Trump's full-throated approach to denuclearize North Korea and the Charybdis of domestic desiderata for some form of reconciliation. Such deft steering of the ship of state is what differentiates a statesman from a mere politician.

For now, the cycle of on-again, off-again thawing and freezing, without a genuine vision of détente, rapprochement, or normalization, will age rather than tenderize the meat of diplomatic statecraft. The next few months will determine whether the statesmen of our time can put us on a path that aspires to denuclearize North Korea, as the first real step toward reconciliation, or drag us stumbling towards the road to war.

Talking to North Korea is a Risk Worth Taking*

History is sometimes made in sudden, unexpected bursts. Upon his return to Seoul from his meeting with North Korea's Kim Jong Un, South Korea's national security advisor, Chung Eui-Yong, announced on March 6, that South Korea's President Moon Jae In and Kim Jong Un would hold a summit by the end of April. Just 48 hours later at the White House, Chung stunned the world with the announcement that President Trump had agreed to accept Kim Jong Un's invitation to meet by the end of May.

And history sometimes conjugates. On June 15, 2016, 16 years to the day after the June 15th North-South Joint Declaration failed to herald a new era of inter-Korean cooperation, then Presidential candidate Donald Trump made portentous off-the-cuff remarks at a political rally in Atlanta, Georgia. It is worth quoting him at length:

> "One of the papers called – 'would you speak to the leader of North Korea?' – I said, absolutely, why not, why not? ... Who the hell cares, I'll speak to anybody. Who knows? There's a 10 per cent or a 20 per cent chance that I can talk him out of those damn nukes because who the hell wants him to have nukes? And there is a chance. I'm only going to make a good deal for us. But there is a chance... What the hell is wrong with speaking? And you know what, it's called opening a dialogue, it's opening a dialogue... I wouldn't go there [North Korea], that I can tell you. If he came here, I'll accept him. But I wouldn't give him a state dinner.... We shouldn't have dinner at all. We should be eating a hamburger on a conference table..."[2]

---

* This essay was published in *CapX* on March 12, 2018. The original essay has been edited for clarity and standardization of vocabulary.

Thus, the vernacular tag of a "hamburger" summit stuck. South Korea's Moon administration is euphoric. Japan is stunned by the turn of events. China and Russia are ostensibly supportive of direct talks given that it is exactly what they have called for since the beginning of this crisis. In a twist of irony, it is the United States that seems uncertain and internally conflicted. U.S. experts were wrong-footed by Trump's decision. They rationalize their shock by reflexively adhering to the mantra that the devil is in the details.

Leaving to one side the logistics of the two upcoming summits, how serious issues will be addressed and what formidable obstacles will be faced requires deeper scrutiny. What good will come from these summits and what are the risks involved?

By agreeing to the meeting, President Trump has upended decades of standard operating procedures of summit diplomacy and arms control negotiations. There are risks and benefits associated with this move.

In March 2016, President Obama met Cuba's President Raul Castro. Except for vocal but minor hardliners on Cuba, many in the international community hailed the meeting as a breakout development. But after the euphoria faded, there was little to no progress.

The exact same risk lingers for the April Moon-Kim summit. The importance of the April summit is for South and North Korea to avoid making any deals or announcements that may undermine the Trump-Kim summit.

The United States and its allies should not get ensnared in the language of momentum, a tactic that has been used by previous negotiators to justify talks under any conditions. Experienced negotiators like Trump know that interrupting momentum can sometimes garner more leverage in future negotiations.

Some have cited the precedent of President Nixon meeting with China's Mao Zedong. But this analogy falls flat. Nixon's overture to China was a strategic gamble to divide and split the USSR-China alliance, not to denuclearize China. To be sure, North Korea wants to be treated as a co-equal, but they are far from that status, and nuclear parity remains a fantasy.

But sometimes fantasy influences behavior. North Korea holds a different definition of denuclearization. For Pyongyang, denuclearization is the demilitarization of the Korean peninsula. That means the absence of U.S. military forces.

Because North Korea views the upcoming meeting with Washington as an arms control meeting, Pyongyang will do all it can to retain what they have developed already. For them, denuclearization means that they will not develop any more than what they currently have. That may be a North Korean fantasy. But the expectations of North Korea dismantlement by American and allied decision makers are equally delusional. Though the goals of complete, verifiable, and irreversible dismantlement (CVID) are laudable and desirable, the reality that the U.S. and its allies confront is grim.

Only four countries that possessed, controlled, and maintained nuclear weapons have surrendered them – Ukraine, Belarus, Kazakhstan, and South Africa. The first three chose to eliminate their weapons in exchange for security assurances from Russia. But it was only South Africa that had developed and controlled its own nuclear weapons, and then made the subsequent decision to abandon them. The nuclear ambitions of South Korea and Taiwan were thwarted in their inchoate stage by determined and resourceful American diplomatic efforts.

On December 19, 2003, Libya announced that it would eliminate its weapons of mass destruction program.[3] Though it had a nuclear program, Libya did not have a nuclear weapon mated to an ICBM at that juncture.

North Korea is in a category of its own. Even South Africa's nuclear weapons program had not reached North Korea's level of technical mastery. Though experts differ in their assessment, North Korea's sixth and last nuclear test indicates that it has a thermonuclear weapon. And its ICBM tests demonstrate that North Korea only has the reentry problem left to perfect in their ballistic missile program. It is a matter of time before they succeed in mastering this final detail.

Because of the advanced level of North Korea's nuclear and missile program, interim, half-measures by North Korea will be futile and counterproductive. If a big deal is in the making, then the U.S. and its allies should "go big." Among the talented inspectors of the U.S. nuclear weapons laboratories, there is a growing concern that verification of an agreement will go the way of past attempted North Korea "agreements" and the Iran "agreement," without a strong and preeminent verification process integral to the negotiations. The contention over verification led to the collapse of the Six-Party Talks in 2009 and it may lead to the deflation or collapse of the upcoming summits.

But even with the imperative of including sampling in any verifiable agreement, we need to acknowledge that verification, like sanctions, is a tool of policy, not the policy. The larger policy framework requires statesmen doing what they should do best - thinking at a strategic level.

The model should be South Africa. The guideline should be Britain's deal with China for a 99-year lease on Hong Kong. South African senior leaders made the strategic decision that the continued possession of nuclear weapons would not be in its larger national interest. Trump's major homework is to convince Kim of that logic. North Korean military hardliners may oppose any diminution of its nuclear arsenal. But Kim Jong Un can override that opposition.

If, however, North Korea is developing nuclear weapons to ensure regime survival, then the goal of denuclearization isn't feasible. But if North Korea's pursuit of nuclear weapons is guided by the desire to become a respectable regional power seeking to join the international community in some manner, then an incremental arrangement of dismantlement may be attainable.

As with the 99-year Hong Kong lease, stretching out the timeline over a generation creates ample political "space" for the time being which allows both the U.S. and North Korea to claim that they have emerged victorious out of negotiations. The U.S. can claim that it has received a firm commitment by North Korea to denuclearize (even if it takes 99 years). North Korea can claim that its nuclear weapons program provided the leverage to sit down with the most powerful nation in the world (the North Korean people won't need to be told about giving up nuclear weapons).

Under this plan, a number of weapons can be dismantled every few years. This would give both sides what they need even if they cannot get what they want. Time may not heal all wounds, but it can mollify contemporary grievances.

In 1982, Paul Nitze had his "walk in the woods" with the Soviet Ambassador, Yuliy Kvitinsky, during which they were able to outline possible concessions which President Ronald Reagan and Soviet Secretary General Leonid Brezhnev could discuss at a later summit.

Who will emerge as the contemporary equivalents of Nitze and Kvitinsky? General Mattis and Lee Yong-Ho?

The risk involved in a summit that has such a short planning period is that critical details will be cast aside in favor of a larger symbolic victory. If either or both of the summits lead to a permanent peace treaty to replace the 1953 armistice, the details of such a peace treaty remain that much more important.

Any consideration of a peace treaty will be forced to tackle the issue of the drawing down of U.S. military forces, for symbolic as well as substantive reasons. Candidate Trump consistently harped on the disproportionate defense outlays that the U.S. expends on South Korea. Talks of a possible normalization between Washington and Pyongyang would exacerbate those fissures. Manpower and money remain the difficult meat of statecraft.

There are those who bemoan talking for the sake of talking. They rightfully point out that North Korea has reneged on every promise and commitment over the past two decades of nuclear talks. They argue that a Trump-Kim summit would give North Korea what they have sought since its existence, a conferring of legitimacy by the United States of America.

But to Trump's credit, his pronounced reversal of years of ineffectual diplomacy and perfunctory military maneuvers has led to the greatest chance for talks – with military assets ensconced around Korea to maximize pressure to negotiate. All nations boast that they don't negotiate under threats. But the opposite is true.

To be sure, the summit may not happen. But suppose it does. If Trump can avoid the pitfalls of personal summits (ingratiation followed by self-flagellation) then he may go down as a consequential statesman. If all goes well, the amateur Trump and the amateur Kim may end the Korean War once and for all, sign a peace treaty, and set forth the road to normalization. Moreover, even if Trump and Kim fail to agree, just as Reagan and Gorbachev did at Reykjavik, the collapse may lead to unexpected results such as a major arms control agreement.

But there are a few things Trump should do to maximize the chances of success.

Don't underestimate the 34-year-old leader. You don't rise to the top of a ruthless regime like North Korea by being a soft touch.

Exploit your age. Though there are exceptions, Koreans are taught to respect authority. You don't have to treat him like your son, but you do need to comport yourself like an authoritative father.

Lay down a few, key serious markers. An inspecting team needs to conduct verification to assess past discrepancies in North Korea's nuclear weapons program and stockpile of sensitive nuclear materials. Such assessments will provide a more accurate rendering of the actual state of its nuclear weapons program. Such information would be critical to formulating and assessing a policy to ultimately dismantle NK's nuclear program.

Ask him questions. How does Kim Jong Un want the U.S. to guarantee its security? Will North Korea open up its economy and society to seek true modernization?

Trump and Kim may share a hamburger in May. But meaningful progress on denuclearization will take a lot more than one meeting. But Trump's job is to make sure the first meeting is at least a step in the right direction.

Bring a Long Spoon: The Korean Deal*

Historic, undoubtedly.
Historical, undetermined.
The April 27, 2018 summit between South Korean President Moon Jae In and North Korean Chairman Kim Jong Un is forever recorded in the annals of history. Will it change the course of history? North Korea is the last frontier of the Cold War. If Trump is somehow able to completely denuclearize North Korea, then he will go down as one of the most consequential leaders in history.

But before we put Trump on the pedestal of history, and at the risk of crashing the party, let's not gloss over an inconvenient fact: with or without nuclear weapons, North Korea remains one of the most repressive and criminal nations in the world. That it wields and threatens the world with nuclear weapons is more reason to despise it than to respect it. This is a regime that is currently governing, supervising, and operating a modern Holocaust, perpetrated against its own people. That it is not televised live on CNN does not make it untrue. What a grotesque use of that term to describe an ongoing situation in which real "lives" are being snuffed out "live." Otto Warmbier and the millions of North Koreans who perished under the Kim family must be turning over in their graves.

There is an old English saying: "He who sups with the devil should bring a long spoon." Aghast at Kim's pomposity and the world's conferring of legitimacy to his murderous regime, the hundreds of thousands who are currently languishing in Kim Jung Un's gulags know just how long that spoon needs to be.

In the midst of a celebration, it seems improper to cast aspersions.

---

* This essay was published in *War Room* on May 30, 2018. The original essay has been edited for clarity and standardization of vocabulary.

Symbolic gestures are moving: an unexpected reaching out of a hand, stirring rhetoric that pulls at the heart, tears that are the byproduct of decades-long division. However, other gestures are also powerful, like a middle finger, or a loaded gun – which essentially describe Trump's Korean approach. Reduced to its raw essence, foreign policy is still about the calculation of power. No more euphemisms. Blunt words backed by blunt power have to be the order of business from now until a real deal is reached.

The U.S. has demanded, in Trumpian diplomatic speak: 'get rid of all your nukes and I got a huge deal for ya. Open up every suspect site. Undergo intrusive verification with unlimited sampling or we walk, and you continue to face maximum pressure. It's simple. Your nukes or your regime. Take it or leave it. You lose. I win.'

The timing seems to be the crux. The Trump administration is honing in on the word "immediate." To be sure, phased negotiations have been tried before, with no success, because diplomacy was not adequately backed up with military force and diplomatic officials were too eager to attain a deal (see Banco Delta Asia). But an intrusive verification regime cannot be established immediately and certainly cannot produce results immediately. The *sine qua non* of verification is sampling and it takes time to gather, assess, and determine what activities have taken place in the past and what/ if activities are taking place now, and in this regard, assess compliance with any agreement.

But if we set aside the question of immediate versus phased approaches, a larger picture emerges that may render the distinction moot. Whatever you think of Trump's style and tone, his verbal bombast and military preparations for war have yielded the opportunity for peace. Presidents Johnson, Nixon, Ford, Carter, Reagan, Bush, Clinton, Bush, and Obama all failed to do what Trump is doing. Vegetius would approve. Kim Jong Un may make the right decision. But he won't make that decision without the United States and its allies instilling fear. Hope comes and goes. Fear stubbornly stays.

Peace may indeed be possible, but the political credibility surrounding the peacemaking remains questionable. There is no South Korean equivalent to a Nixon who has the credentials and standing to go to China. There is no South Korean equivalent of a Thatcher who has the audacity and integrity to make the case for the supremacy of South Korea's freedom, democracy, human rights, and capitalism. Moon put up no such defense of South Korea's values.

Twenty years ago, in 1998, Chung Ju Yung, South Korea's Andrew Carnegie, drove 500 head of cattle across the Demilitarized Zone (DMZ) between North and South Korea. But he had credibility. Chung was conservative by nature, a capitalist to his core, and a common man with an uncommon touch. Moon has none of these qualities. Rather, he groveled to a Panmunjom statement that smelled as if the South merely edited a statement written by the North. Moon agreed to cease, as of May 1, "hostile acts" such as "broadcasting through loudspeakers and distribution of leaflets."[16] But he received no written commitment from the North to make any similar concessions, such as withdrawing some artillery units near the DMZ. Reading the Joint Declaration, one gets the unsettling sense that South Korea is the one that has been engaging in hostile acts and is the obstacle to peace.

If the road to hell is paved with good intentions, then the road to denuclearization is littered with discarded promises and ephemeral hopes. The United States and South Korea must keep the knife at the North Korean throat while Pyongyang denuclearizes.

Trump has successfully pressured China by linking better relations with Washington in return for reining in North Korea. While the empty mantra of "China, China, China" has echoed in the halls of Foggy Bottom for the past three decades, no North Korea expert or policy official suggested that the United States bring its power to bear on China or to force China to actually do something meaningful. These so-called experts said "China is the key" while never turning the key. Trump did more than turn the key. He put the screws to them. Trump's decisive actions proved that it was the "U.S., U.S., U.S." all along.

This is the deal that Trump and anyone serious about North Korea can accept: no nuclear weapons in either North or South Korea. Thus, if North Korea collapses and South Korea absorbs it in unification, then there is no need for China to worry. In this vein, Japan will also not go nuclear. China won't have to worry about the duality of a nuclear South Korea and a nuclear Japan. In return, China will have to continue to keep North Korea on a tight leash until complete denuclearization can be verified and confirmed. The United States may reward China with favorable trade deals in return.

While efforts to denuclearize are to be commended, I worry that our generation will be harshly judged by history for ignoring the plight of – and failing to liberate – North Korea's slaves. Lest we forget, North Korea is a prison state with ICBMs.

The U.S. and its allies may or may not succeed in denuclearizing North Korea over the next few years. But this cannot absolve the denuclearization acolytes of their moral obtuseness regarding the human tragedy that is North Korea. If they can denuclearize the peninsula, it could be a first step to alleviating this human disaster rather than letting it go on. The advanced nations of both West and East share an ultimate dereliction of duty – the duty to their fellow human beings. If that does not unite the Left and the Right in any society, then what will?

Kim Jong Un resorted to some skillful rhetoric to tug at the hearts of Koreans to soften his image. In his remarks at Panmunjom, he repeatedly underscored the "oneness" of the two Koreas: "one blood, one brotherhood, one people."[5] Elsewhere, he cited "one bloodline, one language, one history, one culture." George Orwell, in his 1940 review of Hitler's *Mein Kampf*, warned about such appeals to "blood and soil" sentiments.[6]

But Kim never once uttered the phrase "one value-system." That absence points to the gulf between those who appeal to our darker instincts and those who seek the better angels of our nature. It is emblematic of the larger battle between those who value primitive tribalism, and those who value our basic shared humanity.

We must choose. Kim must choose.

This is the deposit of my sour voice in the sweet soup of peace and reconciliation. But for me, the time has come, time to unfold the folded lie.

No more promises to be reneged on. No more false hope. No more lying. Let's hold North Korea to account. And let's prepare to "fight tonight." The ultimate maximum pressure is war. Trump, Mattis, and Pompeo have never taken that option off the table despite the euphoria. For example, the deployment of the 3rd Battalion, 4th Marines from 29 Palms to Camp Mujuk would send a strong signal that maximum pressure will be applied till the very end.

Such a stance may be just enough to convince North Korea, once and for all, to come to its senses and join civilization and modernity, warts and all.

Origen of Alexandria said: "the power of choosing good and evil is within the reach of all."[7] Here's to hoping that Kim chooses good over evil, and to being prepared to confront him if he does not.

That's the deal.

Trump Huffs and Puffs, But Doesn't Bluff*

The current tariff trade fight between the United States and China is a harbinger of the struggle for mastery of world politics. A metaphor best captures the current fight over tariffs. Both nations are in a desert. The U.S. has a bottle of water while China has a bowl of rice. The one with the water will outlast the one with the rice. There will be no clear winners and losers in this fight, but we know who will fare the worst – China.

China will ultimately lose. They know it. Trump knows it. And Trump knows that China knows that the U.S. will win. China just needs a face-saving gesture in the tit-for-tat exchange of tariffs. After the initial exchange of strikes, China will fold and concede. That is in their best interest despite the rhetoric.

China is dependent on the U.S. market for its exports. China cannot feed itself. It imports food products including soybeans from the U.S. To be sure, China can devalue its currency. It can shut down factories crucial to the global supply chain. China remains a huge source of profit for Apple, Boeing, General Motors, Starbucks, and other major corporations. But devaluation also hurts the Chinese portfolio of dollar holdings. If China retaliates against corporations, they may move elsewhere. A Chinese scholar admitted as much in his speech.

On May 5, 2019, Trump posted a tweet at 1:08 am: "The 10% will go up to 25% on Friday. 325 Billion Dollars of additional goods sent to us by China remain untaxed, but will be shortly, at a rate of 25%."[8] After China responded with the threat to impose tariffs on $60 billion worth of American goods by June 1,[9] Trump issued an executive order on May 15, 2019, that prohibited transactions involving information or communications technology that "poses an unacceptable risk to the national security of the United States."[10] In short,

---

* This essay was written on June 4, 2019 but was not published.

Huawei. Marco Rubio and Mark Warner surprisingly offered bi-partisan support.[11]

But this shouldn't be surprising at all. On November 10, 2017, at the APEC CEO Summit speech at Da Nang, Vietnam, Trump clearly laid out what he would do with China: "The current trade imbalance is not acceptable... We can no longer tolerate these chronic trade abuses, and we will not tolerate them... previous administrations... did not, but I will... We are not going to let the United States be taken advantage of anymore."[12].

Actually, on April 28, 2011, Trump, in more colorful language, said exactly what he did 8 years later: "I'd drop a 25% tax on China... Listen you motherfuckers, we're going to tax you 25%."[13] Because of his pedestrian rhetoric, many pundits fail to see that Trump actually has a strategy. Trump is not a politician; he's a businessman. He focuses on outcomes over process whereas politicians and diplomats adore process. Most direct their ire at John Bolton but they should focus on Robert Lighthizer, a no-nonsense hawk on trade.

In the recent renegotiation of NAFTA (the trade deal with Canada and Mexico), the U.S. included article 32:10, the core linchpin of the new U.S.-Mexico-Canada Agreement (USMCA) deal. This grants the U.S. the right to veto Canadian and Mexican purchase agreements with "non-FTA market countries" – that is China. The goal was to block China from dumping its products into the U.S. through the backdoor of Canada and Mexico. Failing to reach a trade agreement with the U.S. means that China will remain a "non-market-based economy."[14]

China was the U.S.' top trading partner at 16.9% in 2017.[15] But the figure is misleading. The combined trade percentages of Canada Mexico, Japan, Germany, South Korea and Great Britain constitute 44.5%. Moreover, Trump fractured the BRIC economic network by carving out Brazil and India, leaving Russia and China alone. Trump is engaged in a multi-frontal agreement with Brazil, India, and Japan.[16]

Trump is making sure that China will not overtake the U.S. as a superpower any time soon. In a May 20, 2019 interview with Fox News, Trump was unequivocal: "China is a major competitor of ours. They want to take over the world, ok? They have China 2020 - you know they have 2025.

Right, China 25 - now, I said to President Xi that's very insulting because it's not going to happen... It was very insulting to me, because it's not going to happen. Not with me." When asked if China would replace the U.S. as the superpower, Trump was unequivocal in his usual bluntness: "Not going to happen - not going to happen with me."[17] Trump is putting further pressure on China via Iran.

He knows that China imports some 613,000 barrels of Iranian oil per day. That is about the equivalent of the Iranian oil imported by South Korea and Japan combined. Trump has taken aim at containing Iran by threatening its oil lifeline.

On May 13, 2019, Trump warned: "If they do anything, it would be a very bad mistake. If they do anything, they will suffer greatly." He added: "It's going to be a bad problem for Iran if something happens, I can tell you that, ... They're not going to be happy. Asked to clarify what he meant, Trump responded: "You can figure it out yourself. They know what I mean by it."[18]

Trump has also sanctioned Li Fangwei, also known as Karl Lee. Described as a figure as dangerous as A. Q. Khan, the U.S. has accused Li of supplying Iran with "the full range of materials required to construct ballistic missiles - everything from highly accurate guidance and control components to the raw material ingredients needed to produce missile propellant." The FBI has put a bounty of $5 million for information leading to his arrest. According to the U.S., China has taken no action to stop him, despite Chinese protestations that Li is under control, and they are watching him. A U.S. official fumed with rage: "China is going to have a choice. They can stop him. They can turn him over to us, or we will continue to raise the cost to them, both in terms of political and diplomatic pain and economic pain."[19]

Bret Stephens, the *New York Times* columnist and no friend of Trump, predicted on November 29, 2018 that the elite opinion of the inevitable rise of China may be as misguided as the erroneous predictions of the prowess of the Soviet Union in the 1950s and 1960s, Japan in the 1970s and 1980s, and the European Union in the 1990s and 2000s. Though he failed to give Trump credit, Stephens inadvertently underscored the point that this visceral hatred of Trump has paralyzed clear analysis of what is happening today in foreign affairs.[20] Unfortunately, Donald J. Trump is still dismissed with ridicule, incredulity, and animus. Trump can insult then praise, be playful then threatening, all the while continuing to negotiate. For Trump, it's one and the same – that is, it's all part of negotiation. The insults and carping are leverage that he employs as part of his overall negotiations. Anyone who knows New York knows this "contradictory" pose and stance. It is not an either/or for Trump; it is both/and. But the losers will be those who underestimate Trump.

The recent rhetorical broadside against Iran and his array of actions against China demonstrates the cost of misreading Trump. One of the men who misread Trump is Xi Jinping. He and his country will pay a heavy price for the miscalculation. Underestimating and misreading Trump bodes ill for his detractors and enemies. Trump does not bluff; he says what he means. I hope Kim Jong Un will pay close attention.

From Berlin to Panmunjom*

On June 12, 1987, President Ronald Reagan delivered one of his finest speeches at Brandenburg. Reagan's full-throated entreaty to Mikhail Gorbachev: "Mr. Gorbachev, tear down this wall" is most well-known. On the eve of President Trump's visit to Korea and his expressed desire to visit the DMZ, I am lulled into imagining that Trump could deliver a speech that is just as eloquent, stirring, and important as Reagan's speech.

The DMZ in Korea is Asia's Berlin Wall. It is the last symbol and remaining architecture of the Cold War. Most pertinent for Koreans, it represents Korea's physical and emotional division. It is a permanent scar that time will not heal. For Koreans, the DMZ is a tangible national memory that cannot fade away with time. Whether denuclearization happens or not, this real symbol of division must be dismantled, eradicated, and expunged somehow.

There is a part of Reagan's speech that is less well known, but just as moving as the "tear down this wall" line. Actually, if I substitute a few words of that paragraph, the speech is something that one imagines Trump could deliver at the DMZ in June 2019. Here is the excerpt from Reagan's speech:

> "Behind me stands a wall that encircles the free sectors of this city, part of a vast system of barriers that divides the entire continent of Europe. From the Baltic, south, those barriers cut across Germany in a gash of barbed wire, concrete, dog runs, and guard towers. Farther south, there may be no visible, no obvious wall. But there remain armed guards and checkpoints all the same – still a restriction on the right to travel, still an instrument to impose upon ordinary men and women the will of a totalitarian

---

* This essay was published in the Sermo Institute of International Studies on June 26, 2019.

state. Yet it is here in Berlin where the wall emerges most clearly; here, cutting across your city, where the news photo and the television screen have imprinted this brutal division of a continent upon the mind of the world. Standing before the Brandenburg Gate, every man is a German, separated from his fellow men. Every man is a Berliner, forced to look upon a scar."[21]

I substitute the following italicized words and the juxtaposition is striking.

"Behind me stands *'barbed wire'* that encircles the free sectors of Korea, part of a vast *'artificial line'* that divides the entire *'Korean Peninsula'*. From the *'West Sea to the East Sea'* these *'dividing lines'* cut across the *'Korean Peninsula'* in a gash of barbed wire, solders, dog runs, and guard towers. Farther *'north'*, there may be no visible, no obvious *'division.'* But there remain armed guards and checkpoints all the same – still a restriction on the right to *'pass'*, still an instrument to impose upon ordinary men and women the will of a totalitarian state. Yet it is here in the *'DMZ'* where the *'line'* emerges most clearly; here, cutting across your *'country,'* where the news photo and the television screen have imprinted this brutal division of a *'peninsula'* upon the mind of the world. Standing before the *'DMZ'*, every man is a *'Korean'*, separated from his fellow men. Every man is a *'Citizen of Korea,'* forced to look upon a scar."

The parallels and similarities are strikingly eerie. It sends chill down my spine. And so I thought I might just as well imagine some more.

Reagan's speech was considered too provocative and belligerent. But the speech triggered a flood of developments that became unstoppable. Two years later, in November 1989, East Germany issued a decree for the wall to be opened, allowing people to travel freely into West Berlin. In some cases, families that had been separated for decades were finally reunited. Two years after, on December 26, 1991, the Soviet Union collapsed.

Trump may put an end to my reverie and just make a short helicopter trip to Panmunjom. But it doesn't cost anything to imagine that Panmunjom may meet the fate of the Berlin Wall. And that Korea may also, finally, become one, once again.

With High Accuracy and Sophistication: The Abqaiq Strikes*

Nearly 50% of Saudi's ARAMCO oil refineries at Abqaiq were destroyed in a bold and professional attack that made a mockery of Saudi's air defenses.

The attack shocked Mohammed bin Salman and the Saudi defense establishment. How they will respond is anyone's guess. But it is highly unlikely Riyadh will act unilaterally.

We do not know the culprit with absolute certainty. But Iran is largely suspected to be behind the attack even as the jury is still out on a definitive material and visual evidence link to Tehran. Former Obama official Ben Rhodes fingered the Houthi rebels in Yemen. But this is specious reasoning. The Houthis are backed by Iran.

Most of the analysis surrounding current developments revolves around Middle Eastern politics. But that remains, at best, conjecture.

What we can assess and deduce is based on the nature of the strike operations.

What we do know is that the strikes employed drones and cruise missiles. At least 17 points were impacted. Having worked on strike operations, I recoil in astonishment at the precise nature of these strikes. "High accuracy" is an understatement. In the images provided by the White House and Digital Globe, one can see the high level of accuracy and the quality of precision through the designated mean point of impact (DMPIs). The DMPIs are incredibly narrow and tight.[22]

I doubt a rebel group has the technical understanding or equipment to plan and execute such strikes. Only a state sponsored group or program would be capable of such a sophisticated attack. Only a nation state would

---

* This essay was published in the Sermo Institute of International Studies on September 23, 2019.

have the command and control (C2) capability to possess and coordinate real-time intelligence, precise guidance systems, and target acquisition required for such strikes.

We are waiting for the precise launch points of the attacks as we sort through the debris and data technology. One key point that argues against the Houthi rebels in Yemen launching such an attack is that the cruise missiles could not reach the Saudi oil facilities had they been fired from Yemen.

The Saudis may be contemplating a military retaliatory response but that would need an explicit or implicit endorsement from Washington. Trump's reluctance to launch strikes against Iran is colored by his excoriation of Bush's decision to invade Iraq on a faulty WMD intelligence assessment.

Any response from the Saudis or the Americans will be a political decision. But the technical assessments of the strikes are not swayed by domestic or international politics.

Trump's Impeachment Brouhaha: The Primacy of Primary Sources*

The term, fake news, is an oxymoron. There is no such thing. Either something is fake, or something is true. News is either news or it is not news. The fashionable juxtaposition of the two words doesn't render the term legitimate.

The hoopla surrounding the impeachment inquiry of President Trump is an opportunity for experts and observers to pause and reflect on the ramifications of "fake news."

A recent CNN poll shows public support for the impeachment of Trump.[23] But this poll over- sampled Democrats. Just like in 2016. The Korean media parrots what the U.S. media peddles. As such, it appears that the Korean media doesn't really know what is going on in America because the U.S. media doesn't really know what is going on in the American heartland.

Yet, in that heartland, the Trump campaign was able to raise some $125 million for the current quarter. This shattered all previous records of fundraising.[24]

Moreover, why did Speaker Pelosi and the Democrats rush into impeachment? She has, to this day, not taken a full House vote to authorize formal impeachment proceedings. Not doing so makes it look thoroughly partisan. They will also have no subpoena power for an investigation without a full House vote.

Secondary sources are for secondary minds. What one must do to get at the heart of the matter is to examine the actual primary sources: the July 25,

---

* The Korean version was published in the Sermo Institute of International Studies on October 7, 2019. This is the original English version.

2019 memorandum of conversation between Trump and Ukrainian President Zelenskyy,[25] the whistleblower's August 12, 2019 letter of complaint,[26] former Vice President Biden's 2018 oral video interview,[27] and the September 4, 2019 sworn affidavit by former Ukrainian Prosecutor-General Viktor Shokin.[28]

In the Trump-Zelenskyy conversation, Trump does ask for "a favor" but it is in reference to the overall public effort to get to the bottom of how the Mueller investigation began and specifically about CrowdStrike, the cyber security company that looked into the alleged hacking of the Democratic National Committee by Russia. There was no quid pro quo as the Democrats accused. There was no threat to withhold military aid to Ukraine. There was no secret "deal."[29]

The whistleblower's letter of complaint is an odd document. First, the author admits that he/she "was not a direct witness" of the President's transgressions. Throughout the document, he/she claims that he/she was told by other officials or made aware that the information was obtained through public sources (with the attendant footnotes, mostly consisting of media reports). In short, the person had no first-hand information.

Second, the author says "I don't know" 6 times throughout the document. Third, the author's assertion that the transcript was put into a separate "lock down" apparatus was not an arrangement that was made specifically for this conversation. The practice had been instituted in 2017 when the White House became wary of leaks of conversations between Trump and the Presidents of Mexico and Australia.

Third, a glaring error demonstrates that the whistleblower did not hear the actual conversation or see the actual transcript. He refers to Trump's praise of Lutsenko when in the transcript Trump is obviously referencing Shokin.[30]

Former Vice President Biden in 2018 gushed to an audience at a Council on Foreign Relations event about what happened in 2016. It is on videotape:

> "I remember going over (to Ukraine), convincing our team…that we should be providing for loan guarantees… And I was supposed to announce that there was another billion-dollar loan guarantee. And I had gotten a commitment from (then Ukrainian President Petro Poroshenko) and from (then-Prime Minister

Arseniy) Yatsenyuk that they would take action against the state prosecutor (Shokin). And they didn't... They were walking out to a press conference. I said, nah...we're not going to give you the billion dollars. They said, 'You have no authority. You're not the president.' ... I said, call him. I said, I'm telling you, you're not getting the billion dollars. I said, you're not getting the billion... I looked at them and said, 'I'm leaving in six hours. If the prosecutor is not fired, you're not getting the money.' Well, son of a bitch. He got fired. And they put in place someone who was solid at the time."[31]

There is no ambiguity here. There are no words that are subject to a hermeneutical interpretation here.

Lastly, there is the formal sworn affidavit by former Ukrainian Prosecutor-General, Viktor Shokin: "On several occasions President Poroshenko asked me to have a look at the criminal case against Burisma and consider the possibility of winding down the investigative actions in respect of this company, but I refused to close this investigation. Therefore, I was forced to leave office, under direct and intense pressure from Joe Biden and the U.S. administration. In my conversations with Poroshenko at the time, he was emphatic that I should cease my investigations regarding Burisma. When I did not, he said that the U.S. (via Biden) were refusing to release the USD$ 1 billion promised to Ukraine. He said that he had no choice, therefore, but to ask me to resign."[32] Shokin continues:

> "After my dismissal Joe Biden made a public statement, saying – even bragging – that he had me fired. This is when it became clear that the real reason for my dismissal was my actions regarding in Burisma and Biden's personal interest in that company, which was demonstrated by the following:
> a) It was Biden's order and wish that I be removed from office, not Poroshenko's decision;
> b) The reason was because it was precisely the state officials from the US administration of President Obama – and Joe Biden in particular – who were telling the heads of the Ukraine

law-enforcement system how to investigate and whom to investigate... so I had to be removed from office;

c) It was not Poroshenko being patriotic, it was Poroshenko submitting to the demands of state officials from the U.S. administration of President Obama for reasons of political economy and the personal interests of the U.S. vice President Biden, amongst others."[33]

Someone is lying – Shokin or Biden. Trump or the whistleblower. You be the judge.

The rush to impeach Trump just ended up leading the public and the media to look deeper into the Obama Administration's dealings with Ukraine. The examination of primary sources should extinguish the appetite for "fake news" or innuendos that proliferate on the internet. More information is not necessarily better information. As T.S. Eliot said, "Where is the knowledge we have lost in information?"[34]

Impeachment is a serious matter. It must be taken seriously because it is essentially overturning a national election. To overturn the will of the people who elected Trump in 2016, the highest legal and political standards must be met.

Impeachment must be deliberate, transparent, and evidentiary. But democracy cannot be governed or sustained by mob rule. Popular passions must be dampened through the sober vetting of democracy.

To be sure, being impeached will stain Trump's reputation for the history books, just like it did for Andrew Johnson and Bill Clinton.

If Trump is impeached but not convicted, the real loser will not only be the Democrats but also Congress as an institution.

Planning for the Failure of Deterrence*

The current debate about North Korea revolves around denuclearization. While laudable, the content and context of denuclearization rests on precarious assumptions. If the purpose of North Korea's nuclear weapons is regime survival, then denuclearization has zero credibility and is meaningless – unless its adherents believe that a regime would destroy that which ensures its survival. If the purpose of North Korea's nuclear program is for increasing its national power for the region, then denuclearization or partial denuclearization has a chance, however small that possibility may be.

But let's step away from the current obsession with denuclearization and take a panoramic view of national security fundamentals that surround Korea. If we do so, we see that the issue of war underlies these fundamentals. Peace may be in the air, but war always looms. We have to think about the unthinkable: a possible war with North Korea. Such thinking may be appalling to some. Such thinking may be unpopular. But such thinking is required if we are serious about the formulation of a South Korean national security policy for this point in time and for the future.

It's been 2 years since a North Korean ICBM flew for 53 minutes and 2,800 miles into space on November 29, 2017.[35] Lofted on a standard trajectory, the missile would have a range of over 8,100 miles. New York and Washington, D.C. are now within the range of a North Korean ballistic missile. Though doubts remain as to North Korea's technology of re-entry survivability, there is little doubt that American and South Korean military professionals take the ICBM program seriously. The prospect of a breakout of military hostilities increased, as the military option that had been on the lips of hawkish policy makers gained traction and credibility. U.S. UN

---

* The Korean version was published in *Joongang Exclusive* on November 15, 2019. This is the original English version.

Ambassador at the time, Nikki Haley, warned, "If war comes, make no mistake, the North Korean regime will be utterly destroyed."[36]

The true debate about the North Korean problem divides into many denominations but congregates at the altar of how war may commence on the Korean peninsula. Words like miscalculation, confusion, accidents, out-of-control spirals, belligerent rhetoric, misperceptions, and "lessons" of World War I blanket discussions on how war may begin and how war can be averted with North Korea. But if the military option is being contemplated, then it is equally incumbent on policy makers and analysts to rigorously and thoughtfully think through how war may be brought to an end, after hostilities have broken out. Such an obligation is that much heavier because of the presence of nuclear weapons and must be considered now, before deterrence fails.

The question of North Korea turns largely on our characterizations of Kim Jong Un, which range from cold-hearted murderer to crazy young punk. But such contradictory and inaccurate assessments were also made by the CIA in October 1948 about another Korean – South Korea's first President, Rhee Syngman. But how can someone be "vain, shallow, irrational and even childish, yet remarkably astute."[37] The same mischaracterization can be applied today to how the world views the young North Korean leader.

Fortunately, contradictory personality assessments do not obviate the calculus of deterrence. The logic of deterrence holds even as policy prescriptions differ.

Proponents of a deal and advocates for a military solution both share the same assumption – that Kim Jong Un is not deterrable because he is unpredictable and irrational, and crazy enough to use nuclear weapons against Seoul, Tokyo, or New York.

The deal-seekers emphasize Kim's *unpredictability*. Their logic is that the U.S. must avoid military hostilities by recognizing North Korea's nuclear program and make a deal because a military option is too horrendous to contemplate. The U.S. can deter him after the world community recognizes North Korea's nuclear arsenal and stockpile.

The weakness of this argument is similar to the shortcomings of the Iran deal. Any nuclear deal that calls for a "pause" or curtailment presupposes that the deal itself would moderate the regime. But does Kim Jong Un's unpredictability vanish with a peace treaty and formal diplomatic recognition? If he could not be deterred from the acquisition of nuclear weapons, can Kim be deterred from threatening the world with nuclear weapons in the aftermath of such a deal?

Advocates of a military option emphasize Kim's *irrationality*. In their view, North Korea is not deterrable in light of his madness. But after hostilities have broken out, firepower is exchanged, and North Korea lies in ruins, does Kim become more deterrable? Champions of regime-change ride this coattail. They assume that the removal of Kim will yield a more reasonable and rational North Korea. The dilemma remains, however. A North Korea, without Kim Jong Un in charge but still retaining nuclear weapons, would not automatically be any more deterrable.

Because the question of whether Kim Jong Un can be deterred remains unsettled for the time being, we need to envision the ultimate strategic objective if deterrence has failed and we are at war. If North Korea and the U.S., Republic of Korea, and Japan were to engage in military hostilities, do the U.S. and its allies go for the head of the snake as Colin Powell famously declared in the first Gulf War? In the execution of such a war campaign, the temptation for the removal of the Kim regime would be nearly irresistible. U.S. OPLAN 5015 and South Korea's Kill Chain and the Korea Massive Punishment and Retaliation (KMPR) initiative, as reported by responsible media outlets, accentuate, and even boast of "decapitation" strikes against North Korean leadership targets.

But in a war that may involve nuclear weapons, the ability to terminate war may be more important than the ability to start one. The last North Korean nuclear test in September 2017 was estimated to be between 140 to 250 kilotons.[38] Though estimates vary, there is little doubt that North Korea has at least a boosted-design device or at most a thermonuclear weapon.

Because of this demonstration of explosive capability, and the success of the recent ICBM test, it will be difficult for the U.S. and its allies to contemplate taking the risk of Kim Jong Un or the North Korean military 'going all the way' in a nuclear exchange, even as the prospect for military confrontation increases. Going all the way is tacitly admitting to the rejection of fear, a fear that underpins the impetus for war termination. That awesome fear must never be completely eliminated especially in a war involving nuclear weapons.

Though the desire to remove Kim Jong Un is politically, strategically, and morally tantalizing, the termination of hostilities can only be negotiated by those who have the power and authority to do so. Even in the fog and passion of war, clarity and sobriety do not – and cannot – dissipate. While a highly unpopular proposition, it may behoove us to preserve Kim Jong Un's existence and give him the space and option of terminating hostilities after his forces have been largely decimated. I think he is capable of managing such a defeat. However, if he is unable or unwilling to sue for peace, then a North Korean military leader could take over, remove Kim, and assume the mantle of managing North Korea's defeat. In either case, someone with authority has to end the war. In a war that may involve nuclear weapons, considerations of terminating hostilities after decimation should be a critical element of any U.S.-ROK-Japan strategic planning on North Korea. Wars are often started by emotion but always concluded by reason.

Such exploration of the unthinkable may be deeply uncomfortable. But I believe it is necessary. Denuclearization is a laudable goal, but it cannot be a policy. The Roman General Vegetius said, "If you want peace, prepare for war." Planning for war doesn't automatically propel nations to war. Planning doesn't dampen the euphoria of peace. Planning for war actually increases the prospects of peace because planning deters war and allows South Korean policy makers to think ahead about terminating such a war if deterrence fails. Thinking the unthinkable *now* is preferable to scrambling for termination amid the pandemonium of devastation after war is underway. That is the moral imperative.

TRUMP 2020
Part 1: Revisiting the Lessons of 2016*

It's déjà vu all over again.
Yogi Berra[39]

A year removed from the November 3, 2020 Presidential election, the Democrats, the media, and the pundits are repeating the same mistake they made in 2015 and 2016 - underestimating Donald Trump.

Poll after poll, report after report, anecdote after anecdote, and an avalanche of information, facts, and data all point to a resounding defeat by Trump. So they say. While it is easy and comforting to believe that, experts and opinion leaders are paid to assess reality as it is not as they want it to be.

Hatred and disdain for him cloud rational judgment. It looks like the mistakes of 2016 are déjà vu all over again for 2020.

Trump is the product of popular resentment against established politicians, both Democrat and Republican. He is not the cause of it, as his critics maintain.

The roots of that resentment began on September 15, 2008, with the mass panic ushered in by the collapse of Lehman Brothers. It gained traction with the passing of the Emergency Economic Stabilization Act on October 3, 2008, a $700 billion bailout couched in Orwellian language as the Troubled Asset Relief Program (TARP). In December 2011, James Felkerson estimated the true cost of the bailout at $29 trillion.[40]

This near-nationalization of the American economy was lauded by experts and pundits as a stabilizing measure since large corporations were "too

---

* The Korean version was published in *Joongang Exclusive* on November 27, 2019. This is the original English version.

big to fail" - too big to go bankrupt, as a small flower shop would have under similar circumstances; too big to ignore given the hundreds of thousands of dollars in political contributions they provided politicians; and too big to go under since Wall Street is the engine of the United States.

But these "experts" were wrong.

While Wall Street was being saved by the government, Main Street was left on the sidelines, scratching its head and asking: 'What about us?' No one answered their plaintive cries. Not the President. Not the Congress. Not the media. Not the public intellectuals. While the media applauded former U. S. Treasury Secretary Henry Paulson's foresight, no one stood up for the common man. No one.

That is, until 7 years later, when a flamboyant billionaire from Queens, who had fought his way up in the tough real estate market of New York, threw his hat in the ring - none other than Donald Trump.

He is the epitome of excess. He is not well mannered nor of high society. He is not a polished politician. He is raw and blunt. He uses simple language. He tends to repeat. And exaggerate.

That is exactly what the American people - that segment of the population that felt forgotten - were waiting for. That initial connection with voters in 2016 remains largely intact. Even so, the lessons of 2016 are still lost on most.

It is worth re-examining the dynamics, context, and content of how nearly everyone got it wrong in 2016, so we don't make the same mistakes and misread the reality of what is happening in the lead up to the 2020 election.

Class Struggle and the Forgotten

The 2016 election was the first salvo in the American populist class struggle. More precisely, it was and is about class snobbery. The condescension, the arrogance, the dismissal of the common man. The forgotten man.

In accepting the Republican nomination in July 2016, Trump said: "These are the forgotten men and women of our country. People who work hard but no longer have a voice. I am your voice."[41] He gave voice to the voiceless: the veterans, soldiers, police, firemen, paramedics, groundskeepers, farmers, truck drivers, factory workers, janitors, maids, coal miners.

Trump's 2016 victory was due to millions of fed-up, blue-collar Americans angry at coastal elite condescension and failed policies that flowed from that conceit.

Trumpism

Trumpism is an anti-elite, anti-establishment movement against BOTH parties and against globalization writ large. Globalized capitalism brings many benefits. But not everyone benefits equally. Global capitalism is like salt. The problem - like salt - is that we put it on everything. It tastes good, but too much of it ruins your heart.

A neglect of that heart, lack of empathy, sense of belonging, or regard for the common good, stemming from such greed and selfishness can foment a powerful political force, that in the right hands, wins elections.

Trump instinctively understood Tip O'Neill's (a former Speaker of the U.S. House of Representatives) adage - that all politics is local.[42] He and his campaign managers targeted specific counties. He understood that wounded pride can best be cured by a good job not by a government handout. He may never have read *Rerum Novarum* (1891), but he tapped the essence of Pope Leo XIII's masterful encyclical on capitalism's duty to protect labor. Trump offered to soothe the pains of those who were left behind by capitalism run amok via globalization and bottled it for political victory.

J.D. Vance foreshadowed Trumpism in his breakout book, *Hillbilly Elegy*. It would take a reader without a heartbeat not to be moved by the plight of the forgotten men and women that Trump appeals to.[43]

Vance described with poignancy, the depth of the coastal elite's condescension toward Middle America. Vance was a hillbilly, an unsophisticated person, from the mountainous area of the U.S. He recalled bitterly how other students at Yale Law School made him feel like a second-class citizen as they belittled his background.

Raised by his grandmother after being abandoned by his father and the drug abuse of his mother, he grew up in rural Ohio, a place with little opportunities for jobs or social status. He was white, lower middle class, and had no whiff of racial discrimination or experience with immigrants.

White lower middle-class workers, who were mainly in the Mid-western states, also were not treated fairly, even though they played an irreplaceable role in industrial development.

The fact that coastal "white" elites have ignored "white" workers has been going on for decades. To me, it was a cultural and economic divide between white elite and white working-class that the media largely ignored. Vance represented those who had no voice, and now, Trump was eager to embrace them.

Nearly all the media and experts largely ignored this phenomenon, but there was an exception - Salena Zito, a freelance reporter for the *New York Post*. She found that these Americans felt neglected and forgotten, and that only an outsider and billionaire like Trump, who they perceived as not being owned by any special interests, could speak for them. She reported on the massive size and enthusiasm of Trump's outdoor rallies, events that the mainstream media hardly covered.[44]

I decided to look deeper into this phenomenon. I watched one of Trump's rallies on YouTube. With my own ears, I heard words coming out of Trump's mouth that acknowledged and validated J.D. Vance's pain. I saw the composition of the crowds – whites, blacks, Hispanics, Asians. I could not believe it. There were no racists or angry white men clinging to their guns as Obama so labeled and demeaned them. There were no deplorables as Hillary Clinton labeled and belittled them. And the depth of enthusiasm – one does not drive 300 miles to wait 8 hours outside in the rain to hear someone speak if they are not going to vote for that person. Trump was their hope, their role model of success.

I dug deeper into Trump's message which resonated with this segment of the population. I concluded that most Americans wanted health insurance and that most would even pay a higher cost to get it. But the single most pernicious fact about Obamacare was the enforcement mechanism.

Of course, no one liked the high cost of Obamacare's premium but what they truly despised and feared was the Internal Revenue Service (IRS), which oversaw the enforcement of the collection of premiums. You see, the U.S. Supreme Court had ruled that the Obamacare health insurance was a "tax" and thus constitutional.

A tax is involuntary. If one failed to pay, then one is audited by the IRS. There is no government institution more hatred and feared by Americans than the IRS.

Underscoring support for Trump and embedded in American culture is a belief in merit. Americans admire success – what they call "winners" (more so if they started as underdogs). Americans do not attribute nefarious motives to someone's merit and success, especially self-made millionaires.

An example. There are homeless people in Manhattan and some of them park themselves right in front of Trump Tower on 5th Avenue and 57th Street. If you asked that homeless person whether they hate Trump, they would say, 'No, no, no. I want to become a billionaire like him. He must have worked really hard to get to where he is.' They want to be like Trump and wish they had his successes.

I also assessed that, for most Americans, the notion of the "American Dream" applied not to them but for the newly arrived immigrants who had skipped the line in the immigration system. Americans detest people who cut in line and don't play by the rules. Such behavior cuts against Americans' deeply ingrained sense of fair play.

Working class Americans deeply resented this unfair exploitation of rules. Actually, illegal immigration hurts blacks most, as most of them lost their jobs to illegal workers who would work for less. The Democrats were lazy and arrogant to presume that the black vote would go Democratic. They were wrong.

Given his strident immigration rhetoric (which most misread as anti-immigration; Trump is anti-*illegal* immigration), one could surmise that Trump had negative support from Hispanics. The data failed to support this conjecture. Actually, Hispanic Americans who arrived in the United States *legally* were supportive of Trump. Only recent immigrants were opposed to Trump, and they counted for little since many of them did not register to vote or were prohibited from voting due to their non-citizenship status.

A Cultural Divide

One factor that remains an obstacle to understanding Trumpism is the very reason for his popularity: the social-cultural gulf between his supporters and his detractors.

Most academics and media personnel lean progressive and Democratic. Even if they have originally hailed from rural America, by the time they finish graduate school in the elite universities and climb the corporate ladder of success in major cities, they emerge as liberal progressives who espouse identity politics and social equality.

They tend to view those who do not adhere to this cosmopolitan, sophisticated global view as backwards, nativist, and racist. The most common rejoinder is - how can anyone actually believe what Trump says? These elites live largely in coastal urban cities, and they socialize amongst themselves. It is rare for them to travel to rural or Middle America - it is viewed as just flyover country between the coasts.

Trump the Individual

To be sure, the other, perhaps, most decisive factor, is Trump himself.

Trump is a billionaire from New York City. He has an apartment in Manhattan, but he grew up in the outer boroughs of New York City - in Queens. The outer boroughs of the Bronx, Brooklyn, Staten Island and Queens harbor a chip-on-the-shoulder mentality. Even with all his experience in global business, Trump still sounds like a guy who grew up in Queens.

Outer borough New Yorkers literally exaggerate to accentuate their remarks. For example, if I had been waiting for the city bus and it arrived a bit late, the outer borough New Yorker would playfully insult the bus driver by saying - "Why did it take you freakin' 400 years to get here?" Put downs and compliments alike are conditioned by exaggerations and overstatements. It's not just a good burger. It's the best burger anywhere in the world, ever.

The way Trump talks and carries himself is thoroughly outer borough as anyone from New York will tell you. The style of speaking is self-promoting. Trump exaggerates or overstates to make his points. His narrative is full of braggadocio rhetoric and prone to colorful insults.

Trump does not – perhaps cannot – talk in the watered-down, cautious phrases and measured tones of a smooth politician. He uses colorful language and is repetitive to underscore an important point, often literally rephrasing the previous word or phrase but with added emphasis. He is rough around the edges – and it is this very quality that many of his supporters find refreshing and endearing, and abominable to his critics, especially in the media.

Salena Zito made a great point when she said, "the press takes him literally, but not seriously; his supporters take him seriously, but not literally."[45]

To this day, many people say, 'I do NOT understand Trump, at all.'

But to understand Trump, we must understand his tone, his accent, his background in Queens, and how this plays to his supporters, that "forgotten" segment of the population in difficult social and economic circumstances.

These observations may be dismissed as anecdotal. Yes, many of them are. But as American political scientist Raymond Wolfinger quipped, the plural of anecdotes is data. And the last time around, this type of "data" was accurate and the number crunchers were flat out wrong. When those anecdotes are confirmed by numbers, we call that facts.

After conjectures, sound bites, clichés, and superfluous cotton-candy observations are put to bed, serious students of politics must come face to face with facts and evidence. Facts and evidence are important because, as author Christopher Hitchens noted, "That which can be asserted without evidence, can be dismissed without evidence."[46]

Those in the media and political pundits who had predicted Trump's failure had relied excessively on "numbers" derived from skewed public opinion polls at the expense of listening to the actual stories of common Americans. These "stories" are the flesh of facts and evidence to the bone of politics. They failed to notice the voices of the forgotten Americans that whispered behind the curtain of global capitalism and elitism. They could not see the rudimentary cultural and economic gulf between Trump's supporters and his critics. Lastly, they could not grasp how Trump's characteristics as an individual reflected and captured the sentiments of these forgotten Americans.

To analyze and offer a prognosis on the 2020 presidential election, it was necessary to revisit what many overlooked in 2016. The lessons of 2016 still retain their validity and luster for 2020.

TRUMP 2020
Part 2: The Road to 2020[*]

The lessons of 2016 remain valid for 2020. But there are differences. It appears that Trump may have expanded his base with a solid performance as President. If elections are about the economy, then it is difficult to ignore the following data.

Economic Numbers

The average median income under President Bush rose only $400 over an 8-year period. Under President Obama, it rose $975 over an 8-year period. Under President Trump, it rose $5,000 over slightly more than just 2 1/2 years. You can hate Trump. But you can't ignore numbers like these.[47]

Job openings of 7.6 million in January 2019 outnumbered the unemployed by one million[48] – when was the last time in the U.S. that more jobs were available than the number of unemployed? In 2018, around 155.76 million people were employed in the United States.[49] For 2019, an increase by almost 2 million employed people is expected. The jobless claim of 203,000 was the lowest since December 6, 1969.[50] National unemployment is at a 49-year low of 3.6%; two years ago, it was 4.9%.[51] Blacks, Hispanics, and Asians enjoyed a new low unemployment rate.

The U.S. median household income climbed to a new high of $61,372. A record 149.5 million people have jobs (the non-farm labor number); that is up 4.4 million. Wages are up 5% to a record high average of $27.24 per hour, up from $25.88. The net worth of all Americans hit a record $100 trillion in June 2019 with a $97,300 median net worth of the average U.S. household.

---

[*] The Korean version was published in *Joongang Exclusive* on December 6, 2019. This is the original English version.

The corporate income tax is 21% - down from 35%. The Standard and Poor's 500 index is up 32%.[52] The U.S. became a net oil exporter for the first time in 75 years and is now the largest global crude oil producer.[53]

That is an economic record that any politician would relish.

Key Bellwether States and Counties in the 2020 Election

Wisconsin, Iowa, Ohio, Pennsylvania, Michigan, and Indiana will be the bellwether states in 2020. Some counties within those states will be critical.

Wisconsin. A November 20, 2019 Marquette Law Wisconsin poll reveals who Wisconsin voters would support, as of now, in the presidential election:[54]

Trump: 47% vs Biden: 44%
Trump: 48% vs Sanders: 45%
Trump: 48% vs Warren: 43%
Trump: 47% vs Buttigieg: 39%

Iowa. Obama twice carried Lee County in Iowa by landslides. It flipped to Trump in 2016 and will remain so in 2020.

Ohio. Ohio is **THE** bellwether state; Clark County is critical. Since Lincoln's election in 1860, only Grover Cleveland and John Kennedy won without Ohio. Ohio today is Trump country.

Pennsylvania. Luzerne and Chester Counties are key.

Michigan. Macomb County is key.

Indiana. Vigo County is key.

I expect Trump to carry these counties.

Impeachment[55]

July 25, 2019	Trump/Zelensky phone call
July 26, 2019	Volker and Taylor meet Zelensky
August 27, 2019	Bolton meets Zelensky
September 1, 2019	Pence meets Zelensky
September 5, 2019	Senators Johnson (R) and Murphy (D) meet Zelensky

That's 5 meetings in 2 weeks. Five. And not one mention of linking aid and political investigations. On November 14, 2019, the Ukrainian Foreign Minister, Vadym Prystaiko, verified: "I have never seen a direct relationship between investigations and security assistance."[56] On December 2, in an interview with *Time* magazine, Ukraine President Volodymyr Zelensky was crystal clear: "I never talked to the president from the position of a *quid pro quo*... It's not about a *quid pro quo*."[57] Because most Americans don't understand Latin, Democrats changed the word from *quid pro quo* to bribery. But this also will fail.

You want to see a real *quid pro quo*? Here is Barack Obama in March 2012 asking Russia for a campaign favor – to stop criticizing him on missile defense (for Poland) so he could be re-elected.

> Obama: "This is my last election... After my election I have more flexibility."
> Medvedev: "I will transmit this information to Vladimir [Putin]."[58]

I haven't read anyone writing that Obama should have been impeached over asking a foreign government for a favor to increase his political advantage and personal interests.

Some argue that special envoys such as Rudy Giuliani are a problem. It would behoove these experts to crack open a book and read a bit of history. Special envoys have been used by Presidents since the beginning. George Washington drove Thomas Jefferson crazy with envy when he tapped John Jay to negotiate on his behalf with Great Britain and France. Franklin Roosevelt had Harry Hopkins live in the White House quarters so that he could be sent to deal with Winston Churchill on lend-lease and Josef Stalin on post-war settlements. Secretary of State Cordell Hull was not consulted. Perhaps Washington and Roosevelt should have been impeached too.

Lastly, the President can fire ambassadors at any time for any reason. On December 3, 2008, newly elected President Obama fired every single one of Bush's ambassadors.[59] No one tried to impeach Obama over that.

Twelve witnesses in 2 weeks of testimony produced nothing that came even close to a smoking gun. In a recent Emerson College poll, 49% of independents opposed impeachment, while 34% supported it.[60]

Impeachment Process

Articles of impeachment MAY not go to the Senate for trial. One primary reason is that Trump will get acquitted in the Republican controlled Senate. The last thing Speaker Pelosi and the Democrats want is for the Senate to declare that Trump is NOT GUILTY in an election year.

If the articles of impeachment go to the Senate, there is another problem. The Senate will hold the trial as it is constitutionally mandated. Majority Leader Mitch McConnell is a master tactician. If the House impeaches in January or February, McConnell will carefully and craftily schedule the Senate trial at the most inopportune time. The trial is scheduled to take some 6 to 8 weeks. During the impeachment trial, all Senators are required to attend as they are jurors in fact. That means, Senators Bernie Sanders, Elizabeth Warren, Cory Booker, Kamala Harris, and Amy Klobuchar cannot campaign for 6 to 8 weeks. The only persons benefitting from this may be former Vice President Joe Biden who has stumbled with verbal gaffes and underwhelming debate performances and Michael Bloomberg, a late entrant to the big show, who is perceived as representing a nit-picking nanny state and has a charisma deficit.

The coalescing of Trump loyalty

It helps to put oneself in the shoes of Trump supporters. This is what they face. Obama called them clingers. Clinton called them deplorables. Biden called them the dregs of society. The Democrats call them "racist." Trump calls them Americans.

At the Conservative Political Action Conference (CPAC) in February 2017, Trump declared that the Republicans stood for the Forgotten. He roared to resounding applause: "there is no such thing as a global anthem, a global currency, or a global flag. This is the United States of America that I'm representing. I'm not representing the globe. I'm representing your country."[61]

While Trump might be a billionaire, he is really a man of the people. Nearly 99 percent of the $30 million in donations for the first quarter of 2019 were for $200 or less, with an average donation of just $34. New contributions are fueled from over a million new online donors since his inauguration, including 100,000 new online donors in 2019 alone.[62]

Now, more than ever, leaders, elites, and experts are more detached from the people they serve. The elites have completely forgotten a critical lesson – that the state must always be the servant of the people and never its master. The problem with the elites is that they are against the "demo" (the people) in democracy. That is their Achilles' heel. The elites may scoff and tut-tut all they want. But many Americans like Trump. Underestimating this fondness engendered by that familiarity is a risky proposition.

In November 2019, Salena Zito revisited the people she interviewed for her book, *The Great Revolt*. These Trump supporters were not swayed by impeachment or Trump's tweets. On the contrary, they were even more supportive of him for 2020. One Rust Belt voter said, "I'd vote for him again in a heartbeat."[63]

With less than a year left till the 2020 election, these portentous words echo and reverberate.

The Essence of Nuclear Deterrence*

Part I
Theoretical Foundations

David Foster Wallace bequeathed us this story: There are these two young fish swimming along and they happen to meet an older fish swimming towards them. The older fish nods at them and says, "Morning, boys. How's the water?" The two young fish swim on for a bit, and then eventually one of them looks over at the other and goes "What the hell is water?"[64]

Is the water something we are so familiar with, like the air we breathe, that we don't notice it? We know it's there and we know it's vital, but we don't even think about it.

Nuclear deterrence can be understood in a similar manner. For most of us, nuclear deterrence remains out of our daily awareness. In other words, most of us don't think about it, yet its impact is profound. It is also unfamiliar because there are so many definitions. The term is imprecise. And thus, there is an inordinate fear attached to the term.

Extended nuclear deterrence expounds the difficulty because it is applied deterrence. Primary deterrence is difficult enough but *applied* deterrence requires even *more* trust in rationality and a *deeper* fear of irrationality. Extended nuclear deterrence lies at the heart of the U.S.-ROK mutual defense treaty. In short, it promises that the U.S. will launch a devastating nuclear counterattack against North Korea if it attacks South Korea. This may have been credible until recently. But with Pyongyang's acquisition of a *bona fide* nuclear and ICBM program, this extended nuclear deterrence comes into question. To wit, will the United States sacrifice San Francisco

---

* This essay was written on January 3, 2020 but was not published.

for Seoul?

To answer this question requires that we reexamine the philosophical, psychological, and historical roots of nuclear deterrence writ large. In order to do that, national security experts in the Republic of Korea will have to become thoroughly familiar and conversant with the *American* understanding of nuclear deterrence. Only in that manner will the Republic of Korea be materially and mentally prepared to manage its national defense.

This overview of nuclear deterrence will be largely American in color and structure. The U.S. has had to think about and agonize over nuclear deterrence more than any other nation besides the former Soviet Union. The logic of nuclear deterrence, forged during the Cold War, retains its prestige and gravitas in the post-Cold War era.

International law and ethics are still wedded to conventional notions of warfare. There are acceptable justifications to engage in war (*jus ad bellum*) and there are limits to acceptable wartime conduct (*jus in bello*). The four basic principles of legal warfare (laws of armed conflict, LOAC) still hold - distinction, proportionality, military necessity, and unnecessary suffering. But do these precepts and concepts hold any meaning in a *nuclear* war? Can we think of nuclear war as just a more devastating conventional war? Or do we need a new definition, standard, and understanding of nuclear deterrence?

What is nuclear deterrence?

Nuclear deterrence posits that the very nuclear conjugation of deterrence *ipso facto* possesses both the power to annihilate and, at the very same time, to prevent such an annihilation. Such an assertion is illogical, and thus, untenable. It haunted me every day when I worked on this issue. It still haunts me now. But it haunts me in different ways than it does for most people. I am not afraid of nuclear weapons. I am not afraid to think the unthinkable. I am not afraid to have formulated policies that call for the considered use of nuclear weapons. I am, however, afraid of human beings. And reduced to the barest of essences, deterrence turns on human rationality.

President Kennedy's former Secretary of Defense Robert McNamara said: "nuclear weapons serve no military purpose whatsoever. They are totally useless – except only to deter one's opponent from using them."[65]

Some argue that Clausewitz's idiom that "war is the continuation of politics by other means" cannot be applied to nuclear warfare unless one is to suspend reason, revel in mass casualties, or is so slavish to theory that one is removed altogether from reality. But is the criticism valid?

To be sure, nuclear war is different. In nuclear war, the military means will *always* exceed the political ends. Strategy means the purposeful application of military means to political ends. If so, Mutual Assured Destruction (MAD) negates strategy. But that begs the question – then what do we mean by the strategy of nuclear deterrence?

The Fallacy of MAD

Some argue that nuclear weapons are a force for stability. Kenneth Waltz goes further and actually pleads for nuclear proliferation:

> "The world has enjoyed more years of peace since 1945 than had been known in this century... Nuclear weapons do not make nuclear war a likely prospect, as history has shown... Much of the writing about the spread of nuclear weapons has this unusual trait: It tells us that what did not happen in the past is likely to happen in the future... A happy nuclear past leads many to expect an unhappy nuclear future... With more nuclear states the world will have a promising future... Nuclear weapons make it possible to approach the deterrent ideal."[66]

Critics of deterrence argue that merely thinking about the use of nuclear weapons makes the use of nuclear weapons that much more likely. In other words: the very consideration of the possibility that deterrence may fail will increase the likelihood of its failure.

Defenders of deterrence counter that an implicit threat of annihilation is an integral part of the doctrine known as MAD. Without this naked vulnerability, without this abject fear, deterrence is not credible. The fear of existential extinction must be preserved because such fear is the ultimate deterrence against any use. In this manner, neither side will have a rational

reason to start a war.
But.
But.
But.
Deterrence might fail. Many can agree with President Reagan who used to say a nuclear war must never be fought. But this debate is about the fragility of deterrence. What to do if deterrence fails is left unanswered.

War Termination

When deterrence has failed and we are in the midst of a nuclear war, the primary driving calculus and objective is to end it. Bernard Brodie made the point before his death: "The main war goal upon the beginning of a strategic nuclear exchange should surely be to terminate it as quickly as possible and with the least amount of damage possible on both sides."[67]

The renaissance of Clausewitz is welcome here. War termination is the result of calculations of benefit and loss. In a nuclear war, everyone gains by terminating war as quickly as possible. No one gains from further escalation.

That is the rational view.
That is the logical choice.
That is the moral imperative.
But the essential problem with the concept of war termination is philosophical. Everything turns on human rationality.

In a way, this primer about nuclear deterrence has culminated in a discussion about individual self-control. That is right and proper. The beginning and end of any discussion of deterrence, or any real human endeavor, starts and ends with the individual.

Like water.
Indeed, that is the water.

Part II
Practice of Nuclear Deterrence

In Part I, we covered the theoretical foundation of nuclear deterrence.

We now unfold the theory.

The North Atlantic Treaty Organization's (NATO) policy of nuclear deterrence was encapsulated in MC-48. This policy was the basis of Article 5.[68] In the United States, this doctrine of nuclear deterrence was codified in NSC 162, which called for massive retaliation against the Soviet Union if nuclear war were to break out.

But the policy of massive retaliation lacked credibility. Using a nuclear weapon does not mean that ALL nuclear weapons would be used. Thus emerged the concept of limited nuclear war.

The hydrogen bomb designs of the U.S. Lawrence Livermore National Laboratory were intricate, sophisticated, and nearly impossible to understand. In 1952, the U.S. tested one of its hydrogen bombs in the Bikini Atoll area in the Pacific near the Marshall Islands. One test made an island literally disappear. Such was the frighteningly destructive power of these weapons, the use of which no one could actually contemplate.

A young professor of government at Harvard with a thick German accent made his name by arguing for the use of nuclear weapons in a limited nuclear war. He was vying for a job with the Kennedy Administration. His name? Henry Kissinger.

Though he didn't get the job, his thinking influenced the thinking of a young, untested John Kennedy who quickly became embroiled in the Cuban Missile Crisis. For 13 days, the world teetered on the brink of nuclear war. Following this brush with death, Kennedy centralized ALL nuclear command under U.S. control.

Eisenhower's pre-delegated authority, provided to SACEUR Lauris Norstad, was pulled and Kennedy instituted the permissive action link system (PAL) in which allies with warhead control would not be authorized to use or launch the warheads without explicit American permission. To be an ally of the U.S was one thing. To allow those very allies to have control over the prospect of starting a nuclear war was now prohibited. That was the one key lesson of the Cuban Missile Crisis. If there was to be a nuclear war, it would be America's decision and America's decision alone. So much for trust, commitment, dependability, reliability, and independence. So much for national sovereignty of allies.

Actually, this meant that no one could be trusted to command and control nuclear weapons except the United States. And the allies, satellite states and client states of both the U.S. and USSR learned a harsh lesson - that Washington and Moscow would not necessarily honor the commitment to defend their allies in the event of a nuclear war.

One can make the reasonable argument that this was what inspired North Korea to pursue its independent nuclear capability as Pyongyang saw how Moscow effectively abandoned Havana in the name of nuclear stability. The foundation of the Yongbyon nuclear reactor, "discovered" by U.S. satellites in 1985, was actually laid in 1965, three years removed from the conclusion of the Cuban Missile Crisis.

During the late 1960s, the Soviets attempted nuclear parity with the United States. The Soviets also tried to build a limited Anti-Ballistic Missile (ABM) defense system around Moscow. Such a development could potentially allow one side to launch a first strike and then prevent the other from retaliating by shooting down incoming missiles. The concept of a missile defense (MD) was the first time that MAD's mutual vulnerability was challenged. MD sought to alleviate, if not expunge, the underlying fear that gave deterrence its credibility.

The U.S. accepted Strategic Arms Limitation Talks (SALT) which allowed the Soviets to have a higher number of warheads (at that time in 1972) because the U.S. had the edge in Multiple Independently Targetable Reentry Vehicle (MIRV) technology. In short, the Soviet Union opted for *quantity*. The U.S. chose *quality*. It became less expensive to increase offensive capability than to build defenses. Moreover, any acceleration of defense systems would erode the nuclear fear. So, for the time being, no missile defense.

Despite both sides knowing that the world stood at the nuclear brink, for the time being, the fear of mutual vulnerability (stability) prevailed over the comfort of defenses (instability). Defense as a form of stability (i.e. missile defense) had not yet been imagined.

The issues left over from the first negotiations were covered in the second SALT talks. Namely - whether American forward based weapons and Soviet IRBMs should be counted in the overall number of warheads. After SALT I, the two parties had pursued different nuclear strategies. The U.S. focused on building more accurate missiles and the Soviets focused on building larger warheads.

SALT II talks broke down over the different American and Soviet definition of throw-weight and how to count missiles. Throw-weight is the total weight of the total ballistic missile package to include the weight of the warheads, decoys, and the "bus" that 'houses' them. The U.S. claimed that the high throw-weight of the Soviet Union's large, land-based missiles, allowed the Soviets to put extra warheads on the larger missiles such as the SS-18. The U.S. did not need to put extra warheads on larger missiles because of its advantage in small but more powerful nuclear warheads.

How to count missiles was another point of contention. Anticipating that the Soviet Union could develop a new type of missile that could hold more than one warhead (e.g. the SS-25 missiles that carry one warhead each), the U.S. demanded that any new missile have larger throw weight than existing ones. Unsurprisingly, the Soviets rejected this offer as building a new missile would be cost prohibitive than tweaking an existing one. But that was exactly what Paul Nitze tried to do - make the Soviets overspend into bankruptcy.

Yes, that Paul Nitze, the author of NSC-68, the defining policy paper that argued that the only way to deter the Soviet Union was for the U.S. to engage in a massive build-up of both conventional and nuclear arms.

Missile Defense undermines MAD

The greatest of Cold Warriors, Ronald Reagan, called nuclear weapons immoral. To live under perpetual insecurity due to the fear of annihilation was insane, he said. MAD was mad. He did not want to live in such a world. He wanted to be able to protect the U.S. from offensive missiles. Thus, the idea of the Strategic Defense Initiative (SDI) was born. This was the origin of missile defense.

But missile defense undermined the essence of MAD. Its critics argued that, if one was less vulnerable, then the temptation to launch a preemptive first strike that would be fatal to the enemy would become more attractive.

MD attenuated the fear of death engendered by a reduced vulnerability. This would lead to a more dangerous world in which the likelihood of war increased. Critics accused Reagan of warmongering.

Supporters argued that MAD remained largely intact despite MD developments due to the awesome power of nuclear warheads. They argued that MD actually increased security and stability and lowered the probability of war since each party with missile defenses would be secure in knowing it could shoot down incoming offensive missiles and thus would gain no advantage in launching a first strike. They argued that MD actually enhanced the probability of survival and therefore increased second strike capability which would actually deter the first strike. Thus, MD buttressed deterrence by despoiling the attractiveness of a first strike.

U.S. Nuclear Doctrine

Contrary to a profound misconception about American nuclear policy, the United States does not have a 'first use' posture. More accurately, it has the *absence* of a 'no first use' posture. The U.S. does *not* pledge to use nuclear weapons first in a conflict to discourage enemies (or allies) from starting a fight.

So, the question is not whether the U.S. should develop all conventional means necessary to both bolster its promises to its allies and raise the nuclear threshold so that the U.S. does not have to use nuclear weapons. To be sure, the U.S. will continue to bolster conventional capabilities.

The question is whether the U.S. would weaken its assurances to allies if it pledged to never cross the nuclear threshold first in the most extreme circumstances. That probability may be very low. But allies need this assurance. And thus, nuclear deterrence enhances rather than undermines the conventional deterrence value.

The theory and practice of nuclear deterrence is essential and existential. To deeply ponder, critically analyze, and interpret such analysis into actionable policy is the remaining duty of serious scholars of nuclear deterrence. Peace is a hope but war is the reality. Nuclear deterrence does not need international politics. But international politics is empty and meaningless without nuclear deterrence. After all, the central question of international relations revolves around nuclear weapons.

2060 East Asia: A Nuclear South Korea, a Nuclear Japan, a Pacific Alliance Treaty Organization and the New American Extended Deterrence*

The End of the American-made Order

Extraordinary times require extraordinary thinking. It is time to remake and reshape the international order to anticipate the realities of East Asia in the next 40 years. A nuclear South Korea and Japan subsumed under the rubric of a new Pacific Alliance Treaty and undergirded by a new American extended deterrence, holds the best hope for containing a nuclear North Korea and a rising China.

History is the only real "big" data we have even as that data can at times be "messy." The job of the international relations student is to sift through that messy data to excavate lessons for the present and future.

There is no shortage of experts and commentators shedding tears over the collapse of the "liberal international order." But like the Holy Roman Empire, the liberal international order was neither liberal, nor international, nor orderly. Nor is its demise. Like many historical trends which enjoy a lifespan of approximately 100 years, the decline of the Wilsonian international order has been in the making for some time - we are now seeing the effects of its brick-by-brick dismantlement coming to fruition in our time.

About 100 years ago, on June 28, 1914, Archduke Ferdinand, heir to the Habsburg throne of the Austro-Hungarian Empire was assassinated in

---

* This essay was written on March 7, 2020 but was not published.

Sarajevo by Serbian nationalists. This development unleashed the anti-imperial forces of self-determination, codified in Wilson's Fourteen Points, which would topple ancient empires and redraw maps, culminating with the First, then Second World War, and the firebombing of Dresden and Tokyo, stretching the legal limits of warfare, as Little Boy and Fat Man ushered in the nuclear age.

Some 100 years later, on March 19, 2014, Russia annexed Yalta, Crimea, snuffing out the very symbol of the post war international order. It would take two more years, with Trump's victory, for the wave of the "common man" to wash over the banks of the international order.

The end of World War II was the beginning of the American world order. With Yalta touted as the benchmark for international cooperation and the Bretton Woods system promulgated as the global economic arrangement, the Treaty of Paris created the European Coal and Steel Community on April 18, 1951. While the French and German progenitors of the European Union were also the most responsible for the outbreak of the European conflict that engulfed the world, the United Nations, International Monetary Fund, World Bank, and nearly every "international institution" were American-made.

This American-made order was forged in the hills of Kaesong and the waves of Incheon. Harry Truman, an untested hillbilly, demonstrated his mettle and proved his detractors wrong through his decisive actions during the Berlin Crisis and the Korean War. Guided by the cool elegance of Dean Acheson and the sober integrity of George Marshall, Truman kept the peace in Korea. If Berlin and its wall were the symbols of the Cold War, the 38th parallel and the DMZ of Korea were its unrelenting reality. The Korean War cemented European cohesion, putting the "O" in the North Atlantic Treaty Organization.

Six friends, comprised of two lawyers, two bankers, and two diplomats, shaped the post-WWII American order, underwritten largely by the Marshall Plan. They were: Dean Acheson, Charles Bohlen, Averell Harriman, George Kennan, Robert Lovett, and John McCloy. To this mix of ego and talent were added McGeorge Bundy, Eugene and Walt Rostow, and Allen and John Foster Dulles. These white Anglo-Saxon males were the authors of this quintessential American order.

The Cold War was kept from becoming "hot" largely by the deterrence manifested through the posturing of "a mad man" who was advertised as someone who would be crazy to risk nuclear Armageddon. The apotheosis of such calculated irrationality, General Curtis LeMay, commanded the preponderant lethality of the Strategic Air Command to ensure that the Soviet Union would be held at bay. That fear increased tensions but maintained the peace. The hermeneutics of NSC-68, advances in game theory, the pioneering works of Herman Kahn, Bernard Brodie, Thomas Schelling, and Fred Ikle advanced the rhetoric, logic, and argument of nuclear deterrence. The world order that emerged was tested in the jungles of La Drang and Dak To, and challenged in the halls of Bandung. Soon, MIRV, throw weight and SLBMs altered the nuclear algorithm as unequivocal fear and mutual vulnerability buttressed geopolitical stability.

That stability held for nearly 50 years until the Berlin Wall came down and proceeded to pull the USSR down with it. After the end of the Cold War, conspicuous materialism dominated the world even as reductionistic fear of nuclear weapons lingered. And indulge we did. Nations and generations were lifted out of poverty in an awesome display of unprecedented material wealth and tangible improvements in standards of living, health care, and longevity. Malaria was banished to science textbooks.

But hubris accompanied the material progress of globalism. Personal computers, cell phones and financial derivatives fueled the excesses of consumerism. The 2008 financial crisis deepened the fault lines between the elite and the common man. Between 1991 and 2008, Main Street and the middle class were largely bereft of globalism's spoils. And those at the top made sure the masses were kept in their place through cultural and social condescension.

Limited and restrained government was caricaturized as antiquated. But the principles that underpin the Magna Carta and the Federalist Papers still ring true to a large swath of individuals across the world. To wit, that the state must always be the servant not the master of the people. It is this simple and cardinal principle of *a priori* freedom, preceding the establishment of government or religion, which has nourished freedom aspiring people since Spartacus uttered the simple words of "no more." It is a principle that has been vitiated by the global elite's hypertrophied statism.

The air at the top was thin. They breathed only what they wanted and failed to see the gathering storm of populism. The global elites failed to see the 2014 Russian annexation of Crimea as the first salvo against the established order. The election of Trump in November 2016 and the fall of Aleppo in December were the coup de grace that sealed the deal.

Trump tapped into the suffering and wounded pride of the ignored masses. Eric Hoffer alluded to this appeal of mass movements in *The True Believer*,[69] a neat counterpoint to Jose Ortega y Gasset's *Revolt of the Masses*[70] which while flipping such appeal on its head confirmed its prognosis. America retains enormous power but evinces no desire to provide law and order services to the world. Russia and China are making portentous military advances with echoes of the naval arms build-up of the 1920s. This contemporary era has been marked by military power acclimating to the social and cultural revolution instigated by the proliferation of information. Problems of nationalities and territories remain enduring headaches for leaders. The instantaneous nature of information exacerbates these difficulties. The precepts of self-determination archived by Wilson's 14 points spawned the proliferation of democracy and national identity across the world. *Sonderweg* is no longer uniquely German. Now, every nation claims its own "special way."

The European dream of a common identity, driven largely by the memories of war, is also eroding. The rise of *Lega Nord*, the return of "Boulangisme" in France and the emergence of Alternative for Germany (AfD) reek of the nativist nationalism that propelled the world into two wars. The world was unprepared for that then and remains unprepared today.

We are in virgin territory. We are at a turning point in history akin to the September 12, 1683 Battle of Vienna when John III Sobieski liberated Vienna from the Ottomans. 318 years later to the day, on September 11, 2001, 19 Islamic terrorist hijackers avenged that loss and altered the course of history.

The "end of history" has been firmly discredited. History trumps economics and culture. History is here and now.

There is no other place in which "history is here and now" more than the Korean peninsula. It is here that the proverbial rubber of international relations theories, speculations, and prognoses meets the road. It is here that power politics and international issues collide, comingle, and ultimately, coexist. There is no "either/or" here. Only "both/and." It is here where history needs to be made - and urgently.

With the erosion of the post-World War II American-made order, a new order needs to be created in East Asia where ethnic nationalism, economic populism, corporatism, and totalitarianism exist side by side, albeit uncomfortably and awkwardly, with free elections, personal freedom, capitalism, and democracy. The current either/or model of "either" North Korean denuclearization "or" the continued American nuclear umbrella that negates the need for nuclear weapons for South Korea, cannot hold. This is a dichotomy premised on disillusion. Under a truly stable international order, the framework should be both/and. Acceptance of "both" a nuclear North Korea and a nuclear South Korea, "and" the strengthening of America's extended nuclear deterrence. It is this nuclear umbrella, this extended deterrence, that needs a new calculus.

A New Extended Deterrence

In contemporary international relations, there isn't much enthusiasm for hand-wringing debates about Mutual Assured Destruction (MAD) or Missile Defense (MD). But despite the attenuation of fear of an all-out nuclear war, deterrence, that is to say, nuclear deterrence, retains its luster as a symbol for allied unity and as an operating concept for strategy and defense planning. The advantages of nuclear deterrence are pertinent now more than ever.

The nuclear strategist Keith Payne puts it well:

> "For over two decades since the end of the Cold War, U.S. nuclear policy has been based on a general belief that nuclear deterrence, and thus also nuclear weapons, are of rapidly declining value because international relations had moved toward a much more benign and enduring stage of history. Nuclear weapons supposedly had little or no remaining role to play in U.S. security; the only real questions were how, and how quickly could

the United States lead the world to nuclear disarmament. The end of the Cold War, which left the United States as the only standing Superpower inspired this view of history, nuclear deterrence, and nuclear weapons. With the nuclear resurgence of Russia, the rise of China, the mounting nuclear threats from North Korea and potentially Iran, that foundational belief underlying U.S. inattention to its nuclear arsenal is now a manifest fiction, and U.S. nuclear policy must confront, and adjust to a very different reality."[71]

That very different reality is very real on the Korean peninsula. Indeed, the cohesion of the alliance between Washington and Seoul is linked to the credibility of America's extended nuclear deterrence. The 2018 Nuclear Posture Review (NPR) anticipates the considerations of employing low-yield, highly precise nuclear warheads and highly accurate cruise missiles for possible use in a conflict that may not necessitate the use of higher yield, less accurate warheads.[72]

NPR proponents argue that high-yield weapons undermine the credibility of deterrence (primary and extended), and that lower yield, but more accurate weapons, enhance the credibility of extended deterrence.[73]

The political question of alliance credibility, posed by de Gaulle, and more colorfully paraphrased by President Trump in another context, remains difficult to deny: will the United States sacrifice New York for Paris? In the Korean context, will the U.S. sacrifice San Francisco for Seoul?

Under the logic of the new NPR, the U.S. seeks to avoid that dilemma by signaling to friend and foe alike that more layered lethal measures can offer more credible options. This posture obviates the need for a maximalist approach in Korea and buttresses the assurances of extended deterrence.

Critics argue that the NPR would encourage leaders to be less wary of using nuclear weapons in a conflict. They point out that employing lower yield weapons is tantamount to lowering the threshold for nuclear usage and claim that nuclear war has to remain so appalling and unthinkable that any consideration of usage has to be extirpated from the minds of decision makers.

Despite all developments and changes, MAD still holds sway over a vast majority of people who study nuclear deterrence. Accordingly, allies such as South Korea and Japan would be further alienated and alarmed if the employment of nuclear weapons became a much more likely consideration. After all, any nuclear exchange between the United States and North Korea will take place on allied territory. This would exacerbate allies' concerns about the fear of war, thus degrading rather than enhancing extended deterrence.

In some respects, both sides make assumptions that are misguided. Proponents of lower yield accurate weapons assume that the opponent can discern and differentiate between low yield and high yield weapons, and that escalation can be controlled from the beginning and throughout a conflict. Critics of these low yield weapons assume that anything a tiny bit less than MAD invites warfighting and that first strikes lead to full scale, all-out nuclear war. Both assumptions are tenuous and require further examination.

Without defaulting back to the vulnerabilities of MAD and without triggering the aggressive impulses of pre-emption and nuclear survivability via missile defense, is there a way to hold at bay those who may threaten with nuclear weapons?

Perhaps there is.

In 1995, STRATCOM released a little noticed document, dryly titled, "Essentials of Post-Cold War Deterrence" that dazzled with analytical insights, historical details, and psychological acumen.[74]

This document overturns MAD's core assumption of rationality. It argues for the U.S. to understand rationality through the eyes of potential hostile actors, and in so doing, effectively deter them from taking action against the U.S. It targets the enemies' emotions and values and focuses on the leader's decision-making process, which is considered both rational and emotional.[75] In short, it argues that deterrence can best be served when the enemy's values are identified, targeted, and threatened. It is this understanding of and threat to specific cultural "values" that deters aggression.

The example given for this assertion is gruesome. In the 1980s, Lebanon was lawless and multiple revolutionary groups thrived amidst the chaos. One group kidnapped and killed three Russians. Two days later, the Soviet Union delivered to the leader of that revolutionary group a package containing his oldest son's testicle with a message that said in no uncertain terms - "never bother our people again." No Russians were touched for the remainder of the Soviet presence in Lebanon.[76] That's deterrence: the effect of the message sent was clearly understood by the enemy and the enemy was deterred. The absence of nuclear weapons in this example is irrelevant. The threat and action taken went to the heart of what was valued most and thus was instrumental in deterring subsequent acts of aggression or retaliation.

If we apply this new concept of deterrence to North Korea, the pertinent question is - what does Kim Jong Un value? And how do we threaten that value? We assess Kim's nuclear weapons. We analyze Kim's shuffling of personnel. We attribute motive and intent to Kim and his aides. But has there been a study of what Kim Jong Un actually values most? There are no scholarly works or even journalistic accounts of what Kim values and the implications for deterrence.

This novel concept can be applied to allies as well. Without explicitly saying so, this STRATCOM document underscores an important fact. Extended deterrence is about more than treaty commitments. There has to be an emotional and cultural attachment among allied leaders for extended deterrence to work. This does not bode well for America's relationship with allies that are not Anglo-Saxon or Western.

So, how do South Korean leaders become more emotionally and culturally attached to Americans? How do American leaders become more emotionally and culturally attached to South Koreans? Korean and American officials talk breezily about "shared values" and recite "*gatchi-gapshida*" ("let's go together"). That is fine for public relations and diplomatic pieties. But it does not meaningfully build trust nor advance South Korean strategic thinking.

Building real trust is more than a series of conference meetings and sharing meals at which only surface pleasantries are exchanged. Real trust, trust that is essential in a conflict involving nuclear weapons, requires true consultation. Most American officials have little to no language fluency in Korean, let alone a true understanding of Korean cultural idioms. Many Korean officials, on the other hand, are proficient in English but do not have a solid command of American cultural references (especially sports analogies) and are deficient in even a rudimentary understanding of American nuclear deterrence doctrine and strategy. "Breaking bread" may be a cliché but it also happens to be true. Real breaking of bread requires sharing not only food and drink but also sharing personal details about family and professional war stories. Fluency in a common language or an implicit understanding that the other person "gets it" despite linguistical and cultural differences will be instrumental in building real trust required for extended deterrence to have true credibility. The current Extended Deterrence Strategy and Consultation Group (EDSCG) should meet much more frequently and at length to familiarize both parties with their respective sensitivities, priorities, and insecurities.

While the reality of North Korean nuclear weapons and the ideal of a peaceful future in East Asia exist side by side for the time being, it is an unconventional arrangement that is not likely to prove sustainable in the future.

It is time for an evolution in thinking about U.S. extended nuclear deterrence to strengthen security in East Asia and globally. It is time to seriously consider South Korea's pursuit of a nuclear capability. As played out in the context of East Asia, this could include a South Korean and Japanese nuclear capability that *reinforces* deterrence through an even closer relationship with the United States. It is time to up the ante in the alliance with America's top two major non-NATO allies.

The fundamental question needs to be answered – will America's extended nuclear deterrence remain reliable and credible in the next 40 years? If the answer is negative, then Seoul has its work cut out for it. Beyond the military requirements and financial sustainability needed to develop and maintain an independent nuclear capability, Seoul must undergo a huge leap in deep thinking about strategy, deterrence, nuclear doctrine, nuclear use, and rules of engagement. In this matter, Seoul can learn a great deal from Washington's unmatched experience in thinking about nuclear weapons.

Advanced preparation is important, if and when the actual decision to acquire nuclear weapons is made. Before such a decision is made, we must first think about whether the existing concept of American extended nuclear deterrence is a policy that is in Seoul's and Tokyo's national interest or whether it is time to explore a *new* concept of extended deterrence. Thus far, we have avoided that debate in the name of nonproliferation and denuclearization, fueled by the fantasy of regime change via regime collapse. We need to fully and directly consider this issue now.

Here is one novel approach.

The best golfers, such as Jack Nicklaus and Tiger Woods, played each hole backwards rather than the conventional forward manner. That is to say, unlike amateurs, the best strategists in golf envision how long the approach into the green would be, then, calculate how to hit the ball from the tee to that distance spot where the approach would be taken. This approach is apt for North Korea. That is to say, let's play North Korea backwards.

Kim Jong Un was born on January 8, 1984. The 36-year-old is known for his fondness for alcohol and cigarettes. And his heft underscores a robust diet. Though he may face health problems, let us assume that he will rule North Korea for the next 40 years till he is 76 years old. Trump, Abe, Moon, Xi and Putin will be dead by then. Between now and then, there will be other leaders from these nations that will have to contend with a nuclear North Korea.

Playing back from that projected reality of 2060, we can act now to shape a different future. This generation of South Koreans will have to plan strategies for how to cope with a nuclear armed North Korea, as part of a new nuclear deterrent strategy in conjunction with a new concept of U.S. extended nuclear deterrence.

In the next 40 years, the rivalry between the United States and China will be the determining factor in forming the contours of the East Asian geopolitical landscape. The INF Treaty is gone. The New START Treaty may be extended another five years till 2026 but its prospects after that do not look promising. How China perceives this shedding of formal arms control treaties that have been in place since the 1970s will be important for the formulation of nuclear policies by the U.S., Russia, and China. North Korea's nuclear development is the bellwether of U.S.-China relations and any nonproliferation platform for the next several decades.

Absent the effort it will take to imagine and realize a different future, several assumptions will make it to the finishing line in 40 years. Efforts to denuclearize will fail and North Korea will add to its current nuclear inventory, emerging as a middle nuclear power. The U.S. and Russia will find other arrangements besides New START after its expiration in 2026. China will embark on a steady increase in its nuclear and missile capability, tempered only by its economic vitality. China will not overtake the U.S. economically or militarily. The United States will remain the most powerful nation in the world. In that world, South Korea needs to adjust and calibrate. And plan.

South Korea can shape and forge a bright future. In 2019, South Korea was ranked by U.S. News & World Report as the 10th most powerful nation in the world, 12th in nominal GDP with a GDP per capita of approximately $32,000, and the 7th most lethal military.[77]

But these statistics are misleading. Moreover, in comparing South Korea to the United States, one damning statistic stuns. In 2017, the ROK's government revenue was approximately $351 billion.[78] Walmart's revenue in 2018 was $500 billion.[79] South Korea may seek to climb the ladder of global power rankings. But the gap between the United States and South Korea will remain large in 2060.

But these reasons serve as a powerful motive rather than a disincentive for South Koreans to actively pursue an aggressive national security agenda. South Korea should accelerate its conventional military buildup by ensuring that the advanced cruise missile, *Hyunmoo*, becomes the go-to offensive weapon of choice for the South Korean President. South Korea should purchase or develop laser technology that can neutralize North Korean missiles. But all these measures will be irrelevant without nuclear weapons of its own. The South Korean government should immediately create a national commission to study the feasibility of an independent nuclear capability, exploring and shaping its nexus with the U.S. nuclear deterrent and becoming a founding member of a Pacific Alliance Treaty Organization (PATO) along with Japan, India, and the United States.

As long as North Korea continues to exist as a nuclear weapon state (even if Kim Jong Un were to suddenly die or leave office), South Korea needs to remain vigilant in protecting its national sovereignty. Nuclear capability is the ultimate manifestation of national sovereignty. Withdrawal from the Nuclear Non-Proliferation Treaty (NPT) and its subsequent repercussions, such as international sanctions, should be viewed as a cost to the benefit of acquiring an independent nuclear capability. In fact, the NPT is contributing to instability in the region by blocking, as a party to the Treaty, South Korea's nuclear capability, which bolsters North Korea's advantage. Seoul's nuclear acquisition need not vitiate the current alliance with Washington. On the contrary, it may serve to boost existing extended deterrence arrangements by allowing American officials to reduce the number of U.S. troops in Korea.

The pursuit of an independent nuclear capability must be thoroughly examined because the credibility of the U.S.' extended deterrence is attenuated with every North Korean advance in its nuclear capability or inventory. The notion of the U.S. nuclear umbrella as the key to global security is antiquated and needs to be updated to fit the realities of today and the future. Reduced to its most simplistic level, the U.S. has nuclear weapons, North Korea has nuclear weapons, and South Korea does not. If conflict breaks out on the Korean Peninsula, it will likely be a conventional war and South Korea will have to fight with conventional means. In a future scenario in which the U.S. and South Korea both have nuclear weapons, the likelihood of war will be reduced as together they will be able to deter or, if deterrence were to fail, wage nuclear war against a nuclear North Korea. Moreover, if the U.S. were to fold its nuclear umbrella today (a dangerous and short-sighted proposition), a South Korea with nuclear weapons becomes even more important to deter North Korea.

President Trump has complained vehemently for a "fair" alliance.[80] On January 16, 2020, Secretary of State Pompeo and Defense Secretary Esper penned an unprecedented op-ed, calling out Seoul with a backhanded slap that Korea should stop acting like a dependent and step up to be a real ally.[81] So be it. South Korea should pay its own way. But this calls for some reciprocal changes on the part of the U.S. as well. The three hats that the current U.S. commander wears (USFK, CINCUNC, USCFC) can be replaced with a single U.S. commander overseeing both Korea and Japan. American physical presence on South Korean territory can be reduced, but not necessarily eliminated, if South Korea gains nuclear weapons of its own. Moving the U.S. Indo-Pacific Command (USINDOPACOM) to Guam from Hawaii would send a strong signal that America is also committed to rebuilding a "real" and "fair" alliance. Reciprocity cuts both ways.

Washington, Seoul, and Tokyo can negotiate a relationship that joins U.S. nuclear deterrence with a South Korean and Japanese nuclear capability. A nuclear South Korea and Japan should no longer be taboo. American nonproliferation goals are antiquated in light of Chinese and North Korean nuclear advancements. Dissuading a Korean and Japanese nuclear capability in the name of nonproliferation goals that were forged at the height of the Cold War is neither realistic nor desirable. The U.S.-ROK and U.S.-Japan alliance need not be incompatible with a nuclear ROK and a nuclear Japan. New amended treaties can be signed. Alliances are tools not the objective of diplomacy. That logic applies to the United States as well as Korea and Japan.

Japan can make its own decisions about its affairs. But it behooves Japan to work with Korea in anticipation of American adjustments in the region. Historical memories are often painful. But the dangers of China and North Korea outweigh an emotional strategy of denial. Korea and Japan should be natural allies. We shouldn't allow history to stand in the way. Statesmen transcend political expediency and make history by transforming it. A military alliance between the Washington, Seoul, and Tokyo would be an effective counterweight to China and North Korea. Leaders from all three nations can and must think beyond Moon, Abe, and Trump.

In fact, as the forces unleashed by Trump's domestic populism overflow into America's skepticism toward foreign policy arrangements that originated some 70 years ago, America must also think in new ways to build global security. It is time for the United States to forge new and expanded relationships and alliances that envision a nuclear Korea and Japan. Such a policy would buttress Washington's commitment to extended deterrence even as regime change and Korean reunification are deprioritized and effectively sidelined. Over time, such a policy could contribute to creating the conditions for regime change. But until that time, regime change should be suspended and an independent Korean nuclear capability pursued.

The United States will remain the most powerful and formidable nation in 2060. But it will not remain the indispensable nation unless it engages in a meaningful alliance with a nuclear South Korea and a nuclear Japan. In retrospect, the Cold War was an abnormality in the normal course of human history. That history has largely been characterized by each nation making arrangements to advance its own narrow national interests. Despite the onset of AI and big data, we are returning to that pre-Cold War order.

It is now time for other nations to step up to the plate and take responsibility, along with the U.S., for shaping that common history. South Korea and Japan are integral to this undertaking. Denuclearization of North Korea has failed and will fail short of war because the use of force to achieve denuclearization is politically unpalatable and militarily risky. Nonproliferation goals are laudable, but invalid in the face of a nuclear North Korea and the growing nuclear modernization of China. Instead of denuclearization, we must now focus on deterrence. U.S. extended nuclear deterrence joined with a nuclear South Korea, a nuclear Japan, and a Pacific Alliance Treaty Organization would deter China and contain a nuclear North Korea. That will advance extended deterrence to a new level. Such an arrangement heralds a new international order indeed. These are extraordinary times. We need extraordinary thinking that reflects this extraordinary time. The time to consider, debate, and make such changes in thinking and policies is now.

Contracting For Truth*

Mark Ramseyer's "Contracting for Sex in the Pacific War" published by the *International Review of Law and Economics* has raised controversy.[82] But we shouldn't be emotional about it because it is not a serious work. It is superficial, anti-historical. It is an outstanding example of selective history.

Ramseyer's shoddy logical problem is what lawyers call an *ipso facto* argument. "My point is proved by me saying it is." That logical flaw is connected to the larger issue of evidence. It is difficult to evaluate the evidence when there is none. Paragraph after paragraph, words are spilled but there are no sources to back them up.

The "contracting problem" for entrepreneurs? No evidence. "Incentive-based wage contract"? Nothing. In section 2.2.1, he admits "I know of no source detailing how often the upfront payment went to the women herself." He writes "probably" and "should have." That is speculation and conjecture not scholarship. In section 2.2.2, the sourcing problems are even more glaring. Private Korean pimps? No evidence. Women who negotiated higher pay for wartime sex? No evidence. Where are these multiple women? I can't find them. "Contractual dynamics?" No dynamics. Game theory? John Von Neumann and John Nash would roll over in their graves.

The sources that he cites are almost all Japanese sources. There are no Korean sources or allied captured documents. The Northeast History Foundation's four volumes of "The Complete Catalogue of Documents on the Japanese Military's 'Comfort Women'"? Not cited. The "Research Report No. 120: Amenities in the Japanese Armed Forces"? Nothing cited. Hosaka Yuji's works? Nothing cited. He cites numbers of the percentage of licensed *Japanese* prostitutes and *yen* per day but offers no real data that can be fully

---

* The Korean version was published in the Sermo Institute of International Studies on February 19, 2021. This is the original English version.

evaluated. I would have preferred that he resorted to anecdotal data. But then he cites ONE woman's account - Mun Ok-ju. And her account is not credible.

But as bad as the logic and evidence are, his assumptions are his fatal flaws. He assumes that Koreans were sovereign independent agents who had power, leverage, and resources to negotiate on behalf of their party with Japanese officials. This means Koreans (even Korean pimps!) were Japanese equals. Then who were these powerful Koreans? Where are the actual contracts? What were the terms of the contract? Who were the two parties? Who signed it? Does he have names?

The historical facts are thus. There was no entity called Korea. Japan colonized it.There was no Korean racial identity. Japan tried to eradicate Korean cultural customs, mores/standards, and names. But he assumes that weak, lowly Korean women somehow had the power to negotiate their body for money not only with the almighty Japanese imperial forces but with opportunistic Korean male pimps as well. How is this possible? This is laughable if it weren't so grovelingly argued.

This is not scholarship. This is akin to Nazi propaganda of how the Jews of Buchenwald and Auschwitz negotiated the voluntary encampment of their fellow Jews with their equal Nazi counterparts for gold extracted from prisoner's teeth.

This is not history.This is the whitewashing of war crimes through what Hannah Arendt called the banalization of evil. It is a conscious, enthusiastic downplaying, then justifying, then denying of Japanese direct and deep involvement in the sex trade.It is historical denialism in the name of revisionism.

Harvard has also drifted a long way from the standards of excellence in Japanese scholarship, from Edwin Reischauer to Albert Craig to Carter Eckert to Akira Iriye, to now Mark Ramseyer. I guess Darwin was wrong. Harvard is not all that it is purported to be.Ramseyer views historical events through the lens of contract law. Why is a law professor doing history? The etymological root of lawyer is from the Latin *advocatus*, one called to plead on one's behalf. Lawyers are not trained to objectively assess historical facts like a historian. But if an amateur wants to play in the major leagues, then

Ramseyer should be prepared for a hardball thrown under his chin. It is Ramseyer's right to advocate the Japanese view. It is my right to destroy it like Hannibal at Cannae in the intellectual gladiator arena.

Nuclear Deterrence: The Moment of Choice*

It's called 2MTW. The American ability to fight 2 Major Theater Wars simultaneously. Skeptics dismiss the idea as misplaced and dangerous. Champions laud the American preponderance of conventional and nuclear power. Regardless of which side you are on, this concept is the bedrock premise of American operational war planning.

On January 8, 2021, Admiral Charles Richard, Commander of U.S. Strategic Command (STRATCOM) gave a free-flowing interview with the Defense Writers Group, in which he warned about facing "the prospect of two peer nuclear capable adversaries." Russia has always been a "peer nuclear capable adversary."[83] But the Commander who would launch nuclear weapons when President Biden gives the authority was thinking of an additional nation – China. His assessment that the U.S. considers China as a nuclear peer left me scratching my head.

A month later, he penned a column in the U.S. Naval Institute's magazine, The Proceedings, that made me sleepless for several nights even though I have been immersed in strategic nuclear deterrence for over two decades. He was concerned that Russia and China would consider nuclear use to undermine American interests and warned that "a regional crisis with Russia or China could escalate quickly to a conflict involving nuclear weapons, if they perceived a conventional loss would threaten the regime or state." Then came the stunning statement: "Consequently, the U.S. military must shift its principal assumption from "nuclear employment is not possible" to "nuclear employment is a very real possibility."[84] I had to read this sentence three times to make sure I read it correctly. This is deeply disturbing.

---

* The Korean version was published in the *Kookmin Ilbo* on March 8, 2021. This is the original English version.

The use and deployment of nuclear weapons lies at the heart of nuclear deterrence. For the first time since the height of the Cold War when notions such as countervailing and counterforce doctrine insinuated a deliberate application of conventional notions of war to nuclear war, most encapsulated in PD-59, the use of nuclear weapons is a real possibility. The precise and deliberate philosophy of deterrence is shifting to the loose and fluid language of warfighting.

In such warfighting, nuclear doctrine is paramount. China purports a "no first use" doctrine. But this can change in an instant. On the contrary, the United States does not have a "first use" posture. Let's clear the misunderstandings and ambiguities surrounding this issue. The U.S. has the *absence* of a "no first use" posture. It does not pledge to use nuclear weapons first in a conflict to discourage others from engaging in a conflict. It *refuses* to pledge that it will *not* use nuclear weapons *first*, once a conflict has begun, in the event of dire circumstances that threaten its vital interests.

South Korea is the supplicant nation in America's extended nuclear deterrence. The ability to conduct 2MTW is premised on the assumption of two *conventional* wars not nuclear ones. If this portentous shift in strategic thinking is true, then it will directly affect South Korea's notions of defense planning and strategy as we encounter a North Korea with nuclear weapons. If the United States were to engage in a major nuclear war with China over Taiwan, will America be able or willing to defend Seoul from Pyongyang's transgressions?

The Single Integrated Operational Plan (SIOP) was the United States' *first* comprehensive plan for nuclear war that gave the President targeting options for the deployment of nuclear weapons.[85] The SIOP "integrates" the nuclear triad - bombers, ICBMs, and SLBMs. Admiral Richard appears to confirm that China has achieved the nuclear triad even as we remain uncertain whether China has its own SIOP.

If the top strategic nuclear commander is seriously contemplating the use of nuclear weapons, then the likely place for such a conflict is the Korean peninsula. If so, then it is time Korea start, in a serious and principled manner, the prospect and feasibility of an independent nuclear capability. Political willpower may be the indispensable factor in launching such a project but strategic thinking and planning by foreign policy and technical experts will be critical to sustain the initiative. The very first step is a feasibility study to analyze whether Korea can master the nuclear fuel cycle including safe storage with due consideration of the Nuclear Non-Proliferation Treaty (NPT) and other major treaty obligations. There is no room for ruling and opposition bickering. After all, administrations come and go. But Korea's national interest endures.

The Holy Grail of Poison*

We have a China problem. I enjoy and appreciate the complexity and sophistication of Chinese cuisine. I have deep affection for my Chinese friends. But I have a visceral hatred of the Chinese Communist Party. Today, the Chinese government is rewriting history. China claims that the Korean poet Yoon Dong Ju was Korean Chinese. Kimchi, *hanbok* (traditional Korean clothes), and *pansori* (Korea's soulful blues) are culturally appropriated by China as its own.[86] Not only is China slowly but assuredly encroaching on Korean culture, it is trying to re-edit history and is now attempting to proliferate such efforts globally.

One impetus for China's determination to rewrite history is its inferiority complex forged from decades of humiliation at the hands of imperial powers from the Opium War to Japanese occupation. All nations attempt to regain their place to revive a sense of confidence and dignity in their history and culture. Though China's revisionist efforts look immature, it cannot be simply dismissed as amateurish. In international relations, there are invisible forces that go beyond the military, weapons, diplomacy, and economy to explain strategic movements. Such is culture. Korea must not only confront but take forceful actions to rollback such efforts.

Currently, China moves as if it fears no one. That confidence is undergirded by its impressive military buildup. Until 2019, the United States and Russia were bound by the 1987 INF treaty that prohibits Intermediate Range Ballistic Missiles (IRBM in range of 500-5,500km).[87] As a non-member, China exploited this loophole during that period to develop and operationalize this category of weapons.

In the past few years, China has made its military moves. China has built

---

* The Korean version was published in the *Kookmin Ilbo* on April 5, 2021. This is the original English version.

military facilities on artificial islands in the South China Sea and deployed missiles aimed at Taiwan on its adjacent coast. In February 2021, the Chinese defense department announced the test of a ballistic missile which in effect was an anti-satellite missile.[88]

These actions are what the Americans call violations of the liberal international order. In January 2021, "The Longer Telegram," published in the Atlantic Council, asserted that there are factions within the politburo. The author argues that if the U.S. can cultivate and persuade the pro-West faction then China may return to the fold of the international order.[89] This is hope masquerading as policy. China is creating its own world order. But history teaches that overconfidence and arrogance lead to tragedy, not progress. This cultural arrogance, combined with historical revisionism and temporal military enlargement, will constitute the holy grail of poison.

On April 10, 1974, a speaker addressed the 6th Special Session of the United Nations General Assembly, stating: "If one day China should change her color and turn into a superpower, if she too should play the tyrant in the world, and everywhere subject others to her bullying, aggression and exploitation, the people of the world should identify her as 'social-imperialism', expose it, oppose it and work together with the Chinese people to overthrow it."[90] The speaker was none other than Deng Xiaoping. Unfortunately, Deng's portentous warnings are metastasizing into reality. Xi Jinping and the Chinese Communist Party leaders are leading China down this imperialistic road. Deng's admonition 47 years ago was as accurate then as it is now.

All Tears are the Same*

President Biden is considered a bungler. His verbal gaffes during the 2020 campaign were notorious and disturbing. But he made no such mistake when he dismissed the Uighur genocide as part of China's 'different norms' at a CNN town hall on February 17, 2021: "Culturally there are different norms that each country and their leaders are expected to follow."[91] Biden was clear.

One would have expected pundits to take him to the woodshed. But there followed only a piercing silence. If I put on my international relations hat, Biden's choice of words makes sense. Principles and universal values are sometimes limited by reality. The human rights vs. strategic considerations dichotomy is not a debate. It is not a Kierkegaardian *Either/Or*. Striking a balance in a complex world with entangled problems, where nothing seems black and white, is a challenge to say the least.

Ergo, the hat fits awkwardly and uncomfortably. What Biden said leaves a bitter taste in the mouth. The heart pines. The absence of an enduring or eternal truth leaves the modern "realist" longing for something better, something higher, something more dependable. Viktor Frankl called it the search for meaning.

We are taught that international politics is driven by the relentless pursuit of national interests. We have been lectured that human rights considerations must be set aside to acquire the rare earth materials that propel modern industry. The Democratic Republic of Congo holds the largest cobalt reserve with some 3.6 million metric tons.[92] Bolivia has 5.4 million tons of lithium, the largest known concentration of lithium in any country.[93]

Bolivia's lithium and Congo's cobalt fuel the very batteries that are essential to our ubiquitous smartphones, personal computers, and electric

---

* The Korean version was published in the Kookmin Ilbo on May 3, 2021. This is the original English version.

vehicles. But who mines these strategic materials? Congolese children as young as 5 use their small thin fingers to excavate the lethal material that allows our 5-year-old children to watch their favorite entertainment programs in our SUVs.

Surely, the process must be efficient. Undoubtedly such efficiency is the price of modernization. These young children would starve without such a job, they rationalize. But that doesn't seem right. Most of those children die from the disease they acquire by breathing in the lethal toxicity of lithium and cobalt.[94] Burma, North Korea, and Balochistan also possess abundant rare minerals needed for sophisticated weapons systems in advanced nations. Can we see now why the violations of human rights in those places are raised but never enforced? In short, the wealthy nations' military and economic health is being underwritten by the poor and the wretched. Strategic materials trump human rights. Reality beats principles.

At the heart of progressive ideology lies the belief that truth is relative to historical circumstances. The modern world is largely formulated through the secularism of democratic politics, free markets, and pop culture. In other words, our *weltanschauung* boils down to, "it depends." But the very definition of human rights would be vitiated if the clause "it depends" is added. Do we say, "it depends" to North Korean human rights? Are North Koreans not equally as human as we are? Or do we sacrifice North Korean human rights on the altar of denuclearization? If we are silent today, then we will be silent tomorrow. That is unacceptable.

The advocates of human rights for North Koreans can feel like it's a losing game. Realists lecture me that more important strategic considerations such as North-South cooperation and nuclear weapons must be prioritized. Throwing eggs at the wall of tyranny and the oppression of Kim Jong Un and his sycophants seems futile. But the eggs must be thrown. Even if one knows the eggs will never break the wall, one keeps throwing them to delegitimize the presence of the wall, to sully it, and to keep the tragedies of tyranny ever present in our minds. But yes indeed, perhaps I may lose. Probably right. But I would rather lose with Socrates than win with Lenin. In retrospect, the progressive assumption seems to be misplaced. Truth is universal. It always was, and always will be. Because all tears are the same.

Empty Words of Hollow Men*

On May 21, 2021, Presidents Biden and Moon met for three hours at the White House. Except for the lifting of missile range limits, the meeting was a disappointment, wrapped in words like flexible and pragmatic. The joint statement underscored a "calibrated and practical approach" to North Korea.[95] The weakness of the Biden policy is similar to the weakness of the Moon administration who clings to vacuous words like strategic ambiguity, diplomacy, balancing and "flexibility." These are empty words uttered by hollow men. Hemingway said don't confuse movement for action. There are only movements. And they are fake.

Many experts argue that North Korea policy changes with each administration. But this is untrue. There has been no American president who has relaxed sanctions unilaterally in a shift of policy. There has been no one who rescinded the denuclearization of North Korea. Tactics and emphasis have adjusted. Policy tweaks exist due to presidential styles. But policy formed at the working level remains consistent. Consistently wrong.

It is due to personnel. At the joint press conference, Biden appointed Sung Kim as Special Envoy for North Korea. This personnel decision is the key policy implication of the U.S.-ROK summit. This means that there will be no real policy changes.

This is the Sung Kim who with his mentor Chris Hill applauded the destruction of the Yongbyon tower in front of CNN.[96] Experts knew this was absolutely meaningless, as the tower had zero impact on actual reactor operation. Such was touted at the time as a real sign of denuclearization.

Unfortunately, Sung will work with two key individuals to have any real influence or leverage. National Security Advisor Jake Sullivan was Hillary's

---

* The Korean version was published in the *Kookmin Ilbo* on May 31, 2021. This is the original English version.

policy planning director who appeased Iran's mullahs by refusing to support the Green Revolution, sending cash to reach the Joint Comprehensive Plan of Action (JCPOA), and pedaling the Russian collusion hoax for four years.[97] Wendy Sherman, Deputy Secretary of State has never met an appeasement deal she opposed. "Asia Czar" Kurt Campbell is deeply conflicted, with ties to the CCP and Hunter Biden.[98]

T.S. Eliot eviscerated the leaders of post-World War I as hollow men who had "shape without form, shade without color, paralyzed by force, gesture without motion."[99] Empty words sound reassuring to hollow men. But they are devastating for the Korean people.

It is time for the Moon administration to stop prevaricating on words and stop depending on weak personnel in Washington. It must reject subservience to China and stand up for its foundational values – freedom, democracy, and free markets – by joining the Quad. Doing so, the ROK makes its intentions and capabilities clear to the world. To wit, it will defend its national sovereignty with gusto. I wish we had a Foreign Minister with the audacity of the Philippine Foreign Secretary, Teddy Locsin, who told China on May 3: "GET THE FUCK OUT."[100] He was referring not only to the Philippines' exclusive economic zone (EEZ), including its fishing grounds in the South China Sea, but to what he claimed was Chinese overbearance on the Philippines.

Moon is in the last year of his presidency. If he wants to be recorded in history as a consequential President, then he must choose: whether he will place ROK into the Chinese orbit or stand up for the pillars and principles of modern Korea. It is his individual choice. But it is Korea's collective fate. The empty words of hollow men have consequences.

It is the Soldier*

In international politics, what doesn't happen matters as much as what happens. Every June 6th, America celebrates unapologetically the landing at Normandy in 1944 that marked the beginning of the end of Nazism. Operation Overlord is celebrated and immortalized via Steven Spielberg's 15-minute opening scene of carnage, savagery, and bravery in Saving Private Ryan, but also through tear-jerking remembrances by Presidents and opinion makers. Reagan's eloquent 1984 Point de Hoc speech remains the gold standard for honoring the soldier.

But this year, Biden and Harris uttered not a single word about this important event. Actually, Harris took political heat for tweeting that Americans should rather enjoy their three-day weekend.[101] This loss of memory, this loss of history is troubling.

Coincidentally, June 6th in Korea is also Memorial Day. But there was little to no media coverage of the soldiers' sacrifices. I wish that any political leader, left or right, would read out loud each and every name of the 46 soldiers who died in Cheon-an-ham and every other soldier who paid the ultimate sacrifice for his nation. But far from memorializing the soldier, the elites downplay the role of the military. The masses can recall every member of BTS or the national soccer team but can't name three soldiers from the 46. Unification Minister Lee In-young advocates for the continuous delay of U.S.-ROK military exercises.[102] In short, this means the military is training less and less, which I believe, has led to a lax in professional discipline. The recent scandals on sexual abuses demonstrate one dire consequence of that lack of military training.

In our politically correct modern society, notions of virtue and discipline

---

* The Korean version was published in the *Kookmin Ilbo* on June 28, 2021. This is the original English version.

are easily dismissed as anachronistic traits. There are many institutes of peace but not war. But the sharpness of military readiness protects the loose fluidity of a free society. George Orwell said, "People sleep peaceably in their beds at night only because rough men stand ready to do violence on their behalf."[103] Industrialists, intellectuals, journalists, doctors, and engineers have important roles. But without the soldier, none of that matters. I believe what Charles Province said. It is worth quoting the entire, "It is the Soldier."[104]

> It is the Soldier, not the minister
> Who has given us freedom of religion.
> It is the Soldier, not the reporter
> Who has given us freedom of the press.
> It is the Soldier, not the poet
> Who has given us freedom of speech.
> It is the Soldier, not the campus organizer
> Who has given us freedom to protest.
> It is the Soldier, not the lawyer
> Who has given us the right to a fair trial.
> It is the Soldier, not the politician
> Who has given us the right to vote.
> It is the Soldier who salutes the flag,
> Who serves beneath the flag,
> And whose coffin is draped by the flag,
> Who allows the protester to burn the flag.

AI, fintech, the 4th industrial revolution, bitcoin, software apps, cyber learning will all be meaningless and less possible without the existence and protection of the soldier. There is no economy, there is no freedom, there is no nation in the absence of the soldier. It is the soldier. It is always the soldier.

Korea Must Make Its Moves Too*

China and its sympathizers peddle the false narrative of the inevitability that China will overtake the United States. China has ambitions to become the world's largest economy by 2049. It already has the world's largest navy.[105] But there are minor but certain signs that America has started making its moves to counter China.

The Pentagon welcomed Philippine President Rodrigo Duterte's decision to extend the suspension of the Visiting Forces Agreement (VFA) for another six months.[106] Signed in 1998, the VFA makes it possible for U.S. troops, as well as their vehicles and equipment, to move in and out of Philippine territory. The VFA is a keystone in the 1951 Mutual Defense Treaty's Article 4, which commits the signatories to support each other in the event either is attacked by an external party. The Philippine military sees it as a deterrent to Chinese encroachment on Philippine maritime territory in the South China Sea as validated by the International Arbitral Award five years ago. This means that the 23-year-old VFA may survive Duterte's presidency and pave the way for the Philippines to become an integral part of America's frontline defense against Chinese encroachments after Duterte is gone.

Here, the tyranny of geography rules. Subic Bay is a strategic naval base that will soon be leased to the Australian shipbuilder Austal. This development, combined with the expectation of the VFA's ultimate fate, is crucial for control of the Luzon Strait. The Luzon Strait is the strait between Taiwan and Luzon Island that connects the Philippine Sea to the South China Sea. Whoever controls Luzon will control the Bashi Channel, the entry way from the South China Sea to the Western Pacific. Such control will then influence control of the Miyako Strait, a strategically significant international

---

* The Korean version was published in the *Kookmin Ilbo* on July 26, 2021. This is the original English version.

waterway south of the major Japanese island of Okinawa. Access to these connected sea lanes affects major trade and military strategy. This critical area is the battle area for control of the so-called "first island chain." This is where America and China will vie for supremacy and, if need be, clash.

Moreover, many communications cables pass through the Luzon Strait. These cables provide important data services to China, Hong Kong, Taiwan, Japan, and South Korea. As the saying goes, look below the surface. In this case, this is literally true. While people tend to think of satellites and cell towers as the heart of the internet, the most vital component is the 380 submerged cables that carry more than 95 percent of all data and voice traffic between the continents. As U.S. Admiral Jamie Foggo, a career submariner, said: "Underwater cables are part of our critical infrastructure and essential to the global economy."[107]

The U.S. has made its move to oppose a World Bank-led project in the Pacific to lay sensitive undersea communications cables because of Chinese participation. This project was to connect to the HANTRU-1 undersea cable, a sensitive line primarily used by the U.S. government that connects to Guam, a U.S. territory with substantial military assets.[108]

Soon thereafter, President Moon reinforced the strategic partnership with the Netherland's ASML company that produces the machinery to make chips that are vital to every aspect of digital life, from data centers to smartphones. President Biden has upheld former President Trump's prohibition on any ASML equipment being sold to China. Basically, the Netherlands will produce the equipment and South Korea will make it, as the U.S. will seek to exploit its democratic alliance with South Korea and the Netherlands to deny China this critical equipment and chips.

Military hardware, such as advanced missiles, matters of course, in light of the lifting of missile range limits. But strategic considerations for South Korea in the next 50 years will also largely revolve around access to friendly sea lanes, protection of undersea cables, and chips. Those are the new pillars of the new international order.

Position Available: Korea's Cyber Diplomats*

Hitler was responsible for many evil acts. Adding to his dismal resume, he ruined the word, "propaganda." Largely due to him, the word is now tainted to mean political distortions of truth. But the origin of the word is innocuous and comes from a religious context. In 1622, Pope Gregory XV established the *Congregatio de propaganda fide* ("Congregation for propagating the faith") to advance Catholic missionary activity. The word propaganda is rooted in the Latin *propagare*, meaning "to propagate." That is to say, spread the word of God.

In international politics, propaganda on behalf of the nation used to be called public diplomacy. Now it is fashionably called soft power. The words have changed but the objective remains the same – to persuade through the power of reasoning and rhetoric. Moreover, the means have also changed. Twitter, Facebook, and SNS are the new tools of public diplomacy. The old wine of propaganda is now in the new bottles of SNS.

Public diplomacy in the 21st century is the battle for influence in ENGLISH. Look at what China is doing. Qin Gang, the new charismatic Ambassador to the U.S., tweeted in front of the original headquarters of the CCP before departing for his new post in Washington. He tweeted on August 13 that he is out of the two-week quarantine and talked sweetly about "continuing dialogue and communication with American colleagues for a rational, stable, manageable & constructive China-U.S. relationship."[109] He has tweeted a congratulatory message to the Smithsonian Museum and lavished praise on the Tokyo Olympics and the U.S. team. This is the same guy who was a core member of "wolf warrior" diplomats and used to say, "China was once big boss for more than a century," while comparing China's

---

* The Korean version was published in the *Kookmin Ilbo* on August 23, 2021. This is the original English version.

takeover of Tibet to Lincoln's emancipation of slaves.[110] A wolf in sheep's clothing, armed with a powerful Tweeting ability.

Look at the Philippine Foreign Minister Teddy Locsin who is prolific in the cyber world. He sprinkles his tweets with references to Woody Allen. He knows Greek and philosophy. On August 1, 2021, he wrote about a U.S. pharmaceutical company's mistake: "I was promised 30,000 Moderna for my people and the diplomatic corps. My people who are frontliners. I don't know where the f**k that went, but words cannot express my embarrassment and anger. No one endangers my people. No one."[111] Moderna soon expedited the delivery. On August 9, 2021, Locsin elaborated on his nation's foreign policy philosophy: "F**k my country I'll f@@k yours."[112] A small man for a small nation, but he punches above his weight. He is widely sought after for media interviews and his Tweets have earned him a considerable following in foreign policy circles. The Philippines falls behind Korea in nearly every category of the factors of power except one – the employment of English to propagate the national message and advance the national interest.

In 1922, the influential columnist, Walter Lippmann, warned of public opinion that could have a negative influence on the conduct of foreign policy. To counter that, he called for the need to cultivate the opinion of elites.[113] The new type of diplomacy today, be it Twitter diplomacy or digital diplomacy, *combines* elite and public opinion. Thus, this conflation of both has more influence than either by itself.

Unfortunately, Korea is failing and falling far behind other nations. ROK needs to build a team of foreign policy and national security experts who are well read, sharp thinkers with a mastery of English and fluency in western cultures, and savvy with social platforms. In short, the ability to read raw primary material in English and not rely on machine translations of major English newspapers.

One can dream about how great Rhee Syngman would have been with Twitter diplomacy. After Kim Young Chul, the head of the Unification Propagation Department said, "we will let you feel how perilous your security will be if you take the wrong decision," one can imagine the impact Rhee would have as he fired back a tweet in exquisite English. He would eloquently defend and advance Korea's national interests with flair and force, exploiting his Princeton doctorate and penetrating understanding of America, totalitarianism, and world developments. One can dream. But one also must plan.

American Dereliction of Duty*

The falling of two individuals from the sky to their deaths twenty years apart captures the two bookends of calamity. On September 11, 2001, we recall the impeccably dressed man falling from the smoldering World Trade Center. Twenty years later, we see the young Afghan boy falling to his death from the wheel well of the C-17 in Kabul. The two bookends of calamity.

But this calamity was avoidable. No man left behind is an American creed. It is why to this day the U.S. military searches for the remains of fallen soldiers from the Korean War. Lt. Colonel Hal Moore's stirring words to his men captures the backbone of this American ethos:

> "We are goin' into battle against a tough and determined enemy. I can't promise you that I will bring you all home alive. But this I swear before you and before Almighty God: That when we go into battle, I will be the first to set foot on the field, and I will be the last to stop off. And I will leave no one behind. Dead or alive, we will all come home together. So help me God."[114]

That is not what President Biden sought. In his dementia-addled mind, his actions in Afghanistan came down to one simple thing – he wants to be remembered as the President who ended a war. That's it. Legacy was his sole consideration. Lives, reputations, and credibility be damned.

This is not the first time Biden has been wrong on foreign policy. Robert Gates, Defense Secretary under Presidents George W. Bush and Obama, wrote in his 2014 memoir, "Duty: Memoirs of a Secretary at War," that Biden "has been wrong on nearly every major foreign policy and national security issue over the past four decades."[115]

---

* The Korean version was published in the Sermo Institute of International Studies on October 6, 2021. This is the original English version.

Peter Wehner compiles a brutal historical record against Biden.

"In 1975, Biden opposed giving aid to the South Vietnamese government...In 1991, Biden opposed the Gulf War...In 2003, Biden supported the Iraq War but then stated later that he regretted his congressional vote...In 2007, he opposed President George W. Bush's new counterinsurgency strategy and surge in troops in Iraq...In December 2011, President Barack Obama and Vice President Biden withdrew the much-scaled-down troop presence in Iraq."[116]

In his speech to the nation, Biden puffed his chest and hectored that he was a realist while justifying this disastrous evacuation of the U.S. from Afghanistan (it was not a withdrawal) by appealing to America's "vital national interest."[117] In 1949, Hans Morgenthau coined this term in his essay on "The Primacy of the National Interest." Morgenthau presented this notion as a necessary corrective to what he had characterized as legalism, moralism, and sentimentalism in American foreign policy. Foreign policy, he argued, required a cold steely-eyed view of the world based on pure calculations of power.[118]

But there is another powerful tradition in American foreign policy. It is universal morality. This moral strain in the American tradition of American exceptionalism's effect on the world remains strong. In fact, the evocation of America as the "shining city on a hill" by John Winthrop, the first governor of the Massachusetts Bay Colony, runs through the blood of nearly all Presidents.[119] The clash and mixture of these two traditions influences the unfolding of American foreign policy. Americans calculate power but they also care about moral values.

The moral streak of Americans is evident in their reaction to how Biden has handled Afghanistan. Though the results of one poll, may not hold, as Afghanistan recedes from the front pages of newspapers, they are still worth noting A Rasmussen survey, conducted on August 30-31 among 1,000 "likely voters," finds that 52 percent believe Joe Biden should resign because of his Afghanistan policy. 39 percent disagreed. The poll had a 14% tilt towards Democratic voters.[120]

Furthermore, if Biden does not resign (and he won't, of course), 60 percent of those surveyed said he should be impeached. Rasmussen approached that question by quoting Senator Lindsey Graham and asking respondents whether they agreed with him. Graham's statement was: "I think Joe Biden deserves to be impeached because he's abandoned thousands of Afghans who fought with us and he's going to abandon some American citizens because he capitulated to the Taliban to a August 31 deadline."[121]

Leaks from the White House are even more revealing. One White House official told *Politico* that he was stunned by the President's decision to leave Americans stranded as the Taliban solidified their power in the country and reportedly engaged in door-to-door executions: "I am absolutely appalled and literally horrified we left Americans there... It was a hostage rescue of thousands of Americans in the guise of a NEO (noncombatant evacuation operation), and we have failed that no-fail mission." Another administration official said that he didn't consider the mission to be accomplished if Americans were abandoned in Afghanistan. The officials' concerns came the same day that Biden vigorously defended his handling of the withdrawal.[122]

America's closest ally openly questioned the President's sanity. The *Sunday Times* reported. "One minister said the president 'looked gaga.' An aide described the press conference as 'completely mad' and the president as 'doolally'(out of his mind)."[123] The House of Commons held President Biden in contempt for his disastrous Afghanistan withdrawal on September 1 despite his lie at a press conference that no NATO ally had questioned his "credibility." The *Telegraph* reported that the British Parliament delivered an unprecedented rebuke to a U.S. President, condemning the withdrawal as "catastrophic" and "shameful." Members of Parliament across the spectrum accused Biden of "throwing us and everybody else to the fire" by pulling out U.S. troops. Biden's criticism of the Afghan forces for not having the will to fight was condemned as "dishonorable."[124]

Merkel's likely successor, Christian Democratic Union (CDU) Chairman Armin Laschet was even harsher toward Biden: "It's the biggest debacle that NATO has suffered since its creation and it's a change of era that we are confronted with." German President Frank-Walter Steinmeier added, "The images of desperation at Kabul airport are shameful for the political West."[125]

Craig Whitlock's indispensable *The Afghanistan Papers* reveals that blame for the failures of Afghanistan span Democratic and Republican administrations.[126] But it was Biden that chose to withdraw in the ludicrous manner he did. The sole blame for this fiasco lies with Biden and Biden only. No other President would have done what Biden did. His 40 years of wrong and disastrous judgment reached its climax in the incomprehensible abandonment of Bagram air base and the ensuing chaos at Kabul. Instead of compassion and contrition, Biden remains defiant and arrogant that every decision he made was an "extraordinary success."

Korea and Japan are non-NATO major allies. If Biden can't hold NATO together, how would he be able to hold the alliances with Seoul and Tokyo? Both nations would be wise to think through the strategic implications of this devolution of American primacy in international affairs. I am deeply concerned that the current cadre at the helm of U.S. leadership is not up to the task. They will hesitate, equivocate, or excuse, not lead or strengthen alliances. The Republic of Korea must prepare for all contingencies brought forth by this abject dereliction of duty from Joe Biden, Harris, Jake Sullivan, Antony Blinken, Lloyd J. Austin III, and Mark Milley. Perhaps the next administration in 2024 can turn America around. But we can't wait till then. We don't have the time.

There are about three years left in the Biden presidency. Given his deteriorating physicality, Biden may not be able to serve out his term. Harris may be even worse. Harris' national security adviser is Nancy McEldowney, a career foreign service officer. She was a former U.S. ambassador to Bulgaria, former Chargé d'Affaires and Deputy Chief of Mission in Turkey and Azerbaijan, Director of European Affairs on the National Security Council staff in the Clinton administration, and the Principal Deputy Assistant Secretary of State in the Bureau of European and Eurasian Affairs. *Nota bene*: She is a European specialist. She knows nothing about North Korea, China or East Asia.

The Taliban used to tease the Americans – "You have the watches but we have the time."[127] Nothing could have been more apropos and tragic than Biden repeatedly looking at his watch while waiting for the bodies of the 13 soldiers to arrive in coffins at Dover Air Force Base. Now, the Taliban will have all the time to ban music, enforce the sexual slavery of women, reverse 20 years of sacrifice by the sons and daughters of General Massoud, and impose barbaric laws of the 7th century when the Quran emerged in Arabia. Sharia is an Arabic word, literally meaning "the right path." The modern world will now have to face the consequence of the Taliban's march on their path.

Disgraceful. Dishonorable. Contemptible.

I lost four friends on 9.11. That the U.S. has allowed those responsible for their murder to return to power, infuriates me. Biden's disingenuous words need to be thrown back in his face. We will not forgive Biden. We will not forget what Biden did. And we will make sure he pays the price for his dereliction of duty. His all-important legacy will not be the one he wants.

Defeat. Betrayal. Lies.

That will be Biden's legacy.

It is a fitting one.

There is No Snapback*

In September 2021 alone, North Korea test launched FOUR new missile systems. A cruise missile, a rail based Short-Range Ballistic Missile (SRBM), a 'Hwasong-8' with claimed Hypersonic Glide Vehicle (HGV), and a Surface-to-Air Missile (SAM). The Moon administration's blasé response to North Korea's missile tests once again underscores its congenital amateurism in foreign affairs.

South Korean Foreign Minister Chung Eui-yong downplayed the test. Minister Chung - it is a 1,500 km-range land attack cruise missile capable of delivering a nuclear or conventional warhead against targets throughout South Korea and Japan. It is a serious capability that is designed to fly under missile defense radars or around them. North Korea boasted that "The launched long-range cruise missiles flew 1,500 kilometers for 7,580 seconds along the flight track of oval and figure eight set in the territory and territorial air of our state before hitting the targets."[128]

That is serious in-flight maneuverability and terminal guidance. We don't know if they have the Terrain Contour Matching (TERCOM) and Digital Scene-Matching Area Correlation (DSMAC) capabilities of the U.S. Tomahawk missile. But given the above performance, we have to presume they have more than a simple GPS guidance system.

The UNSC resolutions on North Korea only cover ballistic missiles. That's not because ballistic missiles are somehow more threatening than cruise missiles. In September 2010, Dennis Gormley of the U.S. Naval Institute portended the dangerous proliferation of cruise missiles in *Missile Contagion*.[129] The pertinent question is - does North Korea have a nuclear warhead compact enough to put on a cruise missile? If so, then our

---

* The Korean version was published in the *Kookmin Ilbo* on October 18, 2021. This is the original English version.

Hyunmoo-4 is effectively counter balanced since we lack nuclear warheads. Even in the absence of a nuclear capability, North Korea may be able to insert a conventional payload into a submarine or load it onto an airplane. It is that much more ominous precisely because we do not know all the details of its capability.

To such a threat, President Moon uttered not a word at the United Nations. Instead, he called for a worthless end of war declaration and his clueless Foreign Minister glibly called for sanctions relief to revive dormant talks tinged with the arrogance that sanctions can "snap back" at will.[130]

When have so-called "snap-back" sanctions ever snapped back? In 2008, George W. Bush took North Korea off the list of state sponsors of terrorism.[131] An inexperienced first-time amateur Senator named Barack Obama promised that those sanctions would snap back.[132] Four nuclear tests henceforth – where are the snapped back sanctions?

Sanctions *suspension* allows for the re-imposition of sanctions within 90 days. Even that takes serious diplomatic heavy lifting. But sanctions *relief* means the terms of sanctions need to be renegotiated and reinforced. It is neither quick nor snappy. Thus, sanctions relief to gain talks is foolish. Current sanctions in place can work if they are enforced. As the U.S. Panel of Experts noted, not a single major Chinese bank has been held accountable for its violations of NK sanctions.

This lack of understanding of the details demonstrates a lack of seriousness, gravitas, and professionalism. Nothing said more about Moon's frivolity than his appointment of BTS to the UN as special ambassadors. I have nothing against the group. But an aggressor is not going to be deterred by a boy band who thinks they will change the world with words of love and hope. I don't lecture entertainers on how to sing, or act, or dance. I don't second guess a doctor's brain surgery operations. So, stay in your lane. I will stay in mine. Foreign policy is no playground for amateurs.

If Moon had proposed a grand schematic as Kant did in *Perpetual Peace* of a league of peace (*foedus pacificum*) in lieu of a treaty of peace (*pactum pacis*), it would be a worthy debate. But such a breezy utterance of worthless words such as the end of war declaration renders ROK diplomacy to be feckless and amateurish.

The First Corinthians (13:11) admonishes, "When I was a child, I spoke as a child, I understood as a child, I thought as a child. But when I became a man, I put away childish things." It is time to set aside childish notions about North Korea. It is time to get serious and hard-nosed about real deterrence. It is time to conduct diplomacy worthy of a nation that just became the 8th nation to field a Submarine-Launched Ballistic Missile (SLBM).

The Devil is in the Details*

On September 15, 2021, the United States, United Kingdom, and Australia announced the creation of AUKUS, a new trilateral security partnership that provides Australia with a fleet of nuclear-powered, conventionally (not nuclear) armed submarines to ostensibly counter China's influence in the region.

The sharing of sensitive nuclear technology and capabilities with a foreign state raises a number of legal questions. How can Australia, a signatory of the Treaty on the Non-Proliferation of Nuclear Weapons (NPT), obtain a fleet of nuclear-powered submarines while still complying with the NPT?

Nuclear-powered submarines appear to be an exception to NPT rules. States seeking to use nuclear material for a permitted military application would need to remove that material from its International Atomic Energy Agency (IAEA)-monitored safeguards.

Inspired by this AUKUS precedent, many Koreans called for the same lifting of the highly enriched uranium (HEU) restriction on its submarine program. But passions are temporal. It is better to be logical. The devil is in the details. It is surprising to me that ROK foreign affairs and national security experts have not exploited international treaty and law to argue for and advance South Korea's national interest.

Paragraph 14 of the International Atomic Energy Agency Information Circular (INFCIRC)/153 requires an agreement between the member state and the IAEA. It stipulates the following.

> "The Agreement should provide that if the State intends to exercise its discretion to use nuclear material which is required

---

* The Korean version was published in the *Kookmin Ilbo* on November 15, 2021. This is the original English version.

to be safeguarded thereunder in a nuclear activity which does not require the application of safeguards under the Agreement, the following procedures will apply:
(a) The State shall inform the Agency of the activity, making it clear:
(i) That the use of the nuclear material in a non-proscribed military activity will not be in conflict with an undertaking the State may have given and in respect of which Agency safeguards apply, that the nuclear material will be used only in a peaceful nuclear activity; and
(ii) That during the period of non-application of safeguards the nuclear material will not be used for the production of nuclear weapons or other nuclear explosive devices."[133]

In short, no diversion of sensitive nuclear materials for nuclear weapons. But nuclear fuel can be used for peaceful nuclear naval submarines.

No state has ever invoked this paragraph. It was initially inserted for Italy and the Netherlands during drafting due to their (ultimately unrealized) interest in nuclear-powered naval technology. Brazil's current attempt at constructing a nuclear-powered submarine is conducted under a separate four-party agreement. Thus, paragraph 14 has been left dormant since its initial creation. ROK should invoke this clause to argue for its own nuclear-powered submarine.

Paragraph 14 also has to be consistent with ROK obligations under the Nuclear Suppliers Group (NSG). NSG guidelines in INFCIRC/254 encourage states to *only* permit transfers of enrichment technology to states when the purposes of that transfer are peaceful. Paragraph 6b of INFCIRC/254's section on "Special Controls on Sensitive Exports" stipulates that member states "should consult with potential recipients to ensure that enrichment and reprocessing facilities, equipment and technology are intended for peaceful purposes only; also taking into account at their national discretion, any relevant factors as may be applicable."[134]

South Korea may argue that such a purely military investment is a peaceful activity, faithful to NPT and NSG obligations. South Korea can exploit this legal loophole to argue for an HEU fueled submarine under the nonproliferation regime. Such a policy decision may be too late for the current administration. But it is prerequisite homework for the next administration.

Let Them Be*

It is fashionable to criticize the Korean military these days. A movie about orientation abuse, an article about how parents call their son's commanding officers to berate his treatment, a teary news conference by a trans-sexual draftee citing violations of his human rights. It is fashionable to tut tut and gloat at the backwardness of the common soldier.

Recently, I read a surreal *Chosun Ilbo* article about the South Korean military. A Commanding Officer's rueful comment stopped me in my tracks: "For fear of parental petitions, it is impossible to conduct real training."[135]

Korea's problem is not isolated. America's military is showing a similar pattern. Gen. Mark Milley, the chairman of the Joint Chiefs of Staff, declared, in defending the teaching of critical race theory among the ranks: "I've read Karl Marx. I've read Lenin. That doesn't make me a Communist. So what is wrong with understanding... the country which we are here to defend?"[136]

His analogy shows just how ignorant and out of touch top leaders are about cultural Marxism. No, General, cultural Marxists and critical race theory advocates are actually trying to IMPLEMENT the ideas of Marx and Lenin. Defense Secretary Lloyd Austin has also said, "We ought to look like the America we support and defend, and senior leadership should look like what's in the ranks." Austin said the U.S. military needs to be "a bit better" to be "absolutely inclusive."[137]

No, we should not. We should not. Never. The military should never look like the society that it is supposed to defend.

If there is anything the military is good at, it is to take a young civilian male, break them down, and build them back up again, as soldiers.

---

* The Korean version was published in the *Kookmin Ilbo* on December 13, 2021. This is the original English version.

The military inculcates a military ethos and martial virtues such as courage, duty, and honor. Such values seem at odds with the values of a free, democratic, liberal society. Exactly. That is how it should and must be.

In 1957, a young Samuel Huntington wrote that the tension between soldier and statesman is rooted in the essence of professionalism. He described the military mindset as conservative, realistic, and pessimistic about human nature. To achieve "objective control" as the optimum form of civil-military relations, the military must be allowed to be cordoned off and retain autonomy within a clearly defined military sphere – apart from the general society.[138]

In short, the military has to retain its own unique values and way of conducting itself, apart from and at times, antithetical, to the values and priorities of the general society. No more cell phones. No more liberal leaves. The military isn't a daycare center. The military is not a social laboratory to experiment with progressive values. Warriors are the tip of the spears. And that tip has to remain constantly sharp. Soldiers should train till they pass out from exhaustion, not from attending sexual sensitivity classes. The Commanding Officer (CO) has to have absolute command over his men on the field. His authority can't be undermined by a call from a mom or dad complaining about their son's hanging toenail or his allergies to seafood. When your boy is in the military, he is the property of the Korean government. In "The Will to Power," Friedrich Nietzsche observed: "Not the corruption of man, but the softening and moralizing of him is the curse."

Civilian control is paramount in a democracy. But let the military be the military. It needs to do what it does best – fight to win. Everything else is secondary. The military is the ultimate defense. The soldier is the last line. Hold the line. Hold the line. No matter what. Semper fi.

August 15, 2048[*]

Every year pundits make predictions for the new year. That is important and needed. But today I want to be idealistic. I want to imagine what South Korea could look like on its 100-year birthday.

By then, I will be buried in the ground. But for now, this is my strategic imagination.

Realism that paralyzes our imagination is not realistic - or useful. Imagination is not fantasy. It is aspirational. All the pundits failed to predict the collapse of the Soviet Union - except two individuals. Its collapse was predicted by two German Marxists, one of them from the West (Hans Magnus Enzensberger) and one from the East (Rudolf Bahro). Bahro's accuracy was almost uncanny. Their imagination fueled the prediction.

It is the year 2048. North Korea has ceased to exist as a country. Kim Jong Un died of a heart attack in 2035 and his young sister's reign lasted less than a year before she faced the firing squad of the revolting generals. China did not save North Korea. The U.S., China, South Korea, and Japan came together to accept a unified Korea. China completed construction of 150 new reactors by 2027, more than the rest of the world had built in the previous 50 years. China failed to overtake the United States economically. The Chinese Communist Party changed its name to the Chinese People's Party.

I see a unitary powerful Korea, a thriving democracy with economic fortitude and military power. Its per capita income is $100,000. Its military equals that of Japan. Japan has asked for a military alliance with a unified Korea. The U.S.-ROK defense treaty has been replaced with true joint operability with the United States and Japan, as all American forces have withdrawn from Korea and Japan. Korea is an integral part of Ten Eyes,

---

[*] The Korean version was published in the *Kookmin Ilbo* on January 10, 2022. This is the original English version.

along with Germany, India, Brazil, and Japan. The Hyunmoo-10 has replaced the U.S. Tomahawk as the best cruise missile in the world. The National Intelligence Service has a formidable intelligence capability with top grade collection, analysis, and operational competence.

Korea is a vibrant social media influencer as its soft power has dominated the world. Government leaders are of high caliber. The culture of nepotism and patronage has been eradicated. The government is filled with those who can say no to superiors, those who have guts, those who are not opportunists, those who will resign if policy fails, those who are fluent in English and Chinese, and those who are experts on space exploration. Foreign policy principles and strategies are formed by a strategic studies group, composed of the best thinkers and the best practitioners. Bold in imagination. Ruthless in execution.

The world respects Korea's reputation. No better friend. No worse enemy. A man can dream. A man must dream. Hannibal said, "I will either find a way or make one." That should be the attitude of every President from now till then. That is the way we get to the 100th anniversary of the great Korean nation.

The Nightmare*

I imagined an optimistic vision of Korea in 2048. But nightmares also require imagination. The dystopian vision pains the mind. But sometimes pain clarifies the cluttered mind.

The opening line of Virgil's Aeneid - *Arma virumque ca*no - portends that the epic poem will be about man's struggle with arms (weapons) and other precarious factors in life. In 2048, that same struggle continues on the Korean peninsula.

I close my eyes. And I shudder.

On the cusp of a second civil war, a declining United States has passed the 54th Constitutional amendment eliminating due process, the core of democracy. Ruled by a tyrannical majority, beset with financial drain, the U.S. has abandoned its overseas empire.

China has conquered Taiwan, as Chinese nationalism runs amok. China has achieved near nuclear parity with 3500 nuclear warheads. China, Saudi Arabia, and UAE have formed a new Electric Vehicles (EV) cartel on top of their dominance of oil. Sensitive technologies behind American-made switchblade drones have been stolen and reverse engineered by China.

Japan has revived its *kokutai no hongi* (Greater East Asian Co-Prosperity sphere). Japan, Britain, and Australia have formed a trilateral defense alliance that puts Korea under a Japanese sphere of influence.

Korea is unrecognizable. Considering Korea to be an unreliable ally, the U.S. has abrogated its treaty. Korea's frivolous foreign policy elite is engaged in impulsive vacillations of national security policy which culminated in losing the opportunity to gain an independent nuclear capability.

Neutral and weak on foreign policy, Korea is economically devastated

---

* The Korean version was NOT included in the *Kookmin Ilbo* on January 10, 2022. This is the original English version.

after populist leaders, both left and right, rashly broke up the chaebols without supporting small businesses. The Left worships the 61-year-old Gabriel Boric who had come to power in Chile as a 35-year-old self-described moderate socialist. The Right clings to 63-year-old Lee Joonsuk who has retired from politics after his presidency.

Policies touted in the name of "equality and "justice" have led to everyone being equally poor and equally deprived of justice. The culture of victimhood and entitlement in lieu of a culture of accomplishment has eroded social mores. The fertility rate of 2020 (at 0.837 children per female) has led to a cataclysmic "reduction" in population. South Korea wavers between anarchy and utopia as the state dominates all aspects of life.

Having mastered re-entry technology, North Korea has acquired MIRV technology as it sits on a thermonuclear warhead stockpile equivalent to Britain, France, and Brazil. South Korea's atrophied defense capabilities pale in comparison as Seoul regularly pays ransoms to a nuclear saber-rattling North Korea. China uses Kim Jong Un to harass and dominate both Koreas and Japan.

It is so easy to be negative. It is cool to criticize the Pollyannish view and accept the Manichean worldview. But I refuse to yield to pessimism. I am a realist at heart - that is, I see things as they are and can imagine how they should be and how to achieve that reality. The job of the South Korean leader from March 2022 to August 2048 is to balance the difficult tradeoffs and steer the ship of Korea between the perils and dangers of world politics.

The Republic of Korea has a difficult task. But we must do things not because they are easy but precisely because they are hard. Albert Camus said, "real generosity towards the future lies in giving all to the present." Right indeed. We must be determined to give all to the present to never allow such a nightmare to unfold.

Correlation of Forces*

On January 30, 2022, North Korea fired an Intermediate Range Ballistic Missile (IRBM) that flew a distance of 800 km at an altitude of 2,000 km for approximately 30 minutes. North Korea has tested a lot of missiles recently (6 in January), but this is a big step. It looks like the 4,500 km range Hwasong-12 IRBM. The Hwasong-12 test on May 14, 2012 yielded a 787 km range, with a 2,111.5 km apogee with a 30 minute flight time.

North Korea is doing this at this time because of a favorable shift in the "correlation of forces" in the world situation. In 1951, Raymond Garthoff (a prominent Soviet analyst) wrote, "The calculation of the relation of forces is a most convenient means for internally and externally rationalizing the interpretation of Marxian ideology in pure power terms."[139]

The first "force" is South Korea. Kim aims to humiliate a weak President Moon Jae-In. Kim Jong Un wants to take him out of the Korean equation by making South Korea irrelevant in any future negotiations. Kim is acutely aware that these tests may sway the March 9 election. Some have argued that North Korean provocations have a counter effect of electing Yoon Sok Yeol rather than the more accommodating Lee Jae Myung. That seems counter intuitive but actually it has its own logic. If Yoon wins then it shows that North Korean actions can influence South Korean elections.

The next "force" is to increase fissures in the U.S.-ROK relationship. While Washington condemns these tests, Seoul has expressed only different conjugations of regrets. On January 5, "regrets"; January 11 and 14, "strong regrets"; January 17, "extreme regrets." What's next after "extreme"? These tests erode American trust in the fidelity of South Korea as an ally. Moreover, Yoon has raised preemptive strikes if North Korea positions itself

---

* The Korean version was published in the *Kookmin Ilbo* on February 7, 2022. This is the original English version.

to deploy nuclear tipped missiles against Seoul. Laying aside the merits or demerits of this policy, this stance instills discomfort in the American official's mind regarding the possibility of being drawn into a war that is not of its volition. During the Cold War, the U.S. was quietly but firmly worried about unilateral actions towards the North by Rhee Syngman and Park Chung Hee that would draw American forces into another war on the Korean peninsula. These missile tests exacerbate the existing fissures in the alliance.

The third "force" is the state of power of its enemies. North Korean testing raises its leverage with China. Some have argued that North Korea would not do anything provocative during the Beijing Olympics. I disagree. If North Korea conducts another test during the Olympics, then it shows the world that even China cannot control it. Kim's stature rises accordingly. Lastly, Kim Jong Un is testing a weak President Biden. The awful withdrawal from Afghanistan and the mismanagement of the Ukraine situation has emboldened Kim to exploit the current situation.

In 2018, Kim announced a moratorium on intermediate and intercontinental-range ballistic missile launches. North Korea has now broken that moratorium. Here are the big missile tests prior to the 2018 moratorium: July 2017 ICBM test - 933km range, 2,802km altitude; August 2017 ICBM test - 998km range, 3,724km altitude; and November 2017 ICBM test - 960km range, 4,500km altitude. ICBM tests are almost certain to follow. Whether Kim's calculation of the correlation of forces is prescient or foolish depends on the actions of the United States and the next President of South Korea.

Of Arms And Men In Ukraine*

History is complicated. That means, history is for adults not children. Morals are good. Being moralistic feels good. But taking a moralistic approach to history yields neither morals nor lessons from history. There is rarely the convenient and childish good versus evil in history.

On February 24, 2022, on the exact date of the eight-year anniversary of the annexation of Crimea, Vladimir Putin launched his re-invasion of Ukraine. Thus far, the full story is incomplete and fragmented. Can the origin of Putin's Manifest Destiny-nationalism be traced back to Halford Mackinder's 1904 "The Geographical Pivot of History"?[140] We have speculation but no solid theory. We have no story.

Instead, the all too black and white coverage of the conflict inundates us with propaganda and spin rather than facts and rationality.

Thirteen Ukrainian border guards, surrounded on an island scream, "Fuck you!" to the Russian military demanding their surrender.[141] For the first few days, this was played again and again to underscore the defiant resistance of the Ukrainians, as they were willing to die for the cause of Ukrainian sovereignty. Ukrainian President Volodymyr Zelensky himself touted these men as national heroes. Problem? They had surrendered and are alive and well.

A viral story of the "Ghost of Kyiv" about a mythic Ukrainian fighter jet pilot who downed six Russian aircraft? Too good to be true. Indeed, it was a meme.[142]

Those world leaders, including Zelensky, deplored the Russian bombing of Babi Yar, the memorial for the Jews massacred during the German occupation of Ukraine? The memorial remains unscathed.[143]

---

* The Korean version was published in the Sermo Institute of International Studies on March 29, 2022. This is the original English version.

What is the real story beyond the "breaking news" and spinning from both and every side? Instead of speculating about current developments, it is more productive to try to understand why we are in the situation we are in today.

To do this, we have to go back to the end of the Cold War. We have to go back 31 years to 1990.

Again, the month of February resurfaces.

In February 1990, the fate of Germany – the origin and epilogue of the Cold War – was being debated. Reduced to its essence, the complex and intense negotiations over the impending unification of Germany centered around this singular issue – can the Soviet Union accept a unified Germany in return for stopping NATO expansion?

On February 9, 1990, Secretary General Mikhail Gorbachev, Foreign Minister Eduard Shevardnadze, and U.S. Secretary of State James Baker met for two hours at the Kremlin.

Underscoring the participants' bluntness, Baker made this explicit promise: "We understand the need for assurances to the countries in the East. If we maintain a presence in a Germany that is a part of NATO, there would be no extension of NATO's jurisdiction for forces of NATO *one inch to the east*" [emphasis added]. This has come to be known as Baker's "not one inch" memorandum. In short, Gorbachev was willing to accept a unified Germany that was restrained by and anchored to firm American/NATO control, in return for no NATO expansion. There is no ambiguity here. The Ukraine question was not even entertained.[144]

Depending on one's view, this Baker memo is either the original sin or the original covenant. But it cannot be both. Four years later, President Clinton, Vice President Gore, and Strobe Talbott (against the advice of William Cohen) crafted the 1994 Budapest Memorandum in which the United States and its allies would defend Ukraine in exchange for surrendering its nuclear weapons to Russia. If Baker's "not one inch" promise was the original covenant, then the Budapest Memo was its most ostentatious transgression. If his assertion was the original sin, then Clinton washed away the superficial burden. One cannot stand for not moving NATO by one inch AND defend Ukraine. Promising to defend Ukraine is tantamount to NATO expansion writ large even if Ukraine was not a NATO member.

Three years later, the architect of the containment policy, George Kennan, penned a devastating rebuke of the Clinton administration's inexorable arrogance toward a Russia that was undergoing economic and social turmoil.

On February 5, 1997, Kennan noted that "Russians are little impressed with American assurances that it reflects no hostile intentions. They would see their prestige (always uppermost in the Russian mind) and their security interests as adversely affected." He concluded with the ominous warning that "expanding NATO would be the most fateful error of American policy in the entire post-cold-war era."[145]

A few months later, on June 26, 1997, leading Russian and nuclear experts across the political spectrum, including Fred Ikle, Sam Nunn, Robert McNamara, and Paul Nitze, signed a letter to President Clinton opposing NATO expansion that would give rise to Russia's national security concerns. The views of these serious men, who oversaw the management of American foreign policy throughout the Cold War, went unheeded. Among these, in particular, was the sober analysis of Paul Nitze, the author of NSC-68 and arguably the most influential advisor in U.S. history since John Jay.[146]

Two years later, in June 1999, the U.S. engaged in Operation Allied Force, the first Cold War NATO operation against the ethnic cleansing of Kosovo Albanian Muslims by Slobodan Milosevic. A 78-day air campaign ultimately produced Kosovo independence, a feat that was near unanimously applauded, but for a lone international law scholar by the name of Ruth Wedgwood, who presciently warned of the ramifications of the violation of national and territorial sovereignty embedded in Article 2 of the UN Charter, for future conflicts. In effect, it was the United States that set the precedent against violation of national sovereignty. A freshly appointed Prime Minister Putin took scrupulous notes. Putin is on record justifying his invasion of Ukraine – "how is it different from Kosovo?"[147] History never fades away.

The current CIA director, William Burns, a counselor for political affairs at the U.S. embassy in Moscow in 1995, wrote: "Hostility to early NATO expansion is almost universally felt across the domestic political spectrum here." Burns reiterated this Russian opposition to Ukraine NATO membership in his 2008 memo to Secretary of State Condoleezza Rice: "In more than two and a half years of conversations with key Russian players, from knuckle-draggers in the dark recesses of the Kremlin to Putin's sharpest liberal critics, I have yet to find anyone who views Ukraine in NATO as anything other than a direct challenge to Russian interests." Burns warned, "Ukrainian entry into NATO is the brightest of all redlines for the Russian elite (not just Putin)."[148]

On March 5, 2014, Henry Kissinger warned, "The West must understand that, to Russia, Ukraine can never be just a foreign country." This view was not limited to Russian political leaders, he continued: "Even such famed dissidents as Aleksandr Solzhenitsyn and Joseph Brodsky insisted that Ukraine was an integral part of Russian history and, indeed, of Russia." Kissinger concluded on a pessimistic tone: "If some solution based on these or comparable elements is not achieved, the drift toward confrontation will accelerate. The time for that will come soon enough."[149] They don't call him Mr. Kissinger for no reason.

In 2014, University of Chicago Professor, John Mearsheimer wrote in the September/October 2014 issue of *Foreign Affairs*: "the United States and its European allies share most of the responsibility for the crisis. The taproot of the trouble is NATO enlargement, the central element of a larger strategy to move Ukraine out of Russia's orbit and integrate it into the West."[150] Whether one accedes to Mearsheimer's realism or disdains his personal politics, his intellectual foresight is undeniable.

Given the preponderance of these experts' portentous warnings and admonitions over years and decades, how did we arrive at this stage? What is at stake in Ukraine? We must start where all geopolitics begins. By looking at a map.

Ukraine is situated between two greater powers, Russia and the European Union. That makes Ukraine a buffer state. But we cannot look at Ukraine in a vacuum. There are two subjects that many current observers fail to take into account – the Suwalki Corridor and Kaliningrad.

The Suwalki Corridor is a 65-kilometer-wide strip of territory that links Poland with Lithuania. It is the geographical chokepoint that has a direct and immediate impact on any military intervention by NATO against Russia. This corridor is bound to its West by Kaliningrad, a Russian oblast that is detached from Russia but is part of Russia. An area half the size of Belgium, Kaliningrad (known before as Konisberg) was a gift to Russia at the Potsdam Conference as compensation from Germany. It is Russia's only ice-free port.

If Russia gains control over this corridor, the Baltic States would essentially be cut off from NATO assistance. There are only two major highways and one railroad in the Suwalki Corridor. This is NATO's Achilles heel. If Belarus decides to host Russian nuclear weapons in its country (after its Constitutional amendment), the strategic picture will drastically change. It would make the deployment of Soviet SS-20s and the subsequent deployment of Pershing II missiles in the 1980s look like child's play.

Russia knows this. NATO knows this. The U.S. knows this. All military planners know this. But no one is willing to publicly talk about it. They refuse because it is too uncomfortable to talk about the prospect of the Ukrainian conflict metastasizing into a real military confrontation between Russia and NATO. In addition to this 'dark secret,' nuclear rhetoric has begun to seep into the verbal volleys. Putin minced no words on February 24: "To anyone who would consider interfering from the outside: If you do, you will face consequences greater than any you have faced in history. All relevant decisions have been taken. I hope you hear me."[151] You don't need to be a Russian linguist to understand the nuclear threat. To its credit, the U.S. and the West have thus far not directly reacted to this. On the contrary, the Pentagon suspended the previous scheduled decision to test the Minutemen ICBM to avoid any misunderstanding or mis-signaling during this crisis.

This is a welcome development. But the reality is far from sanguine or clear cut. One can condemn Putin. One can impose sanctions on Russia. But the fact of the matter is that Russia possesses the most nuclear warheads of any single nation. While it may be an Italy with a gas station, a belittling comment by former Senator John McCain,[152] it also has a formidable arsenal of nuclear weapons, an inventory that is only matched in quality and quantity by the United States. That means, Russia remains a great power, a power that cannot be dismissed breezily by slogans of 'We are all Ukrainians' and feel-good sanctions.

Sanctions are a tool; sanctions cannot be policy. What is that policy? Is it a Southern policy that works closely with Turkey to close off the Dardanelles and Bosphorus to warships under Article 21 of the 1936 Montreux Convention?[153] Is it a confrontational policy to introduce a no-fly zone over Ukraine that will risk nuclear war with Russia? The flurry of sanctions announced by the U.S. and other nations will take 30-days to come into force. Can Ukraine hold out for 30 days under Russia's steady penetration of Ukraine? Is the ultimate political goal to restore the status quo ante or can the West live with a partitioned Ukraine? There are no clear answers.

What is clear is that the U.S. and Europe still need Russia and China to manage other pressing international issues. The diplomatic trial balloon has been floated – Iran sending enriched uranium stockpiles to Russia on the condition that Russia will return the stockpiles if the U.S. reimposes terrorism sanctions. This would require direct and active Russian assistance and support.

The U.S. will also need China's cooperation to prevent any Chinese temptations to undertake unilateral encroachment against Taiwan. Undoubtedly, China and North Korea are studying every detail of what is unfolding in Ukraine, especially the West's deployment of sanctions. The U.S. and EU lost an opportunity to forestall the Ukrainian conflict by failing to even consider Ukraine neutrality and rejection of NATO membership. China will probe how the U.S. responds to its encroachments into the Taiwan Straits. The U.S. still needs China – and Russia – to work to resolve the North Korean denuclearization effort, especially the enforcement of existing sanctions.

Moreover, the world needs to be keenly aware that Russia is the world's largest producer of ammonium nitrate that is used as fertilizer.[154] Russia and Ukraine are both important grain exporters, accounting for almost a third of the world's traded wheat.[155] Food may become the next weapon in a strategic struggle. Reeling from gas prices, the rise in food prices (already affected by inflation from supply chain problems arising from Covid restrictions) may be the final straw that breaks the American public's patience with the Biden administration.

The Ukraine crisis is directly relevant for Korea. It affects our calculations of deterrence. Accurate analysis of intentions and intelligence becomes more important than ever. Intentions can be ascertained through the study of history, culture, and traditions, but it usually boils down to the individual leader.

Many in the U.S. and West are mis-analyzing Putin's personality. It is amazing how many people seem to believe BOTH that: 1) Putin is crazy, or at least dangerously emotional; and 2) we should implement a no-fly zone since there is no danger of him overreacting and things spinning out of control!

Which one is it? Both cannot be true. This conflicted analysis of intelligence and intentions has a sordid history.

As the Korean War raged on, American officials were perplexed and deeply concerned about the intentions of its main South Korean ally. President Rhee Syngman was considered unpredictable, capricious, vexatious, AND steady, consistent, subdued. Impertinent, intransigent, and dictatorial, he was at times, proper, agreeable, and generous. A CIA report at that time characterized his personality:

> "Rhee has devoted his whole life to the cause of an independent Korea with the ultimate objective of personally controlling that country. In pursuing this end, he has shown few scruples about

the elements which he has been willing to utilize for his personal advancement, with the important exception that he has always refused to deal with the Communists... Rhee's vanity has made him highly susceptible to the contrived flattery of self-seeking interests in the U.S. and Korea. His intellect is a shallow one, and his behavior is often irrational and even childish. Yet Rhee, in the final analysis, has proved himself to be a remarkably astute politician [with the] remarkably accurate estimate of popular attitudes and prevailing political conditions."[156]

But how can one be vain, shallow, irrational, childish and be remarkably astute? In any personality analysis of a leader, it behooves the student to understand that such an analysis is likely more about the portrayer than the portrayed. South Korea must be prepared to have an accurate assessment of Kim Jong Un and Xi Jinping prepared by the best minds.

The accurate analysis of leaders to get at intentions must also lead to an accurate assessment of the military situation. If Putin succeeds in occupying Ukraine, if not controlling it, then the military posture of the United States will likely be affected. These forces have been developing for some time. The forward deployed nuclear warheads in Europe including at Incirlik and Aviano will be reconsidered or revamped depending on whether Putin decides to deploy nuclear weapons to Belarus. If the "buffer" of Ukraine evaporates or is effectively neutered, then the U.S. and NATO will also have to change its military posture within NATO and on the frontline of NATO countries, especially Poland, Lithuania, Latvia, and Estonia. Such changes, in turn, will affect America's defensive postures in East Asia and the Taiwan Straits. Resources, time, and political attention are never unlimited.

The U.S. Marine Corps, under General David Berger, has instituted its offshore retrenchment strategy that calls for swift expeditionary forces rather than reliance on allied bases in Korea and Japan which are subject to local political influence.[157] The absence of a footprint or a tripwire in the form of blood shed by American soldiers has deep national and psychological implications for Seoul. If deterrence fails, then Korea and Koreans must be prepared to react swiftly to defend itself before the arrival of American assistance.

To be sure, the Republic of Korea is not Afghanistan. It is not Ukraine. It is a major non-NATO treaty ally of the United States, with the world's 12th largest economy and 6th ranked military. But North Korea has nuclear weapons. South Korea does not. So, the doubt lingers - would Washington sacrifice New York for Seoul?

I like that the United States and Korea both have formidable soft power. But we have become too enamored of our superiority. It should give one no comfort to wear alligator shoes while listening to BTS on an iPod if we are not strong enough to protect that free lifestyle and liberal values. For me, the formula is simple. If enemies don't fear the United States, its friends cannot trust it. I don't worry about the noise of enemies but the silence of my friends. I can only see one indispensable nation that can assist Korea in this effort to hold this country intact. Will the United States be silent or loud, absent or present, if something awful transpires in Korea?

The first line of Virgil's "Aeneid" notes *Arma virumque cano* - I sing of arms (weapons) and of a man. The Ukraine story is the continuation of this story of men and his struggle with arms. It is the same old story of human folly and limitations. It is the same story. The truth is always the same story.

Source Notes

1 Rolando Vitale, "The Secrets Behind the Legend of Rocky Marciano," *Boxing News*, June 23, 2016 https://www.boxingnewsonline.net/the-secrets-behind-the-legend-of-rocky-marciano/

2 Nick Gass, "Trump: I'll meet with Kim Jong Un in the U.S.," *Politico*, June 15, 2016. https://www.politico.com/story/2016/06/donald-trump-north-korea-nukes-224385

3 "Fact Sheet: The President's National Security Strategy to Combat WMD, Libya's Announcement," *The White House*, December 19, 2003.

4 Mina Lee, "South-North Panmunjom Declaration 'Agreement on denuclearization.. No More wars," *The Korea Economic Daily*, April 27, 2018. https://www.hankyung.com/politics/article/2018042778537

5 Transcript, "Kim Jong Un 'North and South Should Join as One In Order to Enjoy Endless Prosperity," *Yonhap News*, April 27, 2018. https://www.yonhapnewstv.co.kr/news/MYH20180427016800038?did=1825m

6 George Orwell, "Review of Adolph Hitler's 'Mein Kampf,'" *New English Weekly*, March 21, 1940. https://gutenberg.net.au/ebooks16/1600051h.html

7 Origen, *De Principilis*, Book II, Chapter 4, section 5. https://www.newadvent.org/fathers/04122.htm

8 Donald J. Trump (@realDonaldTrump), *Twitter*, May 6, 2019.

9 Reuters Staff, "Factbox: Tariff wars - duties imposed by Trump and U.S. trading partners," *Reuters*, May 14, 2019. https://www.reuters.com/article/us-usa-trade-tariffs-factbox-idUSKCN1SJ1ZJ

10 Donald Trump, "Message to the Congress on Securing the Information and Communications Technology and Services Supply Chain," *The White House*, May 15, 2019. https://www.presidency.ucsb.edu/documents/message-the-congress-securing-the-information-and-communications-technology-and-services

11 Martin Matishak , "Bipartisan bill seeks to toughen Trump approach on China," *Politico*, January 4, 2019. https://www.politico.com/story/2019/01/04/

bipartisan-bill-trump-approach-china-1060974

12 "Remarks by President Trump at APEC CEO Summit," *U.S. Embassy*, November 10, 2017. https://vn.usembassy.gov/20171110-remarks-president-trump-apec-ceo-summit/

13 "Donald Trump Speech in Las Vegas," *C-SPAN*, April 28, 2011. https://www.c-span.org/video/?299259-1/donald-trump-speech-las-vegas

14 "Agreement between the United States of America, the United Mexican States, and Canada," *Office of the United States Trade Representative*. https://ustr.gov/trade-agreements/free-trade-agreements/united-states-mexico-canada-agreement/agreement-between

15 "Top Trading Partners - January 2017," *Census Bureau*. https://www.census.gov/foreign-trade/statistics/highlights/toppartners.html

16 "Donald Trump says 'Tariff King' India Wants Trade eal with US Primarily to Keep Him 'Happy,'" *The Statesman*, October 2, 2018. https://www.thestatesman.com/world/donald-trump-says-tariff-king-india-wants-trade-deal-us-primarily-keep-happy-1502691908.html. See also, Yong-seung Jang, "Trump's Outbursts··· 'Calls out the Tariff Kings of Brazil and India,'" *Maeil Business*, October 2, 2018. https://www.mk.co.kr/news/world/view/2018/10/615426/

17 "Interview: Steve Hilton Interviews Donald Trump," *Fox News, The Next Revolution*, May 19, 2019. https://www.youtube.com/watch?v=H9ys30khGM8

18 "Trump: If Iran Does Anything, It Will Be A Very Bad Mistake," *CNBC*, May 13, 2019. https://www.cnbc.com/video/2019/05/13/trump-if-iran-does-anything-it-will-be-a-very-bad-mistake.html

19 Jeff Stein, "New Donald Trump Sanctions Target the Shadowy Chinese Weapons Dealer in China-Iran Ballistic Missile Deals," *Newsweek*, May 22, 2019. https://www.newsweek.com/donald-trump-sanctions-weapons-dealer-ballistic-china-iran-missile-1433084

20 Bret Stephens, "The Real China Challenge: Managing Its Decline," *New York Times*, November 29, 2018. https://www.nytimes.com/2018/11/29/opinion/china-rise-series-declining-economy.html

21 Ronald Reagan, "Remarks on East-West Relations at the Brandenburg Gate in West Berlin, Germany," June 12, 1987. https://www.presidency.ucsb.edu/documents/remarks-east-west-relations-the-brandenburg-gate-west-berlin

22 For detailed imagery of the attack, see "Saudi Arabia. September 17, 2019. Imagery released September 15, 2019." *Alamy*. https://www.alamy.com/saudi-arabia-17th-sep-2019-imagery-released-15th-sep-2019-the-damage-caused-by-a-drone-attack-on-saudi-aramcos-kuirais-oil-field-in-buqyaq-saudi-arabia-can-be-seen-in-this-image-released-by-the-us-government-and-digitalglobe-on-september-15-2019-the-attack-on-this-and-saudi-aramcos-abaqaiq-oil-processing-facility-has-halted-oil-production-of-57-million-barrels-of-crude-oil-per-day-photo-via-us-governmentdigitalglobeupi-credit-upialamy-live-news-image274651252.html

23 Jennifer Agiesta, "CNN Poll: Support for Impeaching Trump Rises Among Independents and Republicans," *CNN*, September 30, 2019. https://edition.cnn.com/2019/09/30/politics/cnn-poll-impeachment-ukraine/index.html

24 Monica Alba, "Trump, RNC combine for $125 million raised in third quarter," *CNBC News*, October 1, 2019. https://www.nbcnews.com/politics/meet-the-press/blog/meet-press-blog-latest-news-analysis-data-driving-political-discussion-n988541/ncrd1061041#blogHeader

25 Alex Ward, "Read the Transcript of Trump's Call with Ukraine's President," *Vox News*, September 25, 2019. https://www.vox.com/2019/9/25/20883325/transcript-trump-ukraine-president-impeachment

26 Politico Staff, "Read the Trump-Ukraine Whistleblower Complaint," *Politico*, September 26, 2019. https://www.politico.com/news/2019/09/26/read-the-trump-ukraine-whistleblower-complaint-002239

27 "Foreign Affairs Issue Launch with Former Vice President Joe Biden," *Council on Foreign Relations*, January 23, 2018. https://www.cfr.org/event/foreign-affairs-issue-launch-former-vice-president-joe-biden

28 Paul Craig Roberts, "Sworn Statement of Ukraine Prosecutor General Viktor Shokin that He Was Forced out of Office by US VP Joe Biden," *TheAltWorld*, September 27, 2019. http://thealtworld.com/paul_craig_roberts/sworn-statement-of-ukraine-prosecutor-general-viktor-shokin-that-he-was-forced-out-of-office-by-us-vp-joe-biden

29 Alex Ward, *op.cit*.

30 Politico, *op.cit*.

31 Council on Foreign Relations, *op.cit*.

32 Sworn statement of former Ukraine Prosecutor General Viktor Shokin. John Solomon, "These Once-Secret Memos Cast Doubt on Joe Biden's Ukraine story,"

The Hill, September 26, 2019. https://www.scribd.com/document/427618359/Shokin-Statement

33   *Ibid.*

34   T.S. Eliot, *The Rock* (New York: Houghton Mifflin Harcourt, 2014), p.7.

35   Mark Landler and Choe Sang-Hun, "North Korea Says It's Now a Nuclear State. Could That Mean It's Ready to Talk?," *New York Times*, November 29, 2017. https://www.nytimes.com/2017/11/29/world/asia/north-korea-nuclear-missile-.html

36   Pamela Falk, "Nikki Haley says North Korean Regime 'Will Be Utterly Destroyed' if War Comes," *CBS News*, November 30, 2017. https://www.cbsnews.com/news/north-korea-regime-destroyed-if-war-comes-nikki-haley-united-nations-ambassador/

37   Cited in Stephen Jinwoo Kim, *Master of Manipulation: Syngman Rhee and the Seoul-Washington Alliance, 1953-1960* (Seoul: Yonsei University Press, 2001).

38   Michelle Ye Hee Lee, "North Korea Nuclear Test May Have Been Twice as Strong as First Thought," *Washington Post*, September 13, 2017. https://www.washingtonpost.com/world/north-korea-nuclear-test-maybe-have-been-twice-as-strong-as-first-thought/2017/09/13/19b026d8-985b-11e7-a527-3573bd073e02_story.html

39   Scott Stump, "'It's Deja Vu All Over Again': 27 of Yogi Berra's Most Memorable 'Yogi-isms,'" *Today*, September 23, 2015. https://www.today.com/news/its-deja-vu-all-over-again-27-yogi-berras-most-t45781

40   James Felkerson, "$29,000,000,000,000: A detailed Look at The Fed's Bailout by Funding Facility and Recipient," *Levy Economics Institute of Bard College Working Paper* 698 (2011).

41   Politico Staff, "Full Text: Donald Trump 2016 RNC Draft Speech Transcript," *Politico*, July 21, 2016. https://www.politico.com/story/2016/07/full-transcript-donald-trump-nomination-acceptance-speech-at-rnc-225974

42   Quoted in Barry Popik, "All Politics is Local," June 13, 2009. https://www.barrypopik.com/index.php/new_york_city/entry/all_politics_is_local/

43   J. D. Vance, *Hillbilly Elegy: A Memoir of a Family and Culture in Crisis* (New York: Harper, 2016).

44   Salena Zito, "Taking Trump Seriously, Not Literally," *The Atlantic*, September 23, 2016.

45 Ibid.

46 Christopher Hitchens, *God Is Not Great: How Religion Poisons Everything* (New York: Atlantic Books, 2007), p. 258.

47 Donald Trump, "Remarks by President Trump at the Economic Club," *The White House*, November 12, 2019. https://trumpwhitehouse.archives.gov/briefings-statements/remarks-president-trump-economic-club-new-york-new-york-ny/

48 "Job Openings and Labor Turnover Survey Highlights January 2019," *U.S. Department of Labor, Bureau of Labor Statistics*, March 15, 2019. https://www.bls.gov/jlt/jlt_labstatgraphs_jan2019.pdf

49 "Labor Force Statistics from the Current Population Survey," *U.S. Department of Labor, Bureau of Labor Statistics*. https://www.bls.gov/cps/cpsaat01.htm.

50 "Unemployment Insurance Weekly Claims," *U.S. Department of Labor, News Release*, September 6, 2018. https://www.dol.gov/sites/dolgov/files/OPA/newsreleases/ui-claims/20181422.pdf

51 "Unemployment Rate Unchanged at 3.6 percent in May 2019," *U.S. Department of Labor, Bureau of Labor Statistics*. https://www.bls.gov/opub/ted/2019/unemployment-rate-unchanged-at-3-point-6-percent-in-may-2019.htm

52 Erica York, "The Benefits of Cutting the Corporate Income Tax Rate," *Fiscal Fact*, No. 606, *The Tax Foundation*. https://files.taxfoundation.org/20180813165516/The-Benefits-of-Cutting-the-Corporate-Income-Tax_FF606.pdf?_gl=1*g9twb4*_ga*MTg5MzY4NzU3OS4xNjYzMDQwNDU0*_ga_FP7KWDV08V*MTY2MzA0MDQ1NS4xLjAuMTY2MzA0MDQ1NS42MC4wLjA.

53 Javier Blas, "The U.S. Just Became a Net Oil Exporter for the First Time in 75 Years," *Bloomberg*, December 7, 2018. https://www.bloomberg.com/news/articles/2018-12-06/u-s-becomes-a-net-oil-exporter-for-the-first-time-in-75-years

54 Marquette Law School Poll, "New Marquette Law School Poll Finds Shifts in Wisconsin Public Opinion Favorable to President Trump on Impeachment and Presidential election Preferences," *News Release*, November 20, 2019. https://law.marquette.edu/poll/wp-content/uploads/2019/11/MLSP55PressRelease.pdf

55 Relevant dates were selected from Morgan Chalfant, "Timeline: Trump, Ukraine and impeachment," *The Hill*, October 28, 2019. https://thehill.com/policy/national-security/467590-timeline-trump-ukraine-and-impeachment/

56   Adam Taylor, "Amid Trump Impeachment Drama, Ukrainians Ponder a Putin meeting," *Washington Post*, November 14, 2019. https://www.washingtonpost.com/world/2019/11/14/amid-trump-impeachment-drama-ukrainians-ponder-putin-meeting/

57   Simon Shuster, "'I Don't Trust Anyone at All,' Ukrainian President Volodymyr Zelensky Speaks Out on Trump, Putin and a Divided Europe," *Time*, December 2, 2019. https://time.com/5742108/ukraine-zelensky-interview-trump-putin-europe/

58   Reuters Staff, "Obama Tells Russia's Medvedev More Flexibility After Election," *Reuters*, March 26, 2012. https://www.reuters.com/article/us-nuclear-summit-obama-medvedev-idUSBRE82P0JI20120326

59   Charlie Spiering, "Flashback: President Barack Obama Fired All George W. Bush-Appointed Ambassadors in 2008," *Breitbart*, November 15, 2019. https://www.breitbart.com/politics/2019/11/15/flashback-president-barack-obama-fired-all-george-w-bush-appointed-ambassadors-in-2008/

60   "November National Poll: Support for Impeachment Declines; Biden and Sanders Lead Democratic Primary," *Emerson Polling*, November 2019. https://emersonpolling.reportablenews.com/pr/november-national-poll-support-for-impeachment-declines-biden-and-sanders-lead-democratic-primary

61   Glenn Thrush, "Trump's Blistering Speech at CPAC Follows Bannon's Blueprint," *New York Times*, February 24, 2017. https://www.nytimes.com/2017/02/24/us/politics/trump-conservative-political-action-conference-speech.html

62   Zeke Miller, "Trump Campaign to Report $30 Million Haul," *NBC Boston*, April 14, 2019. https://www.nbcboston.com/news/politics/trump-campaign-report-30-million/141582/

63   Quoted in Salena Zito, *The Great Revolt: Inside the Populist Coalition Reshaping American Politics* (New York: Crown Forum, 2018).

64   David Foster Wallace, Commencement Address, Kenyon College, May 21, 2005.

65   Quoted in Tim Weiner, "Robert S. McNamara, Architect of a Futile War, Dies at 93," *New York Times*, July 6, 2009. For his overall philosophy, see his article, "The Military Role of Nuclear Weapons: Perceptions and Misperceptions," *Foreign Affairs*, Fall 1983.

66   Kenneth Waltz, "The Spread of Nuclear Weapons: More May Better," *Adelphi*

Papers, Number 171 (London: International Institute for Strategic Studies, 1981).

67   Quoted in Robert W. Tucker, "The Nuclear Debate," *Foreign Affairs*, Fall 1984.

68   Article V states, "attack against them all and consequently they agree that, if such an armed attack occurs, each of them, in exercise of the right of individual or collective self-defense recognized by Article 51 of the Charter of the United Nations, will assist the Party or Parties so attacked by taking forthwith, individually and in concert with the other Parties, such action as it deems necessary, including the use of armed force, to restore and maintain the security of the North Atlantic area." https://www.nato.int/cps/ua/natohq/official_texts_17120.htm

69   Eric Hoffer, *The True Believer: Thoughts on the Nature of Mass Movements* (New York: Perennial, 2002).

70   José Ortega y Gasset, *The Revolt of the Masses* (New York: Norton, 1993).

71   Keith B. Payne, "Nuclear Deterrence in A New Age: Comparative Strategy," *Comparative Strategy*, February 16, 2018, p.1.

72   "Nuclear Posture Review 2018," *U.S. Department of Defense*, February 2018.

73   *Ibid*.

74   "Essentials of Post-Cold War Deterrence," *STRATCOM*, 1995. https://www.nukestrat.com/us/stratcom/SAGessentials.PDF

75   *Ibid.*

76   *Ibid.*

77   Sinéad Baker, "The Most Powerful Countries on Earth, Ranked," *Business Insider*, March 2, 2019. https://www.businessinsider.com/most-powerful-countries-ranked-us-news-and-world-report-2019-2#10-south-korea-16

78   "Government Posts an 11.3 Trillion Won Surplus in 2017," *Ministry of Economy and Finance, Press Release*, February 9, 2018. https://english.moef.go.kr/pc/selectTbPressCenterDtl.do?boardCd=N0001&seq=4438

79   "Fourth Quarter Fiscal Year 2018 Earnings," *Walmart*, February 20, 2018, p.1. https://corporate.walmart.com/media-library/document/management-commentary/_proxyDocument?id=00000161-b0bf-de73-af67-b2fffe5d0000

80   Donald Trump, "Remarks by President Trump to the 72nd Session of the United Nations General Assembly," *The White House*, September 19, 2017.

https://2017-2021-translations.state.gov/2017/09/19/remarks-by-president-trump-to-the-72nd-session-of-the-united-nations-general-assembly/index.html

81 Michael R. Pompeo and Mark T. Esper, "South Korea Is an Ally, Not a Dependent," *Wall Street Journal*, January 16, 2020.

82 Mark Ramseyer, "Contracting for Sex in the Pacific War," *International Review of Law and Economics*, Volume 65 (March 2021).

83 Admiral Charles Richard, "Interview with the Defense Writers Group," *U.S. Strategic Command*, January. 8, 2021. https://www.stratcom.mil/Media/Speeches/Article/2466803/interview-with-the-defense-writers-group/

84 Charles Richard, "U. S. Navy. "Forging 21st-Century Strategic Deterrence," *US Naval Institute Proceedings*, Vol. 147, No. 2, 2021.

85 Lawrence Freedman, *The Evolution of Nuclear Strategy* (New York: Palgrave Macmillan, 2003).

86 Minwoo Choi, "Yoon Dong-ju is Chinese, 'Claims that Kimchi is also Chinese' underscores distortion," *Kookmin Ilbo*, December 30, 2020. http://news.kmib.co.kr/article/view.asp?arcid=0015375146&code=61131111

87 Daryl Kimball, "The Intermediate-Range Nuclear Forces (INF) Treaty at a Glance," *The Arms Control Association*, August 2019. https://www.armscontrol.org/factsheets/INFtreaty.

88 "China Conducts Successful Land-Based Mid-Course Missile Interception Test," *CGTN*, February 5, 2021. https://news.cgtn.com/news/2021-02-04/China-successfully-conducts-missile-interception-test-XCaJvPO7EQ/index.html

89 ANONYMOUS, "The Longer Telegram: Toward A New American China Strategy," *Atlantic Council*, 2021. https://www.atlanticcouncil.org/wp-content/uploads/2021/01/The-Longer-Telegram-Toward-A-New-American-China-Strategy.pdf

90 Deng Xiaoping, "Speech at the Special Session of the UN General Assembly," April 10, 1974. https://www.marxists.org/reference/archive/deng-xiaoping/1974/04/10.htm.

91 "CNN Presidential Town Hall With Joe Biden," *CNN*, February 16, 2021. https://transcripts.cnn.com/show/se/date/2021-02-16/segment/01

92 "Reserves of Cobalt Worldwide in 2021, by country," *Statista*, 2021. https://

www.statista.com/statistics/264930/global-cobalt-reserves/

93 Diego Ore, "Set to Build Large Lithium Plant in Uyuni," *Reuters*, October 1, 2009. https://www.reuters.com/article/bolivia-lithium-idUKN3021269020090930

94 "Democratic Republic of Congo: 'This is What We Die For': Human Rights Abuses in the Democratic Republic of the Congo Power the Global Trade in Cobalt," *Amnesty International*, January 19, 2016. https://www.amnesty.org/en/documents/afr62/3183/2016/en/

95 "U.S.-ROK Leaders' Joint Statement," *The White House*, May 21, 2021. https://www.whitehouse.gov/briefing-room/statements-releases/2021/05/21/u-s-rok-leaders-joint-statement/

96 "N. Korea Destroys Nuclear Reactor Tower," *CNN*, June 27, 2008. https://edition.cnn.com/2008/WORLD/asiapcf/06/27/northkorea.explosion/index.html

97 "Statement from Jake Sullivan on New Report Exposing Trump's Secret Line of Communication to Russia," *The American Presidency Project*, October 31, 2016. https://www.presidency.ucsb.edu/documents/statement-from-jake-sullivan-new-report-exposing-trumps-secret-line-communication-russia

98 Dale Hurd, "Is Biden in Deep with Beijing? Why Chinese Leaders Believe 'They Can Push Him Around,'" *CBN News*, March 11, 2021. https://www1.cbn.com/cbnnews/world/2021/march/is-biden-in-deep-with-beijing-why-chinese-leaders-believe-they-can-push-him-around

99 T. S. Eliot, "The Hollow Men," *The Complete Poems and Plays* (London: Faber and Faber, 2004), p. 81

100 Teddy Locsin Jr. (@teddyboylocsin), "GET THE FUCK OUT," *Twitter*, May 3, 2021.

101 Kamala Harris (@VP), "Enjoy the long weekend," *Twitter*, May 29, 2021.

102 "Unification Minister Calls for 'Maximum Flexibility' on Joint Military Exercises with US," *Korea Times*, June 6, 2021. https://www.koreatimes.co.kr/www/nation/2021/06/113_310009.html

103 George Orwell, *Brainy Quote*. https://www.brainyquote.com/quotes/george_orwell_159448

104 Charles M. Province, *U.S. Army*, 2005. http://www.pattonhq.com/koreamemorial.html

105 Benjamin Mainardi, "Yes, China Has the World's Largest Navy. That Matters Less Than You Might Think," *The Diplomat*, April 07, 2021. https://thediplomat.com/2021/04/yes-china-has-the-worlds-largest-navy-that-matters-less-than-you-might-think/

106 Idrees Ali and Karen Lema, "Philippines Again Suspends Scrapping of Troop Pact with U.S. amid China Dispute," *Reuters*, June 15, 2021. https://www.reuters.com/world/asia-pacific/philippines-suspends-decision-scrap-troop-pact-with-united-states-2021-06-14/

107 James Stavridis, "Opinion: China a Threat to Underwater Data Cables," *The Post and Courier*, April 10, 2019. https://www.postandcourier.com/opinion/commentary/opinion-china-a-threat-to-underwater-data-cables/article_4c87d528-5bd3-11e9-bcb0-6b4aa8ed0fd9.html

108 Jonathan Barrett and Yew Lun Tian, "Pacific Undersea Cable Project Sinks after U.S. Warns against Chinese Bid," *Reuters*, June 18, 2021. https://www.reuters.com/world/asia-pacific/exclusive-pacific-undersea-cable-project-sinks-after-us-warns-against-chinese-2021-06-18/

109 Qin Gang (@AmbQinGang)," Thank you DeputySecState Wendy Sherman for meeting with me StateDept on my 1st day out of self-quarantine. Look forward to continuing dialogue and communication with American colleagues for a rational, stable, manageable & constructive China-US relationship." *Twitter*, August 13, 2021.

110 Emily Feng, "China's New U.S. Ambassador Pioneered The Foreign Ministry's Brash Tone," *National Public Radio*, July 28, 2021. https://www.npr.org/2021/07/28/991934046/china-new-us-ambassador-qin-gang

111 Teddy Locsin Jr. (@teddyboylocsin), "I was promised 30,000 Moderna for my people and the diplomatic corps. My people who are frontliners. I don't know where the f**k that went, but words cannot express my embarrassment and anger. No one endangers my people. No one" *Twitter*, August 1, 2021.

112 *Ibid*, "F**k my country I'll f@@k yours." *Twitter*, August 9, 2021.

113 Walter Lippmann, *Public Opinion* (New York: Harcourt, Brace and Company, 1922).

114 "We Were Soldiers," Paramount Pictures, 2001. https://atloa.org/ltc-hal-moore-and-the-battle-of-the-ia-drang-valley-14-16-november-1965/

115 Quoted in Robert Gates, *Duty: Memoirs of a Secretary at War* (New York: Vintage, 2015).

116 Peter Wehner, "Biden's Long Trail of Betrayals," *The Atlantic*, August 19, 2021.

117 Joe Biden, "Remarks by President Biden on the End of the War in Afghanistan," *The White House*, August 31, 2021. https://www.whitehouse.gov/briefing-room/speeches-remarks/2021/08/31/remarks-by-president-biden-on-the-end-of-the-war-in-afghanistan/

118 Hans J. Morgenthau, "National Interest and Moral Principles in Foreign Policy: The Primacy of the National Interest," *American Scholar*, No. 18, 1949.

119 Ronald Reagan, "Farewell Address to the Nation," *Ronald Reagan Presidential Library and Museum*, January 11, 1989. https://www.reaganlibrary.gov/archives/speech/farewell-address-nation

120 "52% of Voters Think Biden Should Resign Over Afghanistan Withdrawal," *Rasmussen Reports*, September 1, 2021. https://www.rasmussenreports.com/public_content/politics/biden_administration/52_of_voters_think_biden_should_resign_over_afghanistan_withdrawal

121 *Ibid.* See also, Lexi Lonas, "Lindsey Graham: 'I think Joe Biden deserves to be impeached,'" *The Hill*, August 25, 2021. https://thehill.com/homenews/senate/569351-lindsey-graham-i-think-joe-biden-deserves-to-be-impeached/

122 Alex Thompson and Christopher Cadelago, "Biden Tries to Shift Blame on Afghanistan," *Politico*, August 31, 2021.

123 Tim Shipman and Josh Glancy, "The 2-trillion Afghan Shambles," *Sunday Times*, August 22, 2021. https://www.thetimes.co.uk/article/the-2-trillion-afghani-shambles-58sdwt3t7

124 Ben Riley-Smith, "Parliament Holds Joe Biden in Contempt over Afghanistan," *The Telegraph*, August 18, 2021.

125 Quoted in Vijeta Uniyal, "Germany Calls Biden's Afghanistan Pull-Out the 'Biggest Debacle' for NATO," *Legal Insurrection*, August 18, 2021.

126 Craig Whitlock, *The Afghanistan Papers: A Secret History of the War* (New York: Simon and Schuster, 2021).

127 Sami Yousafzai, "10 Years of Afghan War: How the Taliban Go On," *Newsweek*, October 2, 2011. https://www.newsweek.com/10-years-afghan-war-how-taliban-go-68223

128 Samantha Beech, Jake Kwon and Oren Liebermann, "North Korea Says It Fired New Long-Range Cruise Missiles, according to State Media," *CNN*, September 13, 2021. https://edition.cnn.com/2021/09/12/asia/north-korea-missile-

launch-new-intl/index.html

129 Dennis M. Gormley, *Missile Contagion: Cruise Missile Proliferation and the Threat to International Security* (Washington, DC: Naval Institute Press, 2010).

130 "A Conversation with Foreign Minister Chung Eui-yong of the Republic of Korea," *Council on Foreign Relations*, September 22 2021. https://www.cfr.org/event/conversation-foreign-minister-chung-eui-yong-republic-korea

131 Sue Pleming, "U.S. Takes North Korea Off Terrorism Blacklist, "*Reuters*, October 12, 2008. https://www.reuters.com/article/cnews-us-korea-north-list-idCATRE49A2F020081011

132 "Statement of Senator Barack Obama on the North Korean Declaration," *New York Times*, June 26, 2008. https://www.nytimes.com/2008/06/26/world/americas/26iht-26nuclear-obama.14017843.html

133 "The Structure and Content of Agreements between the Agency and States Required in Connection with the Treaty on the Non-Proliferation of Nuclear Weapons," INFCIRC/153, *IAEA*, 1972. https://www.iaea.org/publications/documents/infcircs/structure-and-content-agreements-between-agency-and-statesrequired-connection-treaty-non-proliferation-nuclear-weapons

134 "Guidelines for Nuclear Transfers," INFCIRC/254/Rev.11/Part 1, *IAEA*. http://www.iaea.org/Publications/Documents/Infcircs/2012/infcirc254r11p1.pdf

135 Sunwoo Won, "Managing the MZ Generation Soldier…'Take Care of the Battalion Commander,'" *Chosun Ilbo*, September 20, 2021. https://www.chosun.com/politics/diplomacy-defense/2021/09/02/PZSNGQYT3NEK3IU6GJ72HRYAKQ/

136 Sarah Betancourt, "America's Top General Defends Study of Critical Race Theory by Military," *Guardian*, June 24, 2021. https://www.theguardian.com/us-news/2021/jun/24/critical-race-theory-general-mark-milley-defence-military

137 Morgan Phillips, "Cotton Presses Defense Secretary on 'anti-American Indoctrination' as Austin Defends Diversity Push," *Fox News*, June 10 2021. https://www.foxnews.com/politics/cotton-defense-secretary-anti-american-indoctrination-austin-diversity

138 Samuel P. Huntington, *The Soldier and the State: The Theory and Politics of Civil-Military Relations (*Cambridge: Harvard University Press, 1957).

139 Raymond Garthoff, "The Concept of the Balance of Power in Soviet Policy-

making," *World Politics*, Volume 4, Issue 1, October 1951, pp.85-111.

140 Halford J. Mackinder, "The Geographical Pivot of History," *The Geographical Journal*, No. 23 (1904).

141 Camille Gijs, "The 'go fuck yourself' Ukrainian soldiers on Snake Island are alive, Navy says," *Politico*, February 28, 2022. https://www.politico.eu/article/ukrainian-soldiers-on-snake-island-are-alive-navy-says/

142 Thomas Novelly, "Ukraine's Fighter Ace 'Ghost of Kyiv' May Be a Myth, But It's Lethal as War Morale," *Military.com*, March 2, 2022. https://www.military.com/daily-news/2022/03/02/ukraines-fighter-ace-ghost-of-kyiv-may-be-myth-its-lethal-war-morale.html

143 Joseph Watson "Babi Yar Holocaust Memorial 'Unscathed' According to Israeli Journalist," *Summit News*, March 3, 2022. https://summit.news/2022/03/03/babi-yar-holocaust-memorial-unscathed-according-to-israeli-journalist/

144 Record of Conversation between Mikhail Gorbachev and James Baker, Kremlin, February 9, 1990. For the full array of primary documents, see https://nsarchive.gwu.edu/briefing-book/russia-programs/2017-12-12/nato-expansion-what-gorbachev-heard-western-leaders-early

145 George F. Kennan, "A Fateful Error," *New York Times*, February 5, 1997.

146 "Letter to the President, 'Opposition to NATO Expansion,'" June 26, 1997. https://www.armscontrol.org/act/1997-06/arms-control-today/opposition-nato-expansion

147 "Putin: "How is it different from Kosovo?," *B92*, February 22, 2022. https://www.b92.net/eng/news/world.php?nav_id=113110

148 Cited in *Congressional Record*, Volume 168, Number 27, February 10, 2022. https://www.govinfo.gov/content/pkg/CREC-2022-02-10/html/CREC-2022-02-10-pt1-PgS632-2.htm

149 Henry Kissinger, "To Settle the Ukraine Crisis, Start at the End," *Washington Post*, March 5, 2014.

150 John Mearsheimer, "Why the Ukraine Crisis is the West's Fault," *Foreign Affairs*, September-October 2014.

151 "Transcript: Vladimir Putin's Televised Address on Ukraine," *Bloomberg*, February 24, 2022.

152 Brett Logiurato, "John McCain: Russia is a 'Gas Station Masquerading as a Country,'" *Business Insider*, March 16, 2014. https://www.businessinsider.

in/john-mccain-russia-is-a-gas-station-masquerading-as-a-country/articleshow/32154817.cms

153 Article 21 states, "Should Turkey consider herself to be threatened with imminent danger of war she shall have the right to apply the provisions of Article 20 of the present Convention." *1936 CONVENTION REGARDING THE REGIME OF THE STRAITS, Adopted in Montreux, Switzerland on 20 July 1936.* https://cil.nus.edu.sg/wp-content/uploads/formidable/18/1936-Convention-Regarding-the-Regime-of-the-Straits.pdf

154 "Ammonium Nitrate Production by Country, 2021" *Knoema.* https://knoema.com/atlas/topics/Agriculture/Fertilizers-Production-Quantity-in-Nutrients/Ammonium-nitrate-production

155 Hanna Duggal and Mohammed Haddad, "Infographic: Russia, Ukraine and the Global Wheat Supply," *Al Jazeera,* February 17, 2022. https://www.aljazeera.com/news/2022/2/17/infographic-russia-ukraine-and-the-global-wheat-supply-interactive

156 Cited in Stephen Jinwoo Kim, *Master of Manipulation: Syngman Rhee and the Seoul-Washington Alliance, 1953-1960* (Seoul: Yonsei University Press, 2001).

157 Gen. David H. Berger, U.S. Marine Corps, "Preparing for the Future: Marine Corps Support to Joint Operations in Contested Littorals," *Military Review,* April 2021.

STEPHEN JINWOO KIM, PH.D.

Stephen Jinwoo Kim is Founder and CEO of the Sermo Group, an educational consulting company based in Seoul, Korea and Zurich, Switzerland. He is also President of the Sermo Institute of International Studies (SIIS), a think tank that conducts analysis of international affairs.

He is Adjunct Professor at Sogang University's Graduate School of International Studies where he teaches national intelligence, American foreign and national security policy, international organizations, and U.S.-Korean relations.

He has worked in the policy, military and intelligence communities across the U.S. government. His portfolio has included China, North Korea, Pakistan, Iran, strategic nuclear deterrence, and WMD issues. He received his B.A. from Georgetown University, his M.A. from Harvard University, and his Ph.D. from Yale University.

You can find him on Twitter @jinwookimsays

Sermo Group

BEYOND SCYLLA AND CHARYBDIS. Copyright @ 2022 by Stephen Jinwoo Kim.

All rights reserved. Printed in Seoul, South Korea. No part of this may be used or reproduced in any manner whatsoever without written permission except in the case of brief quotations embodied in critical articles and review. For information, address Sermo Publishing Company, #202, Eonju-ro 134-gil 6, Gangnam-gu, Seoul, Korea, 06061.

Sermo Group books may be purchased for educational, business or sales promotional use. For information, office@sermo.co.kr

Library of Congress Cataloging-in-Publication Data is available.

ISBN 979-11-980277-8-8(04340)
ISBN 979-11-980277-9-5(04340) (set)